Prince Arthur

ABOUT THE AUTHOR

DR SEAN CUNNINGHAM has worked for The National Archives for twenty years and is currently Principal Records Specialist for the Medieval, Early Modern and Legal sections. His other books include *Henry VII*, *Richard III: A Royal Enigma* and *Henry VII* (forthcoming Penguin Monarchs series). He is a Fellow of the Royal Historical Society and lives in London.

Prince Arthur

The Tudor King
Who Never Was

SEAN CUNNINGHAM

AMBERLEY

For Sam, Dan and Freddie

First published 2016

Amberley Publishing
The Hill, Stroud
Gloucestershire, GL5 4EP

www.amberley-books.com

Copyright © Sean Cunningham, 2016, 2017

The right of Sean Cunningham to be identified
as the Author of this work has been asserted
in accordance with the Copyrights, Designs
and Patents Act 1988.

ISBN 978 1 4456 7117 8 (paperback)
ISBN 978 1 4456 4767 8 (ebook)

British Library Cataloguing in Publication Data.
A catalogue record for this book is available
from the British Library.

Typesetting and Origination by Amberley Publishing
Printed in the UK.

CONTENTS

WHO'S WHO IN PRINCE ARTHUR'S LIFE

The Tudor Royal Family

Henry VII (1457–1509), reigned from 1485

Elizabeth of York (1466–1503), married to King Henry from 1486; daughter of King Edward IV and sister to King Edward V

Prince Arthur (1486–1502)

Princess Margaret (1489–1541), married King James IV of Scotland 1503–13

Prince Henry (1491–1547), reigned as Henry VIII from 1509; married to his brother Arthur's widow, Catherine of Aragon, 1509–33

Princess Elizabeth (1492–95)

Princess Mary (1496–1533), married to Louis XII of France for three months until his death in early 1515

Prince Edmund (1499–1500)

Princess Catherine (b. 1503), lived for eight days, dying the day after her mother Elizabeth of York, who succumbed to an infection after the birth

Elizabeth Woodville (1437–92), married King Edward IV, 1464 until his death in 1483. Mother to Elizabeth of York and grandmother and godmother to Arthur

Margaret Beaufort (1443–1509), mother to King Henry VII and grandmother to Arthur

Catherine of Aragon (1485–1536), married to Arthur in 1501; married to Henry VIII 1509–33

Jasper Tudor (1429–95), uncle to Henry VII and brother to his father Edmund

Godparents

John de Vere, 13th Earl of Oxford (1442–1513)

Thomas Stanley, 1st Earl of Derby (1435–1504), married to Margaret Beaufort

Thomas FitzAlan, 17th Earl of Arundel (1450–1524)

Cecily of York, Viscountess of Welles (1469–1507), younger sister of Elizabeth of York

Elizabeth Woodville, Dowager Queen of England

Nurses and Tutors

Elizabeth Darcy, head of Arthur's nursery at Farnham Palace

Bernard André (1450–1522), poet in the court of Henry VII and tutor to Prince Arthur

John Rede (d. 1557), former headmaster of Winchester School, early tutor to Prince Arthur, later an MP

Ludlow Castle

William Smith, Bishop of Lincoln (1460–1514), President of the Council of the Marches

Sir Richard Croft (1430–1509), steward of Arthur's household

Sir Thomas Cornewall, member of the Council of the Marches

Sir Henry Vernon (*c.* 1445–1515), Arthur's governor and treasurer

Sir William Uvedale, controller of Arthur's household

Sir Richard Pole (1462–1505), Arthur's chamberlain, a close relative of Arthur's grandmother Margaret Beaufort

Friends of Prince Arthur
Anthony Willoughby, son of Robert Willoughby, 1st Baron Willoughby de Broke
John Lord Grey, son of the 1st Marquis of Dorset
Sir Gryffudd ap Rhys (1487–1534), son of Sir Rhys ap Thomas, one of Henry VII's closest supporters
Lord Gerald FitzGerald (1487–1534), son of Gerald FitzGerald, 8th Earl of Kildare
Edward Howard (1476–1513), son of Thomas Howard, Earl of Surrey
Robert Ratcliffe (1483–1542), heir to John 9th Lord Fitzwalter
John St John
Edward Stafford, Duke of Buckingham (1487–1521)
Thomas Howard, Earl of Surrey (1443–1524), chief mourner, Duke of Norfolk after 1513

Pretenders to the throne
Lambert Simnel (1477–1525), claiming to be the Earl of Warwick
Perkin Warbeck (*c.* 1475–99), claiming to be Edward IV's son Richard, Duke of York

The Spanish court
King Ferdinand
Queen Isabella
Don Pedro de Ayala, Ambassador of Spain

A TUDOR TIMELINE

				Battle of
	Henry			Stoke;
Edward	Tudor			Lambert
IV takes	flees to		Battle of	Simnel
throne	Brittany		Bosworth	rebellion
1461	1471		1485	1487

1457	1470	1471	1483	1485	1486	1491
Henry Tudor born	Henry VI restored to throne	Henry VI dies; Edward IV retakes throne	Edward IV dies; Richard III takes crown	Richard III dies; Henry VII takes throne	Henry VII marries Elizabeth of York; Prince Arthur born	Henry VIII born

Arthur moves to Ludlow
1493

Perkin Warbeck executed
1499

Arthur marries Catherine of Aragon
1501

Arthur dies
1502

Princess Margaret marries James IV of Scotland
1503

Elizabeth of York dies
1503

Henry VII dies; Henry VIII marries Catherine of Aragon; Margaret Beaufort dies
1509

Henry VII divorces Catherine of Aragon and marries Anne Boleyn
1533

Catherine of Aragon dies
1536

PRINCE ARTHUR'S GENEALOGY

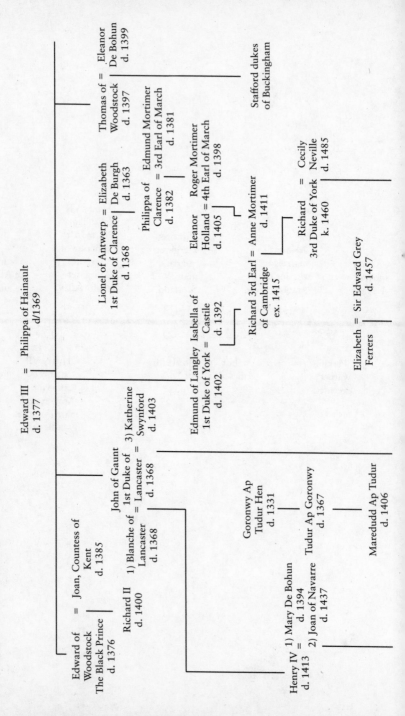

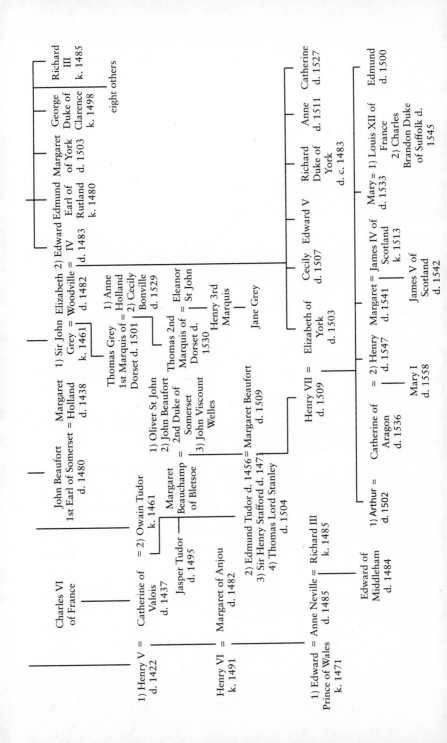

Introduction

ARTHUR AND HENRY

Arthur was the first Tudor prince. His birth in September 1486 promised much for the new royal family; but only fifteen years later, on the cusp of fulfilling his potential to be a king worthy of his given name, he was dead. With his death, the heir to the Tudor crown became his brother, Henry. While Arthur failed to live long enough to take the throne or to make a success of his brief marriage to Catherine of Aragon, Prince Henry went on to rule as Henry VIII. He took Arthur's place on the throne and also took his brother's widow as his first wife. Arthur became a footnote near the start of Tudor histories; the boy who may or may not have consummated his marriage but was gone long before the consequences of his wedding led to one of the most crucial turning points of English history – Henry VIII's divorce and England's break from the authority of the Pope in Rome. Arthur's legacy has been completely overshadowed by the monstrous reputation that his brother would earn. Yet had he lived, a totally different chain of events might have shaped England and Wales under the Tudor dynasty in the first half of the sixteenth century.

Henry was only five years younger than Arthur. Had the elder brother ruled into his mid-fifties, with healthy children to inherit the crown after him, then there would have been no opportunity for Arthur's brother to become king. We cannot say how things would have unfolded under King Arthur's rule; only that the history of England after 1509 is unlikely to have followed the same path as the one familiar to us. The relationship of Arthur and Henry therefore has a very interesting and important influence on how the Tudor dynasty evolved. It is all the more powerful because Arthur and Henry can have spent very little time together in life. Henry was aged only eleven when his brother died. Arthur had been largely absent at his first nursery at Farnham Palace in Surrey and then, from the age of six, as nominal ruler of the Welsh Marches from his base at Ludlow Castle. The brothers met at state occasions and probably at other unrecorded times, but their contact can only have been brief. Arthur was so important to the continuation of the Tudor dynasty that he had a power base created for him which was staffed by some of the king's most loyal servants. Henry, on the other hand, remained in the royal nursery at Eltham Palace with his sisters Margaret and Mary and his infant brother Edmund. By the end of the 1490s it was obvious to Henry that he was the regime's 'spare prince'. Arthur would always be Henry VII's most important focus. The investment in Arthur's future goes some way towards explaining why Prince Henry had a difficult relationship with his father after 1502. Henry was overshadowed by his brother's legacy long after Arthur was in his grave, and he was allowed a freedom that would never have been encouraged if it was thought that he might take the throne.

Although Arthur has been largely forgotten, looking again at the course of his life will reveal an enormous amount about what

Henry VII hoped to achieve as king. Arthur's life was a mirror to his father's hopes and fears and life experiences. If ever there was a grand plan for the Tudor dynasty, it was encapsulated in Prince Arthur's training and visible in the pageantry of the set-piece occasions that marked his progression towards the throne. From the outset, no one could doubt that Arthur would be a rightful ruler. Even his given name carried expectations that grew from the link to the greatest of Britain's ancient warrior-kings. Many of Henry VII's subjects at different levels of society would have understood the link between the mythical King Arthur and the real Prince Arthur. Since the prince would one day sit on the throne, the literary ideal of kingship had a chance of becoming woven into the reality of Arthur's rule. Public events and state ceremonies reiterated Arthur's royal status. No opportunity was lost to remind the king's subjects at every social level that Arthur was the heir to a legitimate ruling dynasty. King Henry had suffered a very uncertain childhood as the ward of a great Anglo-Welsh lord in the 1460s. The aristocratic in-fighting of the Wars of the Roses had forced Henry into exile and isolation at the age of fourteen in 1471. Over half his life had been spent in obscurity overseas by the time he won the Battle of Bosworth. The heir of the first Tudor king would not have to endure such a bleak upbringing, nor would he have to claw his way to power; but he would have to learn how to be an effective king. That could not happen in the way Henry VII wanted if the prince was too close to the centre of power or too strongly attached to the comforts of a metropolitan life. To achieve security and stability in his adult reign, Arthur would have to become accustomed to, and thrive upon, his youthful independence.

Arthur is an essential link between the troubled uncertainty of his father's reign and the opulence and entitlement that typified his brother's time as king. To many people, Arthur's birth as a healthy child in 1486 confirmed God's favour towards Henry VII.

It was a pivotal moment that drew a line under the early setbacks of his life and showed that Henry had much to be thankful for. As Earl of Richmond, he was the last nobleman to share the blood of the Lancastrian kings (his father, Edmund, had been a half-brother to King Henry VI). He posed little threat personally, but as a rallying point in the 1470s for conspirators against Edward IV's Yorkist regime he became a real danger. Unclear about how they might be treated in England, Henry, along with his uncle Jasper, spent fourteen years in Brittany and France awaiting his chance to return to England to recover something of his noble status. Henry's life was so grim that by the start of the 1480s he was ready to return under basic guarantees of life. Yet by the end of 1483, the circumstances of Richard III's usurpation had transformed Henry into a rival claimant for the crown. Soon Henry could also draw upon the experience of those men and women who had been heartbroken and displaced when Richard III took the crown, among them many of Edward IV's loyalists and those connected to the Woodville family. The improbable Tudor victory at Bosworth permitted their reabsorption into national life and gave Henry VII a platform on which to build other pillars of his regime. Arthur's birth allowed the king to look further into the future, but only if his son could be kept healthy and safe. God had looked kindly upon King Henry, but any ideas of the establishment of a dynasty would require a tough prince to survive long enough to follow a tough king.

This could only come to pass after some uncomfortable but necessary years when Arthur might have felt that he was hardly part of the royal family at all. The blueprint for a childhood away from the palaces of the Thames valley existed in the arrangements that Edward IV had made for his heir, Edward, Prince of Wales, in the 1470s. Like so much else about the Tudor regime, King Henry was happy to adapt what his royal predecessors had attempted. The first prince of the House of York had been sent to Ludlow

Castle on the Welsh Marches to learn the craft of kingship. He was guided by a powerful group of royal insiders and experienced officials. Over time, life on the borders of Wales enabled the prince to build up his own power base. He would learn how to assess the skills and loyalties of servants. The legal jurisdictions he presided over revealed how institutions and administrators supported royal power. In short, Prince Edward was given a mini-kingdom in which he could absorb the knowledge of those more experienced in good government. He could test his own learning in an environment where mistakes could be managed. When Edward became king, he would apply this real-world education in ruling the whole country.

Except that Prince Edward never was crowned as King of England. He disappeared in the early summer of 1483 at the hands of his uncle Richard, Duke of Gloucester and was never again seen in public. After the premature death of Edward IV in April 1483, all the planning for the future of his son was rapidly undone. The stability of the Yorkist royal family was broken apart by the swift manoeuvring and ruthless action of one of those royal insiders who were meant to protect Edward V until he was old enough to rule alone. Richard seized the throne for himself and many people presumed that Edward and his brother Richard – the Princes in the Tower – were killed during the course of their uncle's usurpation. Richard III's seizure of the highest office provided a chilling lesson for Henry VII. He dissected the circumstances and failings that had prevented Edward V from becoming an adult king. His response was to carefully plan how Prince Arthur's life at Ludlow would develop. A stronger future awaited the Tudors if the Prince of Wales inherited the throne as a fully formed adult king already up to speed with the rigours of kingship and the techniques required to be an effective ruler. That level of preparation could be achieved on the Welsh Marches, but there could be no possibility that anyone might challenge the succession from within the regime's inner circle or the higher ranks of the nobility. No subject would be allowed to get to a position where they would be able to destroy the king's plans and Arthur's future by getting custody of the prince. Arthur would not be ruled or governed by great men. His upbringing would be entrusted to people who had proved their loyalty by working their way up the ranks of service to Henry VII and his family, people who had been appointed only due to the king's satisfaction with their efforts in office.

Every day of his development took Arthur a step closer towards mastery of the skills that he would need if he was to be the kind of glorious king whom the nation craved after years of civil war and unrest. Henry VII expected his son to become nothing less than a unifier of England. By 1500, Henry had carried through the policies that had kept the Tudor family on the throne during years of danger and uncertainty. The struggle had exhausted him. Surviving portraits show him transformed in a few years into a grey-haired and hollow-cheeked monarch. He looks thin underneath his expensive robes and seems burdened by the pressures inherent in occupying the throne. The circumstances of his reign had heightened the strain, loyalty becoming an obsession as the king sought to pre-empt any opposition. Financial security began to motivate policies built around the transfer of power to an unchallenged heir. Henry was tolerated, respected and possibly feared by some, but he was not loved by many. His reign was a transition laden with sacrifice. His heir would reap the benefits of harsh policies sown in a valiant effort to halt the cycle of civil war that had afflicted much of fifteenth-century England. Only King Arthur could bring about a lasting resolution of the conflict over who had the best right to the crown. He carried none of the personal baggage of the Wars of the Roses that was borne by many aristocratic adults alive in 1486. His birth had already merged the bloodlines of the last direct heirs of the Lancastrian and Yorkist kings. He had inherited the opportunity to rule without looking backwards to past conflict and violence. Arthur represented the future, and it was open to everyone willing to support his kingship.

As the precious first son of a new dynasty, his parents' immediate desire would have been to keep Arthur close and safe with the rest of his family. In the autumn of 1485 the Tudor crown was on shaky ground, under threat from conspirators and with a shortage of truly trustworthy allies. Henry VII knew that serious threats existed and that perilous challenges were heading his way. It made sense to expand the power of the Tudor crown from the small band that had been with him on the road to Bosworth Field. Arthur might have been too young to notice, but he immediately had a role in building the king's authority and in bringing England's subjects closer to acknowledging the loyalty they owed to the new monarch. Against this uncertain background, Arthur was sent away from his parents and brought up completely separately. This decision seems amazingly harsh but also incredibly brave – not least because the people who cared for him were the team that had looked after the children of Edward IV and Elizabeth Woodville. Arthur's mother, Elizabeth of York, had been one of those children, and the decision to reappoint a familiar group of carers suggests her close involvement in planning the early stages of her son's upbringing. However much Arthur was loved by his mother and father, there were bigger considerations at play. The king planned his outline of Arthur's life with a detached calculation of the best route to national security and stability. Achieving this goal meant sacrifice. From the very first weeks of his life, Arthur began to be prepared for an education that would train him to rule. The prince's independence would make it harder for any conspirators to wipe out the entire royal family in a palace coup. A satellite royal household gave the king another space in which to train and develop royal servants.

Later on, it would deliver a powerful military force on behalf of the prince, and, through his Council of the Marches, exercise his legal jurisdiction in the border counties with Wales. Cutting Arthur's physical ties with the tight-knit core of his father's household was a huge risk in uncertain times, but in the long term it would build a stronger regime.

Many books covering this period include the outline of Arthur's story, but not the details. A fuller telling reveals the massive investment that was put into Arthur's future by Henry VII, Queen Elizabeth, the king's mother Margaret Beaufort and all of the prince's advisors, servants and friends. Prince Arthur was, for the first fifteen years of Tudor rule, the most important focus of the whole regime. The increasingly ruthless policies Henry VII devised were part of his aspiration to secure the peaceful succession of the crown to the first heir of the new ruling family. The second Tudor king, when he did arrive on the throne, would be fully formed, experienced and, through his Spanish marriage, ready to take England's seat at the high table of European powers. Henry VII intended that his son would continue the large-scale strategies that had been put in place since 1485, but without the constant background noise of internal rebels and external plotters. They would be swept away or under control. King Arthur would reap the benefits of Henry VII's cleansing of an English political system that had perpetuated a century of infighting and civil war.

When the news of Arthur's death arrived, it was calamitous. The personal and emotional dimension of his loss was shattering to the king and the rest of the royal family. Arthur had hardly been seen in the south-east of England, and as he grew towards manhood he could not have been well known to his family. Now there could be no recovery of lost time. Guilt and regret underscored the outpouring of grief within the royal household. For King Henry and his mother, especially, their political vision lay in tatters. Arthur's death threatened to undo almost twenty years of preparation. His separate education and immersion into the government of Wales was a gamble that had not paid off. Emphasising Arthur's pre-eminence had meant that Prince Henry's position had to be played down before 1501. Henry VII did not wish to breed rivalries by installing and supporting two satellite royal lordships within England. Now the king's attention had to switch to his other son.

Prince Arthur had been on a journey from infancy to the throne along a road designed to expose him to all of the aspects of royal leadership. That same voyage of discovery simply could not now be restarted for Henry, Duke of York. At the age of ten, he was already shaping his character and experiences in different directions. Some elements of the plan for Arthur could be salvaged because they were institutionalised within the regime more generally, but Prince Henry was already a very different person to his brother. He was unlikely to have responded well to being fast-tracked through training for the rigours of kingship. Henry was not transported to the Marches, even after becoming Prince of Wales in February 1503. Whereas details of Arthur's life on the Anglo-Welsh border are shadowy because of the loss of documents, the visibility of Prince Henry around the king's palaces after 1502 is equally obscure but arises because he was thrust into such a stifling and protective existence. His classroom education continued, and he is recorded sitting as a judge in the court of the king's household, but the scale of his experiences and the opportunities to exercise his learning were severely limited when compared to the responsibilities Arthur held in his hands as he approached his teenage years. By looking at Arthur's crucial lost years we can see what the younger son, Henry, had missed, and what had been built around Arthur – so getting a glimpse of Henry VII's plans and Henry VIII's inheritance.

Prologue

PRINCE ARTHUR AND THE WARS
OF THE ROSES

Arthur was born into an uncertain political world. Only one year previously his father had seized power on the battlefield, and he was now locked into a different kind of struggle: to resolve thirty years of civil war and hold on to power. It is essential to understand what had led to this moment in order to fully appreciate how significant this period was for the fledgling Tudor dynasty.

From his long exile in Brittany and France, Henry, as Earl of Richmond, could observe between 1483 and 1485 how acutely changeable the nature of English political power really was. At the root of the unfolding of events during that period was a fluctuation in the way that personal influence was exercised. At the start of 1483, things were as they had been for most of Edward IV's reign since 1471. Prince Edward was learning the intricacies of kingship on the Marches at Ludlow under the guidance of his uncle Anthony Woodville, Earl Rivers. Richard, Duke of Gloucester was refining his northern lordship having triumphed in a grand raid against Scotland the previous year. King Edward, though getting fatter and less interested in the routine business of ruling, had only recently turned forty. His regime seemed confident and in control. Many nobles were comfortable in their spheres of influence. Although squabbling occasionally surfaced, it was contained and not apparently widespread.

What happened next came as a complete shock within England and across Europe. Edward IV died unexpectedly on 9 April 1483. His son, Prince Edward, now King Edward V, was immediately summoned from Ludlow to a coronation planned for 4 May, as the dying Edward IV had wished. On the way to London, however, Richard, Duke of Gloucester, with the help of his ally Henry, Duke of Buckingham, intercepted the prince and took control of him. Gloucester claimed that the Woodville family were plotting to dominate the young king to the exclusion or destruction of other, more established, lords. Duke Richard had the principal officers of Edward's household arrested and sent north. News of his actions caused a rush to sanctuary at Westminster by many others in the Woodville group, including Edward IV's widow Queen Elizabeth and her remaining children. People seemed prepared to accept the allegations of empire-building against the Woodvilles. Edward's coronation was postponed until 22 June since a major state ceremony, held in the difficult circumstances of the protectorate, required a little more preparation time.

Richard's carefully constructed regional power base then supplied the men and intimidation needed to transform an attempt to secure position under a young and impressionable king into a coup to seize the crown outright. On 10 June he mobilised the military steel used in his invasion of Scotland. While the Earl of Northumberland brought forces south, Buckingham worked swiftly to clear Richard's route to the throne. Several of Edward IV's friends who were most committed to seeing Edward V crowned were arrested on 13 June. Some, like Lord Hastings, were singled out for death. Richard moved fast to exert his influence over other peers and to brush all opposition aside. His purpose was apparently still not recognised and right up to 16 June many officials still acted in Edward V's name. Ten days later, on 23 June, Richard, Duke of Gloucester became King Richard III.

Richard's transformation from loyal royal brother to protector and then to king had taken less than three months. This was personal power at its most efficient and ruthless. Richard had divided, outwitted or eliminated everyone who might have stood in his way. He made excellent use of allies who would benefit from his actions while at the same time justifying his decisions through a mastery of propaganda and communication aimed at common citizens. At this stage only the Woodville group was broken. Many other servants of Edward IV and Edward V paused while they considered what to do next. By the end of July, when Richard was on his first progress, some had decided to act against the new king. The first uprising aimed to free Edward V and his brother Richard, Duke of York from their imprisonment in the Tower of London. It failed, and it is probable that the princes died in its aftermath. By October 1483, the next rebellion was organised in Henry Tudor's name – something that would never have happened had the rebels believed that the princes were alive. Once more the rivalries of the roses had risen to the surface and it was clear that twelve years of apparent security was not enough to dissolve old feuds.

Henry was a passive figure in this stage of the conspiracy against King Richard, but he was a rival candidate for the crown nevertheless. He benefited enormously from the failure of the uprising of October 1483, as the Edwardian Yorkists fled to join his court in exile in Brittany. From that point, Henry built momentum at the same rate as he refined his leadership skills. The conclusions he drew regarding the events of 1483 were, judging by his later decisions, filed away in his portfolio of the key skills of kingship. With no one available to teach him how to transform theoretical or abstract ideas into policies, watching Richard III exercise his lordship against other political players must have been very illuminating. There were further lessons to take from Richard's activities during the rest of his reign in England.

Richard's northern resource of hard-working gentry was sufficiently strong for him to try to extend it across the administration of the whole country after southern England rebelled. With much of the class of JPs, sheriffs and other local officials having fled or under suspicion of disloyalty, Richard had little choice but to transplant his loyal followers into the gaps in local government roles. As duke he had achieved an impressive depth in building up his personal service network, or affinity, in this way. Although in the end the northerners did little to support their king at Bosworth, Henry would have recognised how the creation of an intensely personal and reliable following had formed the core of a crown network once Richard became king. Just as Edward IV had planned a similar route to the crown for his own Prince of Wales, so Henry VII was able to use this model to build the foundations of Arthur's regal bearing from the early 1490s.

Henry VII became King of England before he had really tested the depth of his lordship over the supporters who had carried him to victory at Bosworth. A spectacular military campaign called for a different range of abilities to those required for running a peacetime regime throughout the whole country. The Tudor crown's network had to become indistinguishable from the king's own personal affinity. This was the reverse of what had happened in the recent past when aristocrats had become kings, as with Henry IV, Edward IV and Richard III. The servants they cultivated as private lords formed the backbone of their regime as kings. Henry VII had his own core network based around the exiles from 1483 and the servants that Margaret Beaufort and Lord Stanley had attracted during the 1470s. All of these people were compelled to step into central and local government roles after Bosworth; it was part of the deal that restored their estates to them. Nevertheless, an examination of the new Tudor regime would have revealed to the king that very few figures of national prominence were personally committed to him alone and without any former attachment to another figure of importance. The quality of his support had improved by the time his fleet sailed for Wales at the start of August 1485. But Henry remained a proxy figure: a figurehead onto whom support and expectation were projected in hostility to King Richard. Henry became king with a partly artificial fusion of followers behind him. A government formed and then propped up by the convenience of opposition to a previous ruler invited real problems as it sought a new identity. Henry gave that process plenty of attention during his early years. While he was doing this, however, it was vital that the king looked to build the solid foundation of personal loyalty that his heir would need in the long process of transition to adult rule. Even before Arthur was conceived it is tempting to think that Henry was already planning how his first-born son would be educated.

Therefore, at an early age, Arthur's position was built in stages towards the goal of self-reliant lordship with the strongest bonds of loyalty possible. When that came into effect would depend upon a realistic assessment of the point at which Arthur's leadership was sustainable. If the quality and loyalty of his backers was resilient enough, then the prince's age would not be as important as the resolve of those who defended and served him. The key aspect of Henry VII's strategy for Arthur's education and political inheritance was how the training for his life as a lord could overcome the kind of deficiencies that had allowed Edward V's supporters to be so comprehensively outwitted by Richard, Duke of Gloucester in 1483. Careful preparations had to be made before Prince Arthur could be introduced as a new Earl of March and prince in Wales, but once he was accepted in the Marcher region the older structures and precedents were well rooted and capable of carrying him to the throne. His title as Prince of Wales carried national precedence, but it was Arthur's connection with the earldom of March, and the ancestry he could then claim from the Mortimers, that was the essential component of his personal status.

If Henry Tudor's announcement at Christmas 1483 that he planned to marry Princess Elizabeth of York was a naked attempt to build cohesive support for the Tudor cause, the amazing victory at Bosworth allowed Henry to reward those same Yorkist supporters who had stuck with him. It remained a far from perfect victory, however. Richard of Gloucester's coup had fractured the Yorkist elite. Having one enemy to hate and defeat had united them with Lancastrians who had been active but isolated throughout the reigns of the Yorkist kings. Henry's success might have reversed this situation, giving the Yorkists someone to turn against. It was essential that Henry acted to bring all of his groups of supporters into the fold rather than allowing discontent to generate alliances against him. Now that Richard was defeated and dead, the massive body of lords and gentry that had stayed in England to serve his regime also had to be assessed and accommodated by the incoming regime. Very few people moved straight to open resistance and rebellion. True loyalty and allegiance quickly became hidden as many waited to gauge the effectiveness of the new king. By suspending uncertainty over Henry VII's capacity to rule –simply to see how politics unfolded in his first months as king – the political, administrative and publicly active classes made Henry VII's task of building effective support and workable government much harder. Commitment to the new wearer of the crown looked superficially to be solid; but it might not take much to make members of the aristocracy waver if alternative candidates for the throne emerged quickly.

Against this background of stuttering crown authority and rebalancing of lordship, the royal family grasped at any positive development that inched the regime towards stability. Arthur's birth just thirteen months after Bosworth was truly a joyous moment for Henry VII and Queen Elizabeth. It also provided a giant stride towards national acceptance of the Tudor right to rule. The arrival of a prince allowed King Henry to initiate the programme that probably had already begun to evolve as Edward IV's regime unravelled. So Arthur's story is told against the changing nature of personal lordship at the top of late medieval society. Henry VII wanted to re-interpret Edward IV's strategy for his son's rite of passage, since that maintained the interest and backing of the Yorkists who had effectively put Henry Tudor on the throne. Edward IV's plan for his son had been sound; it was its execution and the abilities of some of the personnel responsible that had not been good enough. Henry would learn from the mistakes of others and build a role for his son that would put him at the centre of the political landscape.

THE FIRST TUDOR PRINCE
FROM BIRTH TO INDEPENDENCE

Birth and Christening

On a cold and wet September day in 1486, the aristocracy of England assembled in Winchester, along with most of the people of the city, to celebrate the birth of the first child of a new king and queen. The birth of Prince Arthur allowed for an outpouring of joy and celebration that was a manifestation of how King Henry felt when the queen was safely delivered of a son. The Tudor regime now had a future that was not dependent solely upon the survival of the king himself. Henry VII had already shown by his conduct before and during the Battle of Bosworth that he was a fearless gambler. In 1485, as an unknown king with an uncertain future, he relied upon the status and ancestry of his wife to give his regime a toehold on power. Queen Elizabeth mixed the loyalties of former Yorkists into the cement that was holding the Tudor regime together; but the king was only just in control. In order to break away from this dependency, King Henry needed a healthy male heir as soon as possible. The longer his reign progressed without a son who embodied the unification of the contending houses of York and Lancaster, the less secure Henry VII would be.[1] Queen Elizabeth was aged only nineteen when she married Henry. She quickly became pregnant. It is not difficult to imagine how elated the king and queen must have been at this news. Elizabeth's evident fertility meant that she would escape scrutiny and pressure related to the principal part of her duties as a consort: the provision of children. Henry had a male heir only thirteen months after becoming king. His relief at achieving the first step in securing the succession so early in his reign must have been overwhelming. Historians usually focus on the king's urgency to perpetuate his dynastic future and the fact that his prayers were answered so quickly. For Elizabeth, emotions would have been more mixed. The birth of her first child was potentially a traumatic step into the unknown for the queen. She would have the finest care and could only hope that God would continue to look favourably upon her as the time of her delivery drew near. Elizabeth was young and healthy, but childbirth was the gravest risk to the lives of all medieval women, and it would claim her life seventeen years later. As soon as the queen got through the difficult early stages of pregnancy, there was every chance that nature would take its course successfully. Henry therefore lost no time in planning for the birth of a male heir.

In Henry's mind, there seems to have been every expectation that he would have a healthy son. His actions in planning how to celebrate the delivery of a prince prove that he had built the future of his kingship upon this one key moment. Medieval medical science could not ensure such things, but the king was convinced that God would send him what he needed. Since divine favour had already been demonstrated in Henry's capture of the crown, this was no time for fearing that providence would abandon the Tudors.

The court had probably descended on Winchester by the final week of August 1486. By 31 August, official documents begin to bear dates from the city.[2] King Henry's official court poet, Bernard André, had already written of the joy around the court and throughout the country once it was announced that Queen Elizabeth was pregnant. As the pregnancy advanced without incident, Henry and his advisers were able to devote time and energy into the development of a major state event to celebrate the birth and christening of his first child.

The choice of Winchester was charged with associations linking the new regime to the ancient kings of Britain and to the slightly more recent origins of a unified nation under Alfred the Great and his successors as kings of Wessex. Few outside of the royal family would have known that if the child was a son he would be called Arthur. The intention to name the king's heir after the legendary leader of the British resistance to the Saxon invasions of the fifth century was another of Henry VII's bold gambles – just like his landing and cross-country march towards Richard III's army in August the previous year. Prince Arthur was meant to follow the perfect kingly image that was presented by the literary Arthur in the works of Geoffrey of Monmouth, Sir Thomas Malory and William Caxton: 'a paragon of generosity, affluence, courage, military success, and courtliness'.[3] Arthur had largely been written into the historical record through the popularity of Geoffrey of Monmouth's twelfth-century reimagining of his story. Physical evidence also survived: Arthur's round table was still visible at Winchester according to Caxton's 1485 edition of Malory's account of the death of Arthur, *Morte d'Arthur*. The city was known to be one of a few possible locations for Camelot. In laying all of these associations and expectations on the shoulders of his hoped-for infant son, the Tudor king was broadcasting a strong message to the political elite and the wider population of England and Wales. The themes of that message were venerable lineage, unity in the aftermath of disruptive and divisive civil war, and the shared prosperity that would follow if the prince was nurtured and supported by everyone.

A major prop of this campaign was drawn from history and legend and Prince Arthur's place in a very long story. During his reign, Henry did recruit writers to explore the place of the Tudor royal family firmly within these familiar tales and to blur the boundaries between myth and history.[4] The themes returned in the pageantry surrounding Arthur's wedding. More generally, however, Henry VII's promotion of his connection to Arthurian and Celtic histories did not continue beyond the first few years of the reign. Before the end of the 1480s, as the king continued to struggle to free himself from rebellion and military threat, reliance upon association with a mythological figure as a means to build a stable foundation for his kingship was too passive, even if the truth of Arthur's story was then more readily believed as fact.

Henry VII's spinning of the Arthurian legend carried a major risk of backfiring had Queen Elizabeth's baby been a princess. The queen becoming pregnant so soon after marriage and her safe delivery of a healthy child would have provided some comfort within the royal family regardless, but what King Henry needed was a healthy male heir. The king was already treading a careful path with those male nobles of Plantagenet royal blood who had been pushed aside by the Tudor triumph at Bosworth. The fitness and legitimacy of the new regime had to be supported and promoted by all means available. Ancestral propaganda, repetitive imagery and manipulation of the precedence that the royal family enjoyed were part of a strategy to build and maintain the credibility of Henry VII's kingship.

King Henry and his mother Margaret Beaufort, in their vision for how his reign would unfold, needed to maintain the momentum that had been gained on the battlefield. They would have known that, before committing fully to uphold his rule, some very senior and experienced nobles were probably waiting to see how Henry made the transition from campaign commander to national leader. Had Henry VII's slender grip on power started to unravel within his first year as king then those whose loyalty was not fully assured would surely have looked towards others who might wear the crown more comfortably and in the manner expected of strong medieval kings. Henry's gamble over the birth of a prince in the carefully controlled circumstances of the Winchester pageantry was a calculated risk, and one that aimed to diminish the prominence of his weak royal lineage and the right to rule that followed from it. The king promoted the message that support for Arthur would represent a return to the unifying strength of earlier British rulers. Arthur's current and future position within the political and social structures in which the ruling elites operated was an essential component of a long-term and carefully constructed programme enforcing the dominance of the new king and his heirs.

Arthur was born at Winchester within the first hour of St Eustace's Day (20 September) 1486. Margaret Beaufort's book of hours indicates that he arrived just after midnight but before 1 a.m.[5] Court astrologers would have seen the association as auspicious. Eustace was the patron saint of hunters and people in adversity – something that his father knew well. Eustace was also counted among those Catholic saints who were quick and effective with their intercession in response to prayers (the fourteen Holy Helpers). With all this in mind, Eustace might have been seen as a protector of the young prince.

There are no records of how the court and the city of Winchester prepared for the royal spectacle. We can be certain from later evidence of state events, however, that imagery, heraldry and magnificence were emphasised to the utmost. The queen's early journey to St Swithin's priory allowed detailed arrangements to be made. A warrant later signed by Elizabeth shows how Sir Robert Coton of the king's household (but appointed as master of horse to the queen), organised a litter and chair with appropriate horses for the journey of the queen to Winchester and her return to London – hopefully with her healthy child. The chair was lent by the abbot of Stratford, along with three specialist chariot men and horses to pull it. Many other people at Winchester also lent horses for the removal of the queen's entourage and the equipment of the royal nursery. They included the abbot of Hyde, the prior of Winchester and the prior of Southwick (near Worthing). There was even a reward for the abbot of Chichester's servant for a gift of another horse to the queen.[6]

Arthur had probably been born a little prematurely, hence the gap of almost exactly eight months between his parents' marriage on 18 January and his birth on 20 September 1486. Also, some of the key people required for the christening ceremony had not yet made the journey to Winchester. The ceremony was delayed for four days until Sunday 24 October to allow the ceremony's preparations to be hurriedly completed within the cathedral. The Earl of Oxford – one of the prince's godfathers – was also still at his house in Lavenham in Suffolk. The rainy September weather would have hindered his long overland journey, but he was evidently not expecting to have to leave his estates abruptly when the king's messengers arrived with news of the birth. The earl had been with Henry on his summer progress but had returned to East Anglia to continue the process of rebuilding his regional authority after years of imprisonment and exile. After a brief pause at Westminster, King Henry had travelled to Winchester to join his wife. Arthur evidently made his first appearance before the final arrangements of the meticulously stage-managed ceremony were completed.

Winchester Cathedral had already hosted a procession and service to celebrate the birth, while all other churches in the city had joined in with the traditional popular celebration and public rejoicing, the singing of *Te Deum Laudamus*, the lighting of fires in the streets and heavy drinking. With the royal court and household already in town, the population would have been greatly increased by hundreds of royal servants and hangers-on making the most of the festive atmosphere. The birth and christening of the first-born prince of a new regime was a major event. It was also the first Tudor state occasion to be celebrated outside London and Westminster.

The cathedral was again to be the setting for the christening. It was decorated with expensive arras tapestries and had an elevated stage built to support the font. The font was trimmed with two types of red woollen cloth – worsted around the font itself, and say covering a raised step on which the bishop conducting the ceremony would stand so that the congregation had a better view. This raised stage was covered with a canopy of estate and nearby was a brazier fire to warm the space on what was described as a day of cold and foul weather. Senior yeomen of the crown guarded the access to the dais, but once John Alcock, Bishop of Worcester had blessed the font it was the king's body servants, including Sir David Owen, Sir Richard Woodville, Thomas Poyntz and Thomas Brandon, who set up a guard of honour. They represented the range of former allegiances that Henry VII's regime had already set about refashioning. The process of involving Yorkists, Lancastrians and the king's own family was repeated in other roles assigned on the day. Arthur's christening and its associated feasting was a major opportunity for the Tudor crown to demonstrate publicly just how far it had succeeded in gathering together under a new regime those former enemies who had opposed each other during Richard III's reign and throughout the bloody years of the Wars of the Roses.

With the travelling court came the Chapel Royal. Its *Liber Regie Capelle* set out the course of the religious rites and ceremonies that involved the royal family. The staff, vestments and pomp of the chapel descended in all splendour on the cathedral priory of Winchester, where the queen's household and Arthur's first nursery had by now been established. It was from here that Sir Richard Croft, Lord Neville of Raby, Lord Strange and the Earl of Essex prepared to lead the first stages of the baptismal procession. They received a psalter, a towel, tapers and a pair of gilt basins with another towel folded across them. All four then moved into the cathedral. The procession was led by one hundred unlit torches carried two-by-two by the henchmen of the king's hall, the esquires, gentlemen and yeomen of the crown. Then came the twenty-six chaplains and clerics of the Chapel Royal, accompanied by various other knights and esquires. The kings of arms, heralds and pursuivants in the splendid tabards came next, followed by two lords of high status (and godfathers to the prince): the Earl of Derby and Lord Maltravers, son of the rather ancient Earl of Arundel.

The important materials for the ceremony, the psalter of gold and the basins, tapers and towels, were brought in by their carriers. A chrisom cloth to be wrapped around Arthur's head after his baptism was pinned to the breast of Anne of York, the ten-year-old sister of the queen and one of her attendant ladies. She was escorted by Sir Richard Guildford as constable and Sir John Turbeville as marshal of the day's ceremonies. The honour of carrying Prince Arthur went to Princess Cecily, another of the queen's sisters (who would marry Margaret Beaufort's close relative John Viscount Welles the following year). Arthur was tightly wrapped in a beautiful mantle of crimson cloth of gold furred with ermine. The gown had a train long enough to be supported by Sir John Cheyne and Cecily, Marchioness of Dorset with some help from her husband and John, Earl of Lincoln (who would soon rebel). A canopy was borne over Arthur at all times by more lords, while various ladies of the court, the wives, daughters and sisters of the men already noted, squeezed in at the rear of the procession as it moved through the cloister of the priory. They entered at the south end of the cathedral to avoid the worst of the rain and wind. A rich cloth of estate had been set up there to offer some protection.

Queen Elizabeth, obviously still recovering from the birth, was waiting inside the church when news arrived that the Earl of Oxford was within a mile of the cathedral. The ceremony had already been delayed for three hours, and it was likely that people were beginning to feel cold and uncomfortable. The king, who was not part of the ceremony, as was customary, therefore gave command for the proceedings to start once it was obvious that Oxford would arrive in time to take his part, wet and bedraggled as he must have been. Prince Arthur's christening was performed by John Alcock, Bishop of Worcester in his full vestments (*in pontificalibus*). In attendance were many other bishops, of whom Piers Courtenay of Exeter and Thomas Langton of Salisbury were specially mentioned. It is easy to picture various named doctors of theology and of law, as well as the king's administrators, straining to get a better view as the baptism ritual began. When things did get underway, Derby and Maltravers were the only godfathers at the font while the dowager queen, Elizabeth Woodville, was godmother. Arthur had just been brought to the font and the torches lit when the Earl of Oxford arrived to take his place with the other godparents. Whether he had time to change or came straight in wearing his muddy riding clothes is not recorded.

Having been baptised, Arthur was taken to the high altar where a candle was lit and offered on behalf of the prince. He was handed to Elizabeth Woodville during the part of the service where Bishop Alcock read from the gospel. The popular hymn *Veni Creator Spiritus* was sung by the choristers of the Chapel Royal and accompanied by the powerful cathedral organs in invocation of the Holy Spirit. It was often performed at elections, coronations and consecrations. Another *Te Deum* was part of this service and during that performance Arthur was taken by the Earl of Oxford in his right arm while the Bishop of Exeter confirmed him and a linen band was bound around the prince's neck by the Bishop of Salisbury. The queen was served by Dorset, Lincoln and Lord Strange while her attendants made use of the water and towels offered by other knights of the royal household. A passage was opened through the congregation for the prince's departure, while the gifts of the four godparents were presented – golden cups, gilt basins, a covered psalter and a golden coffer.

An offering was made at St Swithin's shrine while the vesper hymn *Iste Confessor* was performed. Sweet hippocras wine and spice were taken by the elite nobles, with much other wine available to everyone else. Arthur was returned to the nursery in the queen's chambers by Lady Cecily of York, preceded by the lit torches. The king's minstrels and trumpeters were playing as he entered and was received by the king and queen. Arthur was again blessed in the name of God, Mary and St George. The couple set up two pipes of wine (around 240 gallons or almost 1,100 litres) in the cathedral precinct so that all people in attendance might drink to the health of the prince, his parents and the royal family.

Arthur's premature arrival did take its toll on Elizabeth's body, and the queen took some time to recover. The record of the baptism service suggests that she contracted a fever during the long, cold wait for the Earl of Oxford, which would have heightened her weakness after a problematic delivery. By the time she was ready for the rite of her purification she was suffering from an ague. The church normally required a sixty-day period before the ceremony could be performed, which was also set out in the *Liber Regie Capelle*. Elizabeth was with the rest of the court at Greenwich to celebrate All Hallows on 1 November, so clearly endured a shorter period before her churching. Her time with her first child was painfully brief. Elizabeth herself was so young that she barely had time to come to terms with the delivery of a child and motherhood before she was back on the road to London. By 26 October, the mobile court had reached Farnham. Letters issued from there show a pause of a couple of days before continuing onward – without the prince.

Arthur's Nursery and Household

In another bold move that maintained the message of unity and reconciliation, Prince Arthur's care was given over almost entirely to those who had served Edward IV loyally. There was practicality in this decision; by 1486, King Henry's family had no structure to support the raising of children. The king was an only child and the youngest offspring of his stepfather, the Earl of Derby, were well beyond infancy. The queen's numerous siblings, however, were younger. Elizabeth herself was aged only nineteen in 1485, and as a group the siblings were still connected to the nursery set up by Edward IV and Queen Elizabeth Woodville at Eltham Palace. Princesses Catherine and Bridget were still aged under ten when Arthur was born. English expertise in running a royal nursery was limited to those who had looked after Richard III's son Edward of Middleham or to those who were involved in raising Edward IV's children in the 1470s. Nothing specific is known about how Richard's prince was raised in Yorkshire and it was unlikely that Henry would have sought advice in that direction. More accessible were the attendants who had nurtured Edward V, the queen, and her brothers and sisters in the Yorkist royal nursery.

The household infrastructure set up for Edward V was also more acceptable in terms of security. Many of the gentry associated with Edward IV's children in household or other service had been exiled for the previous three years with Henry in Brittany and France. Others had perished in opposition to Richard III. There was therefore a common interest among survivors of the 1483–85 period in seeing the restoration of Edward IV's line through the children of his heir – Princess, now Queen, Elizabeth. That arrangement could not have been sustained had there been any belief that Edward IV's two sons were still alive at that time, or, alternatively, that Henry VII had been responsible for destroying them sometime after 22 August 1485. Those people had demonstrated loyalty, commitment and sacrifice in support of the Earl of Richmond's cause. But their adherence to Henry was the more tenacious because of his intention to marry Elizabeth of York. That recognition of the value of Yorkist support had to be maintained if the Tudor regime was going to survive the threats to its existence after August 1485. Once the decision had been made to base Arthur's nursery and education on the foundations set down for Edward IV's eldest son, the surviving individuals on whom the king would call were probably self-selecting.

Upon this network of individuals who might have been persuaded to accept Arthur as the heir of York must be added the tight group of Margaret Beaufort's own family and supporters. Arthur embodied everything that she had fought for and imagined was possible during the 1470s and early 1480s. Her son Henry had won the crown – that was remarkable enough – but now he and his wife had been blessed with a healthy male heir. Arthur was the personification of the union of the warring noble factions in the struggle between York and Lancaster. He could serve as a magnet for all those willing to look to the future rather than the past; and that included Richard III's loyal friends, should they wholeheartedly abandon hostility towards Henry VII.

As the hope of the Tudor regime, Arthur was also a target for those who would not bend the knee to King Henry's rule. He was vulnerable personally, especially after the king decided that he must have an upbringing independent of the royal household. His father's opponents further hoped to degrade Arthur's status by focussing on the nobles of Plantagenet blood who had been pushed aside when Henry VII became king. When an impersonation of the living Edward, Earl of Warwick failed in 1487, they turned to the unknown fate of the Princes in the Tower as a more powerful means of undermining the basis of Henry VII's Yorkist allegiance. After Perkin Warbeck was declared to be Edward IV's son Richard, Duke of York, Queen Elizabeth's position as the sole surviving heir of the old Yorkist regime was under threat. Since Henry VII had incorporated so many strands of the ancestry of York and Mortimer into his positioning of Arthur at the centre of the polity, any genealogical challenge to it might lead to further fracturing of the groups that were keeping the Tudors on the throne.

The polity was that combination of politics, lordship, law and administration that held society together. Civil disorder and conflict might return to England if the balance of the polity was disturbed and the crown was unable to repair it through its own agencies, or if the lords were unwilling to make sacrifices to ensure it functioned properly. Arthur's custody and education therefore presented an opportunity for the king to demonstrate magnanimity and trust as he continued to include the Edwardian Yorkists in his range of key appointments. What could be more precious than the care of the Prince of Wales and all that he symbolised? Furthermore, the establishment of Arthur's household could, with the proper safeguards, allow the king to experiment with the network of service and security across the regime. The birth of a son provided another outlet for the testing and training of officials and servants.

The 1487 parliament sat between 9 November and 18 December. One of its most revealing statutes was the King's Household Act. The preamble to the Act sets out why Henry VII was so determined to tighten security around the royal family but also why it was essential that he continue to reach out to those who might otherwise drift into opposition to his kingship. The text suggests that there had already been a conspiracy within the king's household during the first year of the reign. It states that the realm had almost been undone by the quarrelling of the great families who advised the crown. A few of those serving in the household had conspired to kill the king's true subjects and even the prince himself, 'as now of late such a thing was likely to have ensued'.[7] The act made it a felony to plan the death of the king, his counsellors or his main household officers. Any servant suspected of such a crime was to be tried by the Court of the Verge. This institution was the court of the steward of the household, and could proceed as a criminal court at common law. The court's jurisdiction fell fully on those in royal service or in the administrative departments of state. It operated within a twelve-mile radius of the palace or house where the king was based at any given time. Its job was to expose the difficulties and mistakes made in appointing servants who were less than loyal or whose fidelity was turned once they were active within the king's private spaces.

The anti-Tudor conspirators sidestepped the force of the Act in the early 1490s by targeting the allegiance of the principal officers of both the above-stairs ceremonial and below-stairs service divisions of the household. The lord chamberlain (Sir William Stanley) and lord steward (John Radcliffe, Lord Fitzwalter) both succumbed to the claims made by the pretender Warbeck. Together, these men were meant to ensure the quality of the service received by the royal family, enforce the ritual and etiquette of the court and household, and protect the safety of the principal royal figures. These responsibilities made their supposed treason all the more damaging, but their visibility could have protected others of lower rank who were even more determined to kill the king or his children. Their control of access might have permitted a determined lone assassin to get into the personal rooms of the royal palaces, or allow the planting of poison, or even facilitate the kidnapping or disappearance of royal children. Henry VII's determined policy to offer an olive branch to partisans from all sides of the civil war since the 1450s meant that his household had to be a melting pot. That brought inherent risks but, superficially at least, the regime wished to be inclusive of those with expertise who could prove their loyalty. Other measures – many of them suspended financial threats – were developed by the king to make individuals think long and hard before breaking conditions or oaths. When people agreed to these bonds and obligations they often had to propose guarantors or sureties who would share the financial cost and penalty in the event of default or the breaking of conditions. Prince Arthur's household is not explicitly mentioned in the Act, but the same principles of protection applied.

After 1473, the provisions made for the conduct of Edward V's household had emphasised aspects of security and moral safety.[8] The gates were shut after dusk. Dishonest people were shut out and excluded from the prince's vicinity. Servants who offended or transgressed were to be placed in the stocks. The prince's governor and/or chamberlain were to control who reached the king's presence or sat with him at meal times. While he was eating he was to hear noble stories. The conversation of those who shared his table had to explore the themes of virtue and honour and the deeds of worship but stay clear of anything that could move him towards vice. Anthony, Earl Rivers, who wore a hair shirt under his fine silk and linen, was just the kind of man to enforce this type of code as his nephew developed. Arthur had no such self-sacrificing guardian, and survived all the better for it. Arthur's household would have followed similar regulations at Farnham and at Ludlow. With Arthur's personal authority as Prince of Wales, Duke of Cornwall and Earl of Chester coming to require an administrative infrastructure, an enormous range of patronage became available to the gentry class right along the border. King Henry could use the seniority of the prince's council in counties from Gloucestershire to Cheshire and Cornwall to stimulate, rebalance, manipulate and dominate the relations between the crown, as embodied by Arthur, and the manorial and parish communities that made local society tick.

By the time he was christened, the first phase of Arthur's care was established. The nursery was to have a lady governor, supported by four female servants known as chamberers or rockers. A chamberlain would be appointed to oversee all the other officials and to swear and hold them to their oaths of loyalty and service. The more menial and physical tasks were undertaken by yeomen and grooms. The relatively small number of officers meant that many of the male servants would have undertaken multiple roles. They would have been found in the chamber and in the hall, especially at meal times. Oher men were appointed to specific posts. A sewer organised meals, arranged precedence and seating and oversaw the serving and tasting of food. A panter was put in charge of bread and food supplies. Of greatest importance was the safeguarding of Arthur's wet nurse. What she ate and drank was key to the health and growth of the baby prince. Her diet and portions were carefully monitored. She would even be watched by a physician as she ate, to ensure that no sudden changes came over her or the boy in her care.

The manager of the Yorkist nursery was Elizabeth Darcy. She had overseen the early upbringing of Queen Elizabeth and all of her royal siblings at Eltham. Darcy was reappointed in 1486 to head a team of nurses and daily attendants that went on to look after the first years of life of all of Henry VII and Elizabeth's children. Darcy brought in her own specialist team – a group of women very familiar to Queen Elizabeth. Arthur's cradle rockers were Agnes Butler, Evelyn Hobbes and Alice Bywymble. The prince's wet nurse was Elizabeth Gibbs. Warrants survive that show regular payment of their generous wages at Michaelmas and Easter. Henry was careful not to let the payments go into arrears, since disgruntled body servants of the royal heir were more likely to fall under other influences if they had to chase payment of the salaries due to them. Henry even wrote from Coventry the week before the Battle of Stoke was fought in June 1487 to ensure that £46 was paid in cash to Darcy and her team. At a time of invasion and perilous threat to the future of the regime, this was a prudent and practical recognition that the duties of these women were as important to the king as the service of others on the battlefield.

There is very little information on how Arthur's chambers were furnished and in what type of surroundings his early years were spent. His first bed was probably a daily cradle of estate – an elaborate infant bed. It was to have five pillars or stolpes, with the king's arms on the middle one and the arms of other members of the royal family elsewhere. There was also a great cradle of estate, which was over five feet in length. It was covered in crimson cloth of gold and had four great pommels of silver gilt at each corner. Various furnishings, sheets, pillows, bolsters and supports were also recorded – all of the finest cloth and many trimmed with ermine or other furs. As was customary, Arthur was swaddled from an early age. Swaddling bands with five gilt buckles are mentioned as part of the furnishing of his nursery. He would have been wrapped tightly in strips of linen cloth for the first nine months of life. Although this practice would be criticised in later centuries for restricting and even deforming infants if applied too tightly, swaddling was considered to be essential to ensure that the child's limbs grew straight.

At a higher level, those who would have a more distant but no less important influence on how the prince developed and grew also shared a strong connection to Edward IV. Peter Courtenay, Bishop of Exeter, is a prime example. He was a member of the Edwardian inner circle who had been exiled with the Earl of

Richmond. He recovered his authority once Henry won the crown. Courtenay had the important role of keeper of the privy seal and was made Bishop of Winchester in January 1487, following the death of William Waynflete on 11 August 1486. His translation to the wealthiest bishopric in England looks like the king's reward for Courtenay's efforts on behalf of Henry before he became king, but also bore relevance to Henry's plans for Prince Arthur. The fact that Courtenay apparently promised, before he took up his responsibilities at Winchester, to surrender the bishop's palace at Farnham so that it could serve as the nursery for the new prince does suggest that some negotiation had already taken place. Waynflete was aged eighty-six and had largely withdrawn from public life during the final years of Edward IV's reign. His death as the court was preparing to travel to Winchester for Arthur's birth gave the king an opportunity to set in motion the changes that would shape the prince's upbringing. Courtenay seems to have taken little persuading that the re-purposing of Farnham palace was not such a difficult adjustment to make in exchange for a major episcopal promotion.

Farnham Palace was first built in the early twelfth century. It had been extensively redeveloped and made very comfortable by Bishop Waynflete. Only a decade before Arthur's birth a new entry tower had been finished. Constructed of highly fashionable red brick, it also housed new living quarters, offices and service rooms and was where Arthur's chambers were sited. Most of the other chambers, a range of guest rooms and the bishop's private quarters and chapel were completed in the mid-fourteenth century. Arthur therefore enjoyed a building that had been maintained and extended by the resources of the wealthiest bishopric in England and by a succession of individual bishops known to be interested in fashionable building projects. Repairs and alterations continued during Arthur's residency. The pipe rolls of the Bishop of Winchester (recording his regular income from the manors of the diocese) indicate carpentry works over several days in the dungeon, chamber and elsewhere in advance of the visit by the king and queen in January 1487.[9]

The 2,000 inhabitants of Farnham also felt that the siting of the royal nursery in their town was a privilege worth commemorating. Around Christmas 1486, they helped Lord Maltravers and the constables of the town to persuade the king to grant a licence for the founding of a chantry chapel in the church of St Andrew. In February 1486, Maltravers, who succeeded to the earldom of Arundel in 1488, also got the king to grant a mortmain licence so that land worth a valuable twelve marks per year could be found to pay for the chaplain. He was to pray for the lives of the king and queen, Prince Arthur and the king's mother, and for their souls after death. Other chantries were licensed to Archbishop Thomas Rotherham in February 1489 to establish a chantry in York Minster to pray for the king and queen, Arthur, the king's mother and her parents John, Duke of Somerset and Margaret his wife. In a cathedral and city with strong connections to Richard III this was part of a determined attempt to impose the new regime in a region that had already caused Henry VII some problems and would do so again in the summer of that year. Arthur's position as heir was to be promoted as part of the package of public measures intended to emphasise the credentials of the regime and the strength and resilience of the new royal family.[10]

In the first parliament of the reign that met from 7 November 1485, the Lords and Commons had voted £14,000 to the king for the annual expenses of his household. On 1 February 1487 the king ordered that 1,000 marks of this sum (£666 13s 4d) should be assigned for the expenses of Prince Arthur's household. This was a staggering sum for an infant's upbringing. It shows the extent of Henry VII's investment in Arthur's future at the very start of his life. £500 of it was to come from the profits of the

Duke of Buckingham's lands in east Yorkshire and the remainder from his estates in Staffordshire. The duke was under age and was a ward of the king's mother Margaret, Countess of Richmond and Derby. Even as an infant, Arthur's income was equivalent to that of a middle-ranking lord, but without the responsibilities of land management, a wide network of followers and crown representation. Without knowing it, the nine-year-old duke was making a strong commitment to the future of the Tudor crown. Buckingham might have harboured some resentment at this. After the prince's death, he refused to take into his service two of Arthur's gentry servants, even though they were recommended by the president of the prince's council, William Smith, Bishop of Lincoln.

After that first period of infancy we know that the prince had a feather bed with a bolster of down. One mattress was stuffed with wool and was two yards long, with four short pillows and various long sheets, one pair of cloth of scarlet furred with ermine and embroidered. The coverture of Arthur's bed was made of fine lawn (linen) with sperners (supporters) of crimson satin embroidered with the queen's arms and other heraldic badges. By the time he was three years old, Arthur's wardrobe had become more diverse. The king's household officers were ordering and delivering robes, tunics and other ornaments to Farnham. Peter Curteys was the keeper of the king's Great Wardrobe. His account for the period 1486–89 contains some evidence of provision for the prince. Arthur's nurses received cloth from which to make new gowns for themselves and the prince as he grew up.[11] The quality was again of the very best – white velvet, damask (multi-coloured silk), satin, sarcenet (fine soft silk), fustian (a coarser flax cloth), fur of ermine, black bogi (budge, or dark lambskin), with sheets of Holland cloth (fine plain woven linen), brushes, crochettes, tapettes (figured cloth used as a hanging), and iron hammers to nail them up in the prince's chamber.[12]

Two of Arthur's male servants were named in this grant: William Wangham and John Hoo. They had nine other companions who together seem to have formed the service part of the prince's household. Their livery uniform was a cloth of russet – the same as that of the yeomen of the crown and garcons of the king's chamber. They probably were on loan from the king's personal retinue, since that was a way that he could be assured of their loyalty and devotion to Prince Arthur. Without further evidence, however, it is difficult to say if otherwise obscure servants like William and John were kept on from the household of the Bishop of Winchester, or if they were vetted and selected from elsewhere in Henry VII's service for the specialist skills they could offer to the prince. Around this time, the identities of some of Arthur's other servants and the posts they occupied begin to emerge from the records. Importantly, the prince's wet nurse, Katherine Gibbs, was paid off in April 1490 with a generous annuity of £20 to come directly from the first monies received at the start of the exchequer year – a notable recognition of how Arthur had been safeguarded in his first thirty months of life. By the time the arrangement of this payment had made its way through the convoluted exchequer system it is likely that Arthur's household had taken on a different appearance. This was the period of transition from nursery to education and service.

In March 1488, Thomas Poyntz, esquire for the king's body, was rewarded with 40 marks per year partly for services to the prince. Poyntz later received a gift of French books of hours from Arthur, suggesting that the relationships forged in that early stage of his life were lasting and would have continued had Arthur become king.[13] These services were likely to have been related to the tightening of security around Arthur in response to the Household Act passed by Parliament before 18 December the previous year. Poyntz's specific role is not recorded but he is the first of the king's more senior officers to be personally attached to the prince. Henry VII's concern for his son's health is apparent from another grant, made with the king's 'cordial affection' a few months after Poyntz received his reward. Arthur's doctor was Stephen Bereworth and the medical attention he had already given to Arthur was enough to earn him £40 each year for the rest of his life. By May 1488, when this grant was made, Arthur would have been a toddler, fully weaned and becoming exposed to the childhood ailments, bumps and bruises that all youngsters experience. He was still too young to have much licence to explore the rooms and grounds of Farnham Palace, and although it has been changed and developed since his brief period of residency there it is still possible to imagine the whole imposing building and the staff in it that became fully devoted to protecting and nurturing the sole heir of the crown. At least one of those newly appointed servants was unable to move from the king's household to that of the prince because of problems with paperwork. In December 1488 Robert Knollys, one of the king's henchmen, was instructed to join Arthur's household with a payment of 100s. He could not be admitted to the name roll of servants because the king had placed his sign manual at the head and foot of the roll and left no space for additions. The check-roll might have been small enough to fit on a single sheet at this stage of Arthur's life (it has not survived), but it would soon expand in parallel to the prince's role.

Once Arthur was considered to have grown and matured sufficiently to cope with the endurance test of the ceremonies of his knighthood and creation as Prince of Wales at the end of November 1489, his household also developed a more formal structure in preparation for this changing role. The age of six or seven seems to have been one at which many royal children moved out of the nursery and into a junior version of the royal household.[14] In Prince Arthur's case, this seems to have happened when he was about three years old. During the late summer of

1489 the impending change in Arthur's status required a step-change in his education and also in the way that he was served and guarded.

John Whytyng was described as Arthur's sewer in grants of annuities in November 1489 and January 1490. The naming of Whytyng in a specific appointment indicates that an element of structure and more formal ritual was entering his household. An important first stage in his development was how the prince began to learn his social role. Mastering the first formal steps of the art of household ritual, etiquette and the hierarchy of social status would lead to a smoother transition into the refined world of court politics and diplomacy. In January 1490 there is first mention of Richard Howell as marshal of the prince's household. Howell's role was to ensure Arthur's security and to monitor the discipline of the other men and women who served him at Farnham. The greater prominence given to household policing might also indicate that the king's heir was developing a less closeted role within his small community. Once his wet nurse and rockers were no longer required physically, the services provided for Arthur had to begin to mirror that of any other senior noble. Within a few weeks of Howell's appointment, King Henry's servant Thomas Fissher was awarded an annuity of 40 marks on 20 April 1490 as yeoman of the cellar to the prince. His appearance points to a greater sophistication in the way that the prince's meals were prepared and served. He was soon followed by John Almor, appointed to Arthur's household on 29 October 1490. Almor was a veteran of the king's hall, one of the main military resources of the royal household. He became Arthur's first sergeant-at-arms; a post that would have incorporated the role of a personal bodyguard with broader responsibility for the security of the household such as the vetting of visitors and servants, guarding doors and access, and setting the watch. Despite these valuable details, a full picture of Arthur's household remains elusive and we may only speculate about its full structure and functions.

Eleven yeomen and grooms of the chamber were recorded in Arthur's service when the king paid their fees at the end of 1491. A decade later four of them were still serving in valuable posts across the estates controlled by the prince. Some men would have died in service, while others moved between the king's household and that of his son. More were able to make the transition from general service to a child-prince to specific roles for a royal heir on the cusp of being able to rule in his own right. These four remaining men took roles as Arthur's foresters, bailiffs, receivers and stewards across the estates of the duchy of Cornwall and earldom of Chester and still held them at the end of the 1490s.[15] Retaining servants in this way was the mark of a good lord. It allowed connections to develop and facilitated the projection of Arthur's influence in areas that he could not regularly visit but in which his presence, even through a deputy, was key to good government. For much of his life, patronage in this regard would have been controlled by his advisors, under the scrutiny of men like the controller of his household, Sir Henry Vernon, and the President of the Council of the Marches, Bishop William Smith. Any continuity in their power to act as the prince's mentors, advisors or guardians stemmed entirely from King Henry's assessment of their effectiveness in mediating and delivering his requirements for Arthur's development.

It is also important to remember that Prince Arthur's estates were spread throughout the country. He was Duke of Cornwall from birth and inherited the *antiqua maneria* of the duchy in Cornwall, as well as estates outside the county and property that had come into the duke's hands since 1337. Arthur owned the honours of Berkhamsted and Wallingford as well as valuable manors like Castle Rising in Norfolk, Kennington in Surrey and Meere in Wiltshire. While the Marcher lands formed a more compact body of estates that could be managed on Arthur's behalf from Ludlow by the Council of the Marches or the steward of the earldom of March, the more scattered possessions of the duchy of Cornwall and earldom of Chester required a different administrative structure. The type of stewards and other officers noted above were coordinated through the prince's and the king's councils. Arthur's council had a clerk based within the Crown's bureaucracy at Westminster. The poor survival of documents makes it very difficult to see how the system was managed in detail, but there was clearly a sophisticated level of coordination between the officers working alongside Arthur in person and a broader administration of his estates that was based in London to take advantage of the communication networks of the king. Arthur's income from land put him in the first rank of wealthy nobles. Managing such a large portfolio of lands and interests, claims and responsibilities was at the core of Arthur's training. Exposure to the practical skills of running estates and understanding the documents and processes that recorded governance in action also obliged the prince to begin to manage the interaction of the people and personalities that made this administration work effectively. His resources and the range of his estates created a huge amount of patronage. Learning how to manage servants and officials was another vital lesson the prince had to master if he was to be a skilled king. The continuance in his service of many officers hints that Arthur's leadership, or at least his interaction with the experienced men that ran his estates, did inspire loyalty and diligence. While the records of his Welsh and Marcher estates appear to be the more important because he spent most of his life living on or near them, his income was drawn from a nationwide collection of lands. When Arthur was being trained in his role as prince and then king it was within this structure of lordship, bureaucracy and the balancing of interests and influences that he learned.

Medieval royal children were not brought up directly by their parents; this was the role of the household infrastructure. The evidence above shows that King Henry continued to take a close personal interest in how his son's life was unfolding. He privately vetted and monitored those admitted to the service of Arthur while at the same time insisting that the prince was independent. There was an inherent risk in handing Arthur's care over to others. Henry VII would have tried to ensure that there were no deficiencies in his son's protection. Yet no matter how well defended he was and how trusted his servants were, an entirely separated household put Arthur outside the direct care of his family and beyond the king's ability to react quickly to any incidents or concerns. That was where the growing prince might have found it difficult to isolate the benefits of an independent existence from the rejection he might have felt at being distant from the centre of his family. Arthur was separated from his mother and father within the first six weeks of his life. This detachment was not a temporary measure for a period of wet nursing, either. Before he could even recognise his parents, it had been decided that Arthur would be brought up at a distance from his relatives. Up until his death at the age of fifteen years and seven months, he would see the rest of his family on a handful of occasions. Even if we allow for visits unknown because of the loss of essential documents, the physical distance that grew between Arthur's household and the king's court made it very difficult, if not impossible, for informal contact to occur regularly. The king's itinerary throws some light on when the court might have had an opportunity be near the Prince of Wales, or at least have been close enough to his residence for a meeting to have been arranged; those times are few and far between.

Of course, Prince Arthur was far too valuable to have been abandoned in north Hampshire. The king was at Farnham in January 1487 and at Winchester in April 1488 but not apparently in between. He was next at Farnham in mid-late March 1489 and finally during Arthur's residency there, in August 1490. Those dates relate to periods when the government was issuing letters and warrants as it travelled around the country. Historians usually use this evidence as proof that the monarch was in a particular place because of the tight control placed on the use of the privy or signet seals to authenticate the issuing of instructions and commands. Arthur was moved from Farnham to Ludlow at some point in the early spring of 1493. Planning for this transfer probably started in earnest after Henry had returned to his London palaces from his military campaign in France around 20 December 1492.[16] So it appears that the king formally travelled to visit his heir at Farnham only four times. Yet the focus of the crown's household records on service to the king's makes it is far harder to track the movements of other members of the royal family. Private household records from other Tudor nobles who might have visited Arthur are lost or otherwise undiscovered. The king's mother and the queen had more flexible but less visible opportunities to travel from London, Sheen or Woking. Woking Palace was Margaret Beaufort's principal residence outside of London. The distance to Farnham was only about nine miles and could have been undertaken as a return journey in one day, even if Lady Margaret travelled by carriage or litter. Nor is it unlikely that Arthur set out on occasion with his entourage of nurses and protectors to visit his parents at one of their palaces around London or elsewhere in the Thames valley. He was at Sheen in the days before he was made a knight and Prince of Wales in October 1489. The possibility of a more mobile household becomes apparent after male servants with specific roles were named in the financial documents of the king's household around that time. Before then, it is likely that Arthur had much more contact with his close relatives and godparents than the surviving records suggest. As the heir to an insecure regime it is inconceivable that

Arthur would have been secluded and left to develop without the constant interest and involvement of the rest of the royal family.

Part of Arthur's destiny as the regime's heir was to have little regular contact with his family. A fact like this is hard for modern parents to comprehend, and it would have been unusual if the prince did not question it at some point, too. His vital role as the future of the crown was obvious in the propagandist badges and heraldry that dominated the public spaces and private buildings of Tudor England. Strong imagery, united family and clear right to the crown were the messages emphasised visually and repeatedly. The initiatives that reshaped courtly service, hierarchy and rank in the court and household (with the Beaufort royals at the top) also placed Arthur in an elevated part of the elite group of society. He was one of the regime's insiders but he was not a presence within the royal family at court. His absence from the centre of the king's power made it more likely that his status would not always be at the front of people's minds. This was part of Arthur's sacrifice. To inherit the crown on the terms Henry VII required, Arthur had to accept that he would build his skills in distant orbit from the royal household. There would be links between personnel and communication by letter to and from Ludlow would have been more regular than with anywhere else in the country. That was the only way that the prince could learn without distraction. Arthur was to be taught alone as he must eventually come to rule alone. There was to be no easy way to begin this process once the child was considered old enough to commence structured learning. The difference was enormous between the training of a boy who would be king and the development of a royal duke, like Arthur's brother Henry, who would be expected to offer a loyal supporting role when King Arthur acceded to the throne.

2

RAISING A PRINCE OF WALES

Knight of the Bath and Prince of Wales

Late medieval power grew from titles and land. Arthur needed both if he was to learn how to rule as the nation expected. The first event in which he had a part that had to be learned and rehearsed was the ceremony that made him a knight and raised him to the top of the peerage as Prince of Wales. The ceremony came after some uncomfortable years for Henry VII's regime. Giving Arthur the dignity of a senior nobleman reflected the growing confidence of the Tudor king as rebellions were defeated and enemies flushed out.

Arthur was created a knight and Prince of Wales in a ceremony on 29 November 1489. At the same event he was also made a knight of the Bath and Earl of Chester. The first years of life were also the riskiest, so surviving beyond his third year was a landmark for Prince Arthur. The bestowing of these titles marked the end of Arthur's infancy and the start of a more structured education for him. From this time, he also began to enjoy an identifiable household once the king's body servants started to give attendance upon the prince alongside his female servants at Farnham. We know the stages of the ceremonies in which these titles were conferred since the rituals were recorded in several copies of precedent books for royal service at court and in heralds' written accounts of major state occasions.

On 26 November, Arthur travelled downriver from Sheen Palace to Westminster. He was rowed in the king's barge. Once he reached Mortlake the barges of nobles and bishops began to join the royal flotilla. Several adults who would have been familiar to the prince seem to have made a ceremonial, if quite daring, jump into the prince's boat from their own mid-stream. Among those on the river that day were Arthur's godfathers, the earls of Derby, Arundel and Oxford, as were the bishops who had supported him at his christening. The mayor of London and representatives of the City companies joined in at Chelsea. By the time the growing fleet of boats and barges reached Lambeth they were met by the Spanish ambassadors and merchants, who fired a great many ships' guns – something that was likely to have delighted or terrified a three-year-old boy.

The river procession landed at the King's Bridge by Westminster Palace. Arthur disembarked towards the Great Hall, passing along ordered ranks of the members of the London livery companies. He was taken through the Court of King's Bench in Westminster Hall to the king's presence in the Brick Tower. There he rested and was allowed to see his mother, who was heavily pregnant with Arthur's first sibling. This encounter might have been only the third or fourth officially recorded meeting between them since Arthur's christening. He would have been prepared for the ceremonies that were about to take place. A few days later, on 29 November, Arthur helped to serve the king's dinner for the first time in his life. Even for such a young boy, the events of these few days must have been memorable. Arthur held King

Henry's towel while other sons and heirs of nobles who were to be created knights of the Bath alongside Arthur carried the water, basin and assay, and brought prepared dishes of carved meat to the king's table. Once the king had eaten, the chamberlain, Sir William Stanley, assigned the esquires Thomas Brandon and Thomas Brereton to wait on Prince Arthur while he took his own dinner. This was a busy and precarious time for the king and his family. Queen Elizabeth was imminently due to be delivered of her second child. Given the perils of childbirth in the late fifteenth century, the king's involvement in the ceremony of the bath was both a distraction and a calculated decision to enhance Arthur's status in full view of the court at what was a crucial moment for the stability of the regime. If the queen or the baby should die, then the prospects for the longevity of the Tudor regime would take a major backward step. Keeping Arthur close at this time of danger would have made sense. His presence might also have been a comfort to his mother as she was about to give birth. If the worst were to occur, Arthur would become the embodiment of the future of the royal family, and would be far more vulnerable to plotters and conspirators if a widowed Henry VII had to begin the search for a second wife.

In the evening, the prince's bath was prepared in the king's closet within the palace. Arthur's fellow candidates from the peerage – the young Earl of Northumberland, the new Lord Maltravers and Lord Grey of Ruthin – had their baths prepared in the entrance between the parliament chamber and St Peter's chapel. The other sixteen prospective knights were to bathe in the parliament chamber itself. King Henry personally made a speech to his new knights, extolling the virtues of the order of knighthood and, no doubt, expressing his high expectations from those who were about to have their status elevated in his direct service. At that same time, Queen Elizabeth had probably gone into labour. The members of the Chapel Royal were reading the psalms and praying for her safe delivery. At about 9 p.m. Princess Margaret was born. She was christened the following day, 30 November, on the same day that Arthur was knighted and made Prince of Wales.

In the morning, after the prince attended Mass, he and his companions were escorted through St Stephen's chapel to the vicar's lodging where his horse was waiting for him. The other knights met their rides at the foot of the Star Chamber stairs. They then rode the short distance to Westminster Hall with the prince at the head of the riders. They all dismounted at the King's Bench and walked into the White Hall where they waited for the king. Arthur was led by one of his godfathers, the Earl of Arundel, while the Earl of Essex, who had carried Arthur's sword and golden spurs, passed them to the Earl of Oxford who awaited the king's instruction. Arundel and Oxford then tied the prince's right and left spur, while the king girded the sword on his son. He was then dubbed a knight, with all his companions being knighted in the same way in their turn only with different lords fastening the spurs for each candidate. King Henry then appointed Thomas Writhe or Wriothesley as Wallingford pursuivant to the prince's service (Wallingford being a castle of the duchy of Cornwall, then in Berkshire). This was only the first stage of Prince Arthur's eventful day.

Arthur returned his new trappings of knighthood and was changed in the king's closet into robes of estate for his creation as Prince of Wales. The parliament chamber had been cleared of its baths, and Arthur was escorted there by the Marquis of Berkeley. The king was again awaiting him. A chair with rich cushions was prepared for Arthur under a canopy of estate. Arundel and Derby were called upon to carry the cape, coronet, sceptre and ring. The Earl of Shrewsbury bore a sword of estate pommel upwards. All were in their parliament robes. By the time Henry, Duke of York was made Prince of Wales after Arthur's death, the protocol for the ceremony had been altered with regard to the status of those supporting the prince. Two dukes were to escort him as he entered the king's presence with his sword born before him. In 1489 only Jasper Tudor, Duke of Bedford and John de la Pole, Duke of Suffolk were adult holders of this rank, Edward Stafford, 3rd Duke of Buckingham was a minor aged eleven, but he was old enough to have played a part in the ceremonies of 29–30 November, especially as he was a ward of the king's mother Margaret Beaufort, Countess of Richmond and Derby. Margaret was the architect of much of the ceremonial and service changes designed to elevate the status of the king's family and connect them to England's established aristocratic elite. Having the old nobility participate in these rituals was a very public display of their service to the Tudor crown.

The prince's cap with a golden circlet around it was carried by Derby and presented before the king on the prince's right side, while his longsword, ring and a gold sceptre or rod were carried by Arundel on the left. At that point the letters patent were read, formally granting the prince his titles as a public proclamation of his right and of the king's free gift of all associated lands and honours. Arthur was Duke of Cornwall at birth and so his father girded his sword around his neck on the left side. King Henry then tied his cape and set his coronet on his head and placed a ring on the third finger of his left hand. The sceptre or rod of gold was held in his right hand.

The accounts are specific about the symbolism of the items used in the ceremony. Arthur was presented with his sword first because as first-born son of the monarch he was automatically a duke without creation and therefore had already assumed the responsibilities of that rank. The coronet was made from gold because that was the noblest of metals and in comparison to its purity any king or prince should be steadfast in doing justice to all his subjects. The ring emphasised that the prince was bound and contracted to offer true justice and equity to all subjects and was to show wise consideration to all parties at law. The golden rod represented the victories that the prince was to enjoy in future, and symbolised how he would deprive and put down his enemies and rebels.

After the patent was read, King Henry departed the ceremony and left Arthur to eat under the canopy of estate. Since this was an unusual but joyous day, all the newly-made knights joined Arthur and several earls and other lords at table. The herald's account specifically mentions that Arthur personally invited them to start to eat their meat; his first recorded solo public ceremonial pronouncement. The king's minstrels played during the courses and when they had finished, the officers of arms received a payment of £20 from the prince by the hands of Sir Thomas Lovell, treasurer of the king's chamber, for their role in accompanying the day's ceremonies. Arthur's largesse was cried by Garter King of Arms, who also proclaimed his style and titles. The new knights also had their largesse cried. The ceremony was conducted at the king's pleasure and maintained his superior dignity and status over all others involved. The newly created Sir William Uvedale was duly elected to thank the king for the dinner and the ceremony. Within a few years he would be one of the most important people in Arthur's life as controller of his household at Ludlow. His promotion shows the importance of these state occasions to the crown. It was rare to have a large body of the nation's most eligible young men in one place, competing for the king's attention as they demonstrated their loyalty by accepting the responsibilities of knighthood. The list of knights created included a number, such as Lord Grey of Ruthin, John St John and Lord Maltravers, who would retain an association with Prince Arthur.[1] In that respect, the bond created by knighthood at this ceremony might be considered as the first stage in building the national network that would serve Arthur as king after Henry VII's death.

Almost at the same time, Princess Margaret was christened in a ceremony that mirrored that of Prince Arthur three years earlier. Some of the senior earls of long ancestry were called upon to maintain the dignity of the service. Shrewsbury, Arundel and Essex played their part in a ceremony dominated by the women of the court, with Margaret Beaufort again pulling the strings in collaboration with the officers of arms. Consistency in the stages of these set-piece occasions was important. They emphasised that the royal family was indeed royal, that they commanded respect and service, and that they had a rightful place in the lineage of English kings. The chamberlain and ushers of the household had crucial roles in ensuring the smooth running of the investiture. The lesser servants were reminded that they would be watched by the entire court and were to look to the chamberlain for their lead.

After four years on the throne, the imminent birth of a second child was another moment of potential joy but real trepidation for the royal family. Joy at the prospect of another prince or princess was tempered by the dangers inherent in childbirth. Henry VII had not yet eradicated his personal vulnerability nor removed his reliance upon loyalists to the queen and her ancestry. Were Elizabeth to die in childbirth, then the king's efforts to strengthen his grip on power would be driven into reverse. Calculation of that risk was surely behind the decision to create Arthur as Prince of Wales just as the queen was coming to term. The youth of the new Prince of Wales would count for little if the worst happened and rebellion erupted after the queen's death; but it might have made some influential men think twice before switching allegiance, or delayed the inevitable desertions. That might have created the strengthened the slender margins by which the king could cling to power. The possibility of a crisis brought the royal family and its allies together at Westminster. The regime held its collective breath in preparation for the birth. When the queen was safely delivered of a princess the relief must have been tangible. Arthur's preparation for kingship could continue according to King Henry's timetable.

Arthur's Education

We know that Arthur could ride from a very early age. He publicly rode to the steps of Westminster Hall on the day of his investiture as Prince of Wales at the end of November 1489. The ability to handle a horse was such a fundamental skill for medieval noblemen that it almost goes without saying that the prince would have been taught to ride almost at the same rate that he learned to walk. It was probably Sir Robert Coton, the queen's master of horse, who trained him at Farnham. Arthur would have been used to a military presence around his household. The years before 1490 were turbulent for Henry VII; with several uprisings, conspiracies and the Irish invasion of June 1487 dominating his attention. As far as is known, Arthur remained at Farnham throughout this period; but steps would have been taken to deepen the military protection around the regime's only heir. As soon as it was feasible, Arthur was probably introduced to the reality of the risks that his father faced. A visible demonstration of force through the loaning of yeomen from the king's household, for example, was an unavoidable part of his young life. Arthur was therefore no stranger to the military and chivalric side of court culture. He seems to have enjoyed the traditional entertainments of the court since tournaments, jousts and fighting at the barriers were part of the celebrations for his wedding

The assignment of his own herald, Wallingford, in 1489 also added a different dimension to his classroom education. All boys destined to be king had an almost overwhelming range of information to absorb and skills to master. An understanding of the genealogies of leading families was essential, as was knowledge of the imagery and badges that were used by the aristocracy, both physically and in literature and performance. The chapter meetings of the Order of the Garter, in which he was installed in 1489, became a living embodiment of heraldic and genealogical knowledge. Arthur might have been involved in a version of the St George's day ceremony for the chapter of the order when he arrived in the Marches in April 1493 – since he was accompanied by several members – although it was not until 1500 that he was fully involved in the Garter ceremonies at Windsor.

A grammar master had been appointed for Edward V when he reached the age of six. He also had a male governor, his uncle Anthony, Earl Rivers, from the age of three. Henry VII installed no governor of noble rank for Arthur, but he did begin to engage with formal schooling between the ages of four and five. John Rede, a former headmaster of Winchester School and 'the best and most learned of preceptors', became his tutor. There is also other evidence that Arthur had a previous tutor charged with even more rudimentary stages of teaching at Farnham, but his name is not recorded. Winchester and Oxford University provided all of Arthur's tutors. Through his Oxford connections, Rede knew churchmen serving Henry VII and his mother like William Smith, William Warham and John Alcock. Alcock had been the leader of the Council of the Marches for the future Edward V and might have been involved in getting Smith appointed to that post under Henry VII. Warham and Smith had both been involved during the 1490s in negotiations with the Spanish for Arthur's marriage treaty and so already knew much of the importance attached to the alliance by King Henry.

By the mid-1490s, after Arthur had moved to Ludlow, the circle of educators and principal advisors around him begins to look more selective, compact and thoroughly aligned with the individuals trusted by the king in building his administration.

Not surprisingly, the men who now began to be associated with Prince Arthur were those same ones who acquired pivotal roles in shaping the future direction of the regime. Whether their route to the king's confidence was through association with Margaret Beaufort, long-term acquaintance with King Henry himself or via Yorkist allegiance to Queen Elizabeth and her heirs, Arthur's inheritance represented the king's hope to blend past loyalties behind a new figurehead who was personally unconnected to the loyalties displayed during the Wars of the Roses. Arthur was a unifying hope for future stability and security.

It is probable that John Rede also continued to be involved in refining Arthur's grammar, since he retained some role in the royal household until 1500. However close his involvement, his contribution during the 1490s came far behind that of Prince Arthur's most influential tutor, Bernard André. Under Rede, Arthur seems to have been a good student who picked up the basics of grammar very quickly.[2] When Bernard André formally took over teaching responsibilities in 1496 he acquired a ten-year-old scholar already capable in Latin and French. It is likely that Arthur received some French language training from Giles Duwes around 1500. By his own recollection in the 1530s, Duwes had served all of Henry VII's children; first as a teacher of the lute and music more generally, and then as a French tutor. His responsibility for formal language training might have arisen only after Bernard André stepped back once Prince Arthur began to prepare for married life in 1500.

The blind scholar André had been appointed to the king's service from Oxford University in November 1486. He came with a reputation as a fine orator and poet; André was initially the author of speeches for many state occasions, but when Arthur's studies had progressed sufficiently, André was charged with bringing his educational abilities to bear on completing the prince's scholarly learning. Arthur's existing levels of knowledge and expertise were to be extended with the introduction of a more rigorous syllabus of classical Latin texts within a more humanistic learning structure. Despite its antiquity, this pre-Christian Latin writing was newly fashionable. Many of the texts and writers that Arthur absorbed had been newly rediscovered within Henry VII's lifetime. Renaissance Europe was experiencing an obsessive revival of interest in the works of history and oratory that underpinned the success of the Roman Republic and Empire. Arthur was therefore receiving the most modern and fashionable education available. Its comprehensiveness was something that his brother Henry eventually benefited from too, and which his near-contemporary François I of France experienced also.

Specialists in Renaissance scholarship see in the publicity given to the works that Bernard André taught to Prince Arthur as a self-conscious demonstration of his knowledge of the latest Italian trends in the education of princes. The recent rediscovery of many of these works and their rapid employment within the royal circle by André is a strong indication of his efforts to connect England to networks of scholars in Italy and France. That was something which the king evidently approved of. These books were also exemplars. Arthur would have been invited to draw on the content of these classical works and reflect on how their content might inform discussions or oratory in council, diplomacy, parliament or court. There is little evidence to demonstrate how Arthur used this training in his daily life as Prince of Wales. We might infer from his surviving letters or from the legal interventions he made in person that he was able to apply the knowledge of his education with some success.

André taught Arthur for four years, and moved into the prince's household at Ludlow Castle and Tickenhill Place in order to focus and concentrate the prince's education. He commented in his *Vita Henrici Septimi*, written after Arthur's death, that the prince was a very literate and noble person who by the age of sixteen had memorised or could recite several of the great works of Roman scholarship and Roman reinterpretation of classical Greek texts. Many of these writers had only recently been rediscovered and printed as part of the developing European Renaissance.

Homer, Vergil, Lucan, Ovid, Silius Italicus (for his long poem about the Second Punic War) and Plautus were noted as authors used in the teaching of Latin language. Terence, whose six plays had first appeared in print in France in 1470, was also favoured for his clear prose and moral insight. André's access to texts also provided the latest materials for Latin grammar. Arthur's public speaking skills would have been addressed through study of Cicero's *De Officiis* (*On Duties*), an idealised view of behaviour for public figures,[3] his Letters and the Stoic Paradoxes. Another important work in this area was Quintilian's *Institutes of Oratory*. Rhetoric and oratory were very necessary abilities for any ruler. The focus on Cicero and other authors who developed his ideas, like Quintilian, puts Arthur's training in this sphere at the cutting edge of the Renaissance revival of antiquarian scholarship. Quintilian's works had been rediscovered in Italy in 1416. André's exploration of their content intended to teach Arthur how to structure and manage arguments; how to listen to another point of view, dissect its key points and set it against his own viewpoint or intentions. Kings had to develop an ability to gauge the quality of the advice they received and the trustworthiness of the people that were giving it.

The major work by Thucydides, his *History of the Peloponnesian War*, first appeared in a printed Latin edition in Italy in 1483. The author's grasp of political realism and the role of human nature in war could have appealed to Henry VII's reflections on his own journey to power. Thucydides' work was effectively a scientific, evidence-based study of politics and war. Arthur's access to books like this, and the deep study that was possible at Ludlow and Tickenhill, placed his learning at the forefront of what European educators were able to offer at the end of the fifteenth century. Analysis of and interest in Livy's *History of Rome* was at the forefront of the European revival of Roman scholarship. Machiavelli's investigation of republics (published around 1517) was the culmination of intense scholarly attention given to Livy's work. The emphasis in the *History of Rome* on heroism and fame through great deeds extended the symbolism of the ceremony of Arthur's creation as Prince of Wales, and would have filled out his learning on how great states functioned. This theme was developed in Arthur's study of Caesar's commentaries on the Gallic Wars and on the Roman Civil War of 49–48 BCE.

The works of Cornelius Tacitus probably included his *Annals* and *Histories*, which continued the history of Rome up to the year AD 70. Also of interest, given Henry VII's exploration of the early history of Britain, was the study Tacitus wrote of Agricola's conquest of Britannia. His precise discussion of politics in a time of war would, with the correct type of interpretation, also have been very instructive to a trainee king. Tacitus was another of Rome's great historians to be rediscovered at the end of the fifteenth century, and another to write an important dialogue on oratory. Suetonius wrote in the second century AD. His most famous writings were his detailed biographical studies of twelve Roman Emperors from Julius Caesar (d. 44 BCE) to Domitian (d. AD 96). This writing covered a similar period to that of Tacitus and provided a formulaic but incisive study of how Rome's rulers had conducted themselves when in power. Pliny the Elder's *Natural History* provided an encyclopaedic snapshot of knowledge at the end of the first century. It is fascinating to speculate on the particular emphasis that was placed upon Arthur's education by the selection of these works. Very few of the materials used by Prince Arthur are known to survive, but their existence is identifiable from an index made by André at Tickenhill in 1500.

André's time with Arthur nurtured a curriculum that was meant to advance his pupil's ability very rapidly between the ages of about ten and fifteen. Even had Arthur and his brother lived in proximity, it is unlikely that it would have been thought desirable or productive to educate them together. Competition between the princes in the classroom might have followed, and Henry VII certainly did not want to encourage any rivalries between his sons that could have formed the basis of something more damaging in later life.

There is no way of knowing if Arthur was actually as accomplished as is suggested by the range and difficulty of the texts he was reported to have mastered. The prince was dead when André circulated this evidence of his scholarly skill, and few people who had known Arthur at Ludlow would have had full knowledge of the material he had been set to study. André himself did produce for Arthur's education some original works as well as commentaries on the writings of Christian thinkers like St Augustine. André's preparation of Augustine's *City of God* included an index to aid the prince's learning. He also glossed existing writings for the education of princes, but seems to have been determined (or had been charged) to explore the works most recently available to Europe's aristocratic elite. William Caxton dedicated his version of Vergil's *Aeneid* to the prince in 1490. This was done with a flourish and one eye on the bounty of royal patronage that would hopefully come when Arthur sat on the throne. André's purposes in securing his position as Arthur's sole tutor were served very well when his curriculum was consciously promoted as highly fashionable. Such marketing presented the tutor as a well-connected pedagogue with his finger on the pulse of European learning at the highest level. That kind of confident self-promotion made it more likely that André's service with the crown would continue once Arthur took up more of the responsibilities of government.

Another long-standing tradition is that the poet Thomas Linacre also secured a post in Arthur's household. Much of the information about Linacre's reputed role as Arthur's tutor comes from second-hand sources of the mid-Tudor period. Linacre was one of the first Englishmen to study Greek in Renaissance Italy and was at the forefront of the transmission of the New Learning back into England. Bernard André's interest and contacts in this area make a link between Linacre and Prince Arthur more plausible. The chief contemporary evidence is the dedication of Linacre's 1499 translation of Proclus's work *On Spheres* (*De Sphera*). Linacre's text is now thought to represent a petition to the king to be allowed some role in Arthur's education. In 1499 André was at the height of his authority as the prince's tutor. Preparations for the prince's marriage were also well underway. He was about to leave the accumulation of classroom theory behind forever as he prepared to rule the Marches alongside his new bride. The humanist scholar Erasmus witnessed Linacre presenting his text at court. His description of the event makes it clear that Linacre's supplication was totally undermined by André, who openly questioned the quality of Linacre's work and his abilities. Erasmus also named André as the worst kind of sycophant and a backbiter who would bear no rivals and no alternative views of how Prince Arthur should be educated, especially in the introduction of new learning from Italy and France.

This courtly spat shows that young humanist scholars recognised that roles within royal education were routes towards career success. John Skelton managed to use his connection with Henry VII's mother to become tutor to Prince Henry around 1499. He is also likely to have had a hand in boosting the grammar and handwriting instruction that the younger royal children had already received, reputedly from Queen Elizabeth herself. Arthur had no access to this communal learning environment based at Eltham. He was stuck with Bernard André at Ludlow, as he had been since the first years of the 1490s.

King Henry was content to continue with André's service up to the marriage of Arthur and Catherine, after which André had more time to begin his eulogistic *Life of Henry VII*. His lengthy period as royal tutor also indicates that Arthur's education was felt to be progressing well in the Frenchman's hands when other tutors like Linacre, Skelton and even Erasmus were beginning to enjoy influence within the royal nursery at Eltham after 1499. There were many other Italian humanists connected with Henry VII's court but few had any links to Arthur's separate household in Ludlow. A requirement to travel beyond the king's Thames-side palaces might explain why figures such as Giovanni Gigli and Pietro Carmeliano (or the likes of Polydore Vergil) were unlikely to have developed influence over Prince Arthur. Bernard André's prickly behaviour in defence of his position in Arthur's service was another contributing factor.[4]

Without detailed descriptions of his daily life in the 1490s modern writers can only speculate about Arthur's character. If André's jealous nature had any detrimental effect on Arthur's learning and on the formation of his personality, it is very difficult to see it in the contemporary descriptions of the prince. André's detail of the works and authors that Arthur read has created the impression that the prince was bookish and cold. But there are no counterbalancing accounts of his physical pastimes or social life. It is probable that Arthur would have learned much about how good government worked and a prince's role within it from the time spent with his counsellors. That experience would have supplemented the examples found in the books he studied. It was a chance to build practical experience behind the knowledge gained in the classroom. From the age of seven he had been a figurehead in Marcher government but this did not exclude the probability that mentors such as Pole, Croft or Smith passed on their expertise and experience at suitable opportunities. It would have been natural for the classroom knowledge gained from Cicero, Tacitus or Suetonius to have been blended with lessons from the active legal jurisdiction of the Council of the Marches, the financial provision for the prince's household and the estate management of the earldom of March. We have no way of knowing exactly how this was achieved. Arthur did, however, have an obligation to learn how good governance was put into practice – that was one of the principal reasons for the establishment of his independent household as an attachment to a fully-functioning agency of crown government.

Henry VII had relied upon a range of whatever texts were available to him during his own teenage education in Brittany in the 1470s. He would have had no direct access to the sessions of Duke Francis's council and so could take little from direct observation. Second-hand knowledge and report were likely to have been the main ways in which Henry learned how personal interaction worked in the context of running a state. It has already been suggested that the structure of Prince Arthur's education and training contained some elements that Henry VII had drawn from his own period of development. His scrupulous personality made it unlikely that any aspect of the progression of his son's education took shape without his involvement and approval. André would not have risked the king's anger by wholly fabricating Arthur's accomplishments or the materials he had studied. Therefore, even if André exaggerated the prominence of texts associated with the new heights of Renaissance learning across Europe, it is likely that they were part of the foundation for Arthur's full education as a future king.

It was at the end of January 1492, when he was aged five, that the king's privy purse expenses record the purchase of an expensive longbow for Arthur. The gift of a bow was one of the few pieces of evidence to show Arthur as a child engaging in anything other than classroom education. The outlay on the gift implies that the bow would have been very welcome within the Farnham household. It is, however, dangerous to associate this present with too many connotations related to military training. There is no evidence so far discovered that suggests that Arthur's martial knowledge was developed in any way but through the classroom study of written histories. Archery was a courtly pastime as well as a practical skill for the hunting field. It was certainly not a military requirement for noblemen to master, although proficiency with the bow and arrow could have been one of the ways in which a commander might understand how archers could best be deployed in the field. Arthur was too young to have any connection to the campaigns of 1497, the last English military activity of Henry VII's reign. Even if he subsequently began to learn how to fight in harness at the barriers or to tilt on horseback, he was unable to take part in the military part of later festivities where tournaments were held; for instance, he was obviously the guest of honour at his own wedding in November 1501. It was not appropriate for him to join in the fighting, and he observed enthusiastically alongside his wife and parents as the Duke of Buckingham, the Marquis of Dorset and many others demonstrated their prowess.

We do not know if Arthur received military training at Ludlow. His armour and warhorse were presented to the grave at his funeral, but there is no evidence that the prince had cause to use them for anything other than ceremonial events. The castle did have a tiltyard and it would have been neglectful of Henry VII not to have insisted on practical as well as theoretical or abstract military training for his son, particularly as his own kingship was directly dependent on his own military victory at Bosworth. Henry VII's vision of Arthur's role was that he be trained to command rather than to engage in the fight. Arthur had to learn what his military resources were, and apply the knowledge of his schooling towards an appreciation of how, ultimately, the monarch would lead troops. From the slight evidence of Arthur's life at Ludlow before his marriage, it does seem likely that this type of training in statecraft and the wielding of all aspects of regal power was to come after Bernard André stepped back from his role as tutor in the autumn of 1501.

Warfare did overshadow much of Arthur's life. His father's reign was born on the battlefield and King Henry was also forced to defend his regime in two more major battles against rebels in 1487 and 1497. Another conflict, the English invasion of France in September 1492, brought Arthur's status as heir into sharper relief. The six-year-old prince was named as lieutenant, regent and governor of the realm.[5] His powers would be exercised through the royal council, mainly to uphold the law and justice while the king was out of the country. Henry VII made very good use of similar arrangements put in place for Henry VI, when eight years old, in 1430 and Edward IV in 1475, the latter having left England in the hands of his five-year-old heir Edward, Prince of Wales. Arthur was far too young to be anything other than a figurehead in the council that ruled in the king's absence. Through the regulations laid down, King Henry did limit the abilities of his officials to make major, lasting decisions, and certainly none that gave away the permanent rights of the crown. It seems that Arthur did sit in person when the council met during the king's three-month absence. A few licences were granted but it is unlikely that anyone expected the government to function in anything but a routine way when the head of state and most of the active and influential men of the country were leading their troops in a fruitless adventure around Boulogne. The importance of this very limited responsibility handed to the Prince of Wales lay in the way that it exposed Arthur to the methods of the royal council and the council's place in the wider system of government. An understanding of the way in which councillors spoke and offered their opinions on the matters in hand was clearly thought valuable to the prince. King Henry might already have thought about the best time to send Arthur off to Ludlow, so this brief period of regency might have been an opportunity for the prince to gain first-hand knowledge of how decisions were made in government. It was a golden opportunity to see how the skills of oratory and rhetoric were put into practice.

Moving from the world of books to the real world of elite decision-making was a big jump for such a young prince. It was, however, directly in tune with Henry VII's intentions for his son. Even if Arthur played no part in reaching the few decisions that his council was able to arrive at, he would have had the processes explained to him and been given expert tuition by professionals such as John Morton and John, Lord Dynham who both stayed in England while the king was away. Morton's role as president of this version of the royal council might also have strengthened the king's plans for the definition and function of the Council of the Marches under Prince Arthur's personal control. This arrangement came into effect just over a year later when Arthur moved from Farnham to Ludlow. The grant of a nominal lieutenancy of the realm in 1492 began in earnest Arthur's transition into the world of big decisions and management and manipulation of strong personalities. The time was drawing near when Arthur would move even further away from his family. However difficult this decision was in family terms, the king knew that it was essential if his son was to be fully equipped to rule in the future.

3

THE KING-IN-WAITING

Training in Isolation

To understand why the decision to educate Prince Arthur beyond the direct comfort and support of his family was so significant, we must look at Henry VII's earlier life. Without any point of reference in the king's own experience and the alliances his family had forged, sending Prince Arthur away to Farnham seems like a harsh decision. Even as part of a strategy to build Arthur's independence and to provide better long-term security for the regime, this was a risky first step for an untried king, which Henry VII still was at the time of Arthur's birth. Yet there was a direct and surprising parallel within Henry VII's childhood that reflects his plan for Prince Arthur.

In September 1486, Henry Tudor had spent little more than a year in England since 1471. During the time since Bosworth the king was focussed on building his government and strengthening its processes. The march to London from Leicester immediately after his battlefield victory and his first royal progress beyond the

Thames valley between March and June 1486 were probably the only occasions since his childhood years when he had travelled in England beyond Westminster and the City. Little about life in England can have been familiar to him. Any anchor points and positive recollections had to come from even further back in time.

It is a step too far to suggest that Henry VII's toughness, determination and focus had developed entirely from the circumstances of his early life; such characteristics were already waiting for opportunities to emerge. Wardship with strangers before the age of fourteen and then another fourteen years of exile did make him the man he was, but it was not an upbringing and education to wish upon his own children. His life had been a precarious struggle. For much of it he would have felt friendless and lonely. Knowing that his mother lived elsewhere and that he could not join her can only have been a source of frustration, if not of despair. The elements of this upbringing that were valuable were self-reliance, independent thinking and close observation of others. The absence of a visible family for the first twenty-eight years of his life also made the connection to his own relatives far stronger once Henry was ruler of England. As king, Henry would apply himself to learn the mechanics of government and master the strings by which subjects were ruled, but any innate ability to assess, judge, predict and manipulate others could only be drawn out by practical application. Princes could read and learn about how to be kings but they would give themselves a better chance of succeeding once power was in their hands if they had been able to test their skills in a practical way. Residence in the royal household would have delivered some opportunities, and direct instruction and repetition might also have helped, but princes needed to be able to make mistakes and see the consequences of their decisions. That could only be achieved if they had an arena where it was safe to learn and to apply experience in the real world. That principle seems to have been at the root of

Henry VII's decision to separate Arthur's upbringing from the royal household. The plan must have been devised and agreed in expectation of his birth, since all of the elements were in place by September 1486. As has already been shown, Edward IV's reign supplied the foundation and personnel for Arthur's nursery environment after 1486. Once that connection to the Yorkist blueprint was established, it was a short step for Henry VII to connect to the rest of the education and training programme set up for Prince Edward in the 1470s. This meant making Prince Arthur the leader of government and society in the Welsh Marches.

To a king whose familiarity with all parts of his new kingdom was poor, one unknown region might have been much the same as another. Curiously, however, the central part of the Welsh Marches was the only locality in England that Henry VII knew well. His memory might have been distant, but as Earl of Richmond Henry had spent the longest part of his childhood in the very neighbourhood at which the Yorkist Prince of Wales would be based after 1476. Young Henry spent most of his pre-teen years, between February 1462 and October 1470, in the household of Anne Devereux, Lady Herbert and Countess of Pembroke. The future king was the ward of William Herbert, Earl of Pembroke. At the age of five, he went to live with his guardian's family at Raglan Castle in Monmouthshire. Henry was only two years younger than Herbert's eldest son, also named William. It is more than probable that the boys spent time growing up together. Their strong relationship was at the root of William's pardon after Henry's accession, coming as it did despite the fact that he had served as chamberlain of the household of Richard III's son Edward of Middleham and had married Richard's illegitimate daughter Katherine.[1] Henry was intended as a bride for his guardian's eldest child, his daughter Maud. That request was made explicit in the Earl of Pembroke's instructions to his wife after his capture at the Battle of Edgecote on 26 July 1469. Herbert's immediate execution quickly changed his ward's circumstances. Henry remained in the household of Lady Anne until Henry VI was put back on the throne at the start of October 1470. At that point Tudor was reunited with his mother until Henry VI's restored regime collapsed after the battles of Barnet and Tewkesbury in May 1471, By then, Henry had reached the age of fourteen. He would have seen how William Herbert, Earl of Pembroke, had come to dominate Wales for Edward IV but then witnessed the spectacular fall of Herbert supremacy after the earl's execution.

His fifteen months living with Lady Anne at Weobley Castle, about eight miles south-west of the town of Leominster, placed the youthful Henry Tudor in the region and community in which he expected his own son to thrive during the later 1490s. The same locality might not have been far from his thoughts as he contemplated Arthur's future by unpicking the provision made for the upbringing of the Yorkist Prince of Wales. It seems clear that some of the earliest lasting memories of the first Tudor king were likely to have been of the English landscape and communities within the border locality of Weobley, Hereford and Leominster. This connection meant that Henry VII knew and was known to members of the gentry families of Herefordshire and Shropshire. The kind of mind that was undaunted by the prospect of running the English state on the basis of an education gleaned from an isolated life in exile would have remembered something of the area where the only stable period of his early life had been spent. These memories are likely to have been brought into sharper focus once he had decided upon the course of action to be taken for his unborn son. That this was a fondly remembered time is demonstrated by Henry's efforts to see Lady Herbert once he became king. She was invited to Westminster soon after Henry made his first entry to the capital. It is unclear if she attended the king's coronation on 30 October 1485, but soon after she became ill. The king's spring progress of 1486 placed him in the vicinity of Hereford and Worcester between 9 and 19 May.[2] The details of his daily movements are unknown, but it is tempting to see him visiting Lady Anne in her final illness. She died on 25 June 1486, so soon after she had the chance to be reunited with Henry. This must surely have been a blow to the king, since at this date he had still spent more time in her company than with his own mother.

The period during which Henry was living with Anne Herbert after Edgecote was a key part of his life. She represented his connection to a family network and a local community that was not repeated until he was almost thirty years old. Henry's conduct towards her when king demonstrated a desire to give thanks for the care and generosity she had offered. Even if Margaret Beaufort ensured that her family loyalties overrode his physical connection to Lady Herbert, there was a legacy to the Yorkist Herbert and Devereux families that was revived at Henry VII's accession. The strength of any individual association should not be overlooked when considering how the first Tudor king sought to find roots for his slender authority in 1485 and 1486. A residual element of this personal and geographical link to the Marcher region was another factor in the choice to send Prince Arthur to live in Ludlow in 1493. Neither Henry VI's nor Richard III's sons had been given any separate status beyond the household of their parents: Edward of Westminster had his household limited to thirty-nine people and he was to live with his father, Henry VI, until the age of fourteen.[3] Edward of Middleham was created Prince of Wales at York Minster in September 1483 and remained based at Middleham Castle in the North Riding of Yorkshire.

It is true that Henry VII did send Arthur away for immersion in the self-reliant world of border politics and government. That training could not be achieved in the same way at Westminster.

After 1493, however, Arthur went to the only part of the country that his father had called home. Sentimentality aside, the king's choice indicates that considerations were made for family and people that were known personally to him. The service connections built through the lordship and landholding of Henry VII's extended family also supplied a very experienced network that supported the creation of Prince Arthur's personal power. Between them, Jasper Tudor, Rhys ap Thomas and Sir William Stanley dominated Wales and the Marches in the decade after 1485. All three closed ranks around Henry VII's son, both in the region and by helping to safeguard at Westminster and at court the prince's widespread national interests. The connection of these powerful men to Arthur supported the king's strategy for his son's development. It was a way to build acknowledgement of Arthur's future personal power, but it also boosted their own influence as representatives and intercessors on his behalf. Backing Arthur's development in this way would have satisfied the king's wish to build a long-term transition of power to an heir trained and experienced to the highest level possible. By the time Arthur became resident in the Marches, the region would already have been prepared in many different ways for his arrival. Having put his life on the line to ensure that his nephew became king, Jasper Tudor became Arthur's champion in the lands of the principality and along the March. Jasper's appointment as justiciar of south Wales revived and exploited the regional connections that he had built up during Henry VI's reign. Sir Rhys was chamberlain of south Wales and succeeded as justiciar there after Jasper Tudor's death in 1495. As steward of Brecon he had a power base close to Arthur's own sphere of influence in the March. His military expertise was particularly useful in confronting rebels and rioters in his lordships and nationally on behalf of his king before 1490. Both of these men possessed the gravity to hold the Welsh and Marcher lands securely while Arthur was shaped for kingship.

On the English side of the March, Sir William Stanley became the prominent representative of the king. Stanley's influence had opened the gates of Shrewsbury to Henry's advancing army in August 1485 and his troops had intervened at the last minute to save Henry's life at Bosworth. At Henry VII's accession, Stanley was already chief justice of north Wales, and although he benefitted materially through service in the new royal household and by grants of lordships in the Marches, his presence was important in establishing a solid regional basis for Prince Arthur's training. It is also likely, if difficult to prove, that Thomas Stanley, Earl of Derby and his wife Margaret Beaufort were regular visitors to Prince Arthur at Ludlow and elsewhere after 1493. Earlier accounts of the shared Stanley/Beaufort household indicate regular communication and travel between Woking in Surrey and Lathom in Lancashire. Once Prince Arthur was living in the Marches, the wily head of the king-making Stanley family would have tempered his power where it connected with the prince's. Sir William Stanley's execution in 1495 made it more and not less likely that his brother the Earl of Derby made accommodation with the prince's jurisdiction as exercised through the Council of the Marches of Wales in Shropshire and Cheshire. Countess Margaret, as custodian of the Stafford lands of the underage Duke of Buckingham until the end of the 1490s, would have been similarly flexible in how her personal influence might have affected Arthur's position in the southern Marcher lands.

This alliance of individuals aligned to support the regime's young heir was at times uncomfortable; not least because each of these powerful figures was as concerned to establish and maintain their own authority as they were to mediate the king's power in the lands they occupied. There was also some turbulence in 1486 that was associated with the change of regime and accommodation of the incoming lords that were strong friends of the new monarch. What seems to have been important in persuading Henry VII to root his heir's education in the Marcher region, however, was that many of the king's key allies were well established and influential there by the time Arthur's household at Ludlow was being set up. Henry's decision to entrust the upbringing of his heir to the nobility and gentry of the land between Hereford, Ludlow and Shrewsbury possibly was made easier by the demonstrable loyalty (before 1492 at least), to the new regime of the dominant personalities on either side of the border. The king's assessment of their capacity to fulfil what was expected from them, and his own personal knowledge of the area, might have assured Henry that sending his son to Ludlow was not a reckless risk to his family's long-term tenure of the crown. The fact that a Yorkist Prince of Wales had resided at Ludlow before 1483 also meant that a precedent already existed in the region for the education of future kings. These factors combined to provide a platform from which Arthur's royal leadership could develop securely.

The hard king that cared little about anything but money and security was not to be found in the first decade of the reign, despite the almost constant wrestling with conspiracy and disloyalty. It was only after his own family was decimated by death between 1500 and 1503 that the character of the king lurched towards paranoia and his policies were tyrannically fixated on achieving restraint. The later loss of his wife and heir altered Henry VII physical and emotionally, and his methods in government followed suit.[4] Arthur, of course, did not witness any of those changes. Any view he had of his father was more positive. From Ludlow, Arthur would have heard about, and occasionally seen, a king who was doing his best to rule well in adversity. Distance did not alter the fact that all of the king's actions were potentially lessons for Arthur. There was value in analysing all situations and the decisions that grew from them – indeed, this had been a theme of the books he had studied. People like Sir Richard Croft, with his role in two royal households, connected the world of the border with the world of Westminster and London. Arthur was not so isolated that he had no opportunity to use national events and the king's role in them as the building blocks of his ruling techniques.

Through the ancestry of the queen, Henry VII promoted Arthur as heir to the York family's inheritance of the rights of the earls of March. The members of the Yorkist establishment returning to power with Henry Tudor would have needed little persuasion to back the continuity in this heritage that Arthur represented. It reactivated their route to the centre of power, which had been broken by Richard III's deposition of Edward V. Whereas the provision for the infant prince at Farnham had carried a greater risk, the king's efforts to smooth the way for his son's arrival at Ludlow ensured that it had more elements of a homecoming than the imposition of an unknown or unwanted lord.

It is very difficult to work out how often Arthur left the Welsh Marches to join his family in Westminster and London. That he is mentioned so seldom in records of events at his father's court does indicate that the personal responsibilities created for him a life that was distinct and separate from the rest of his family. The physical distance between centres of power was an obvious hindrance to a connected family life with his relatives. He was visible and active in the counties of the Marches and slightly further afield in the Midlands. Civic records of welcome show that Arthur visited Shrewsbury in 1494 and 1495. The records of the town corporation also contain examples of letters sent under his signet seal from Ludlow. In one, the prince showed that he was learning to behave as a dutiful lord when he asked the town burgesses to look into issues affecting the Blackfriars there.[5] Arthur was in Coventry in October 1498 and Chester in the summer of 1499. The prince reached Oxford several times between 1495 and 1500, also. The Earl of Shrewsbury's great-uncle Sir Gilbert Talbot carried Arthur's ceremonial sword during a formal entry into London in October 1498.[6] Beyond his home country on the Marches, Arthur's appearance at civic receptions, state events or even visits to the royal court held a special weight. His emergence from the borderlands and into other regions carried many of the trappings of a state visit by a foreign leader or a rarely seen noble worthy of great honour. People of different degrees were perhaps a little wary of his position within the polity. They knew he was a formidable person who was surrounded by people hand-picked by the king to educate him and shape how he was readied to rule.

It was vital for the crown that Arthur was be brought up and educated away from the royal household. The determination of the king on this point is suggested by the benefits that Arthur missed as a result of his removal from the capital. London and Westminster offered a sophisticated metropolitan environment, culture and society that would not be matched anywhere else. The court was the gateway to the Tudor crown. It was a semi-public theatre through which the king's magnificence and authority were projected. International visitors, ambassadors, merchants, petitioners and those with information to sell all made their way to the centre of power – and that resided with the king. Arthur could have learned much by watching and learning how his father and the regime's chief ministers, councillors and administrators conducted state business in this magnified and distorted circus of personalities and influences. Indeed, this was most likely the way that Henry Tudor had developed some of his shrewder traits in Brittany. Within the royal household, the prince could have received a comprehensive scholarly education in exactly the same manner as he did from John Rede, Bernard André and others. Prince Henry, and the princesses Margaret and Mary, were all taught to a high standard in this way. The household-based education system worked well enough to provide Prince

Henry with sufficient skills to take the throne in 1509 with full confidence that he could manage the burden of statecraft (or at least know where to delegate effectively).

The king clearly had a definite goal in setting up Arthur's life as he did, and some of the reasons are suggested elsewhere.[7] The impact on Prince Arthur himself, however, is difficult to gauge. It is important to assess if Arthur knew what he was missing by living in rural Shropshire rather than the bustle of the royal court and household. His isolation did deliberately mirror the conditions in which the king, as Earl of Richmond, had been denied interaction with his mother and other people he knew in England. It might be going too far to say that this was an element of deliberate policy by the king to toughen up his heir. Arthur was not abandoned and dependent upon charity, loans and his own wits, as Henry had been before 1485. He was in an environment where there was the safety net of an experienced council and a community that welcomed and supported his presence. Arthur nevertheless had to establish his authority in his own way and on its own terms.

We should be wary also of applying modern thinking to ring-fence the early years of life as a golden period in which children lead a life entirely separated from adult cares. With life expectancy short and the presence of sudden, premature death familiar across the social scale, late medieval aristocrats achieved many of the milestones towards adult life at a faster pace and in a shorter time. There was no concept of a period of years where play was the dominant pastime. Prince Arthur had to grow up quickly. His father was constantly engaged in the business of holding down the loyalty of his chief subjects. If King Henry were to be struck down by disease or an assassin's blade, then Arthur, his household and council had to be in a position to ensure the continuation of the Tudor regime. From the mid-1490s onwards this was the reality behind Arthur's education.

Life as a royal child was doubly dangerous. The usual threat of illness and disease was partially mitigated by a better diet and access to cutting-edge medical care, but recent history had shown all too painfully that on the battlefield and in the political machinations of a power struggle the heirs of kings and nobles were targets. Henry VII had watched from his exile overseas as other royal children had been subject to the same diseases and perils as the rest of the population. He was also aware of their heightened risks of political manipulation in the struggle for the crown. Life for aristocratic children directly caught up in civil war was uncertain, stressful and dangerous. The killing of Edward IV's younger brother Edmund, Earl of Rutland at the Battle of Wakefield at the end of 1460, or the death of Edward of Lancaster after Tewkesbury in 1471, demonstrated that involvement in politics at an early age could bring disaster as well as glory. In creating an independent household and lordship structure for Arthur, Henry was finding a route to establish as early as possible a means through which his son could define and build his own personal authority and lordship. Edward IV had done the same but had still been posthumously outsmarted by the ruthless skill of his brother Richard of Gloucester. If fortune was to end Henry VII's life before his son was old enough to rule in his own right, the king was determined that any challenges to Arthur's status could be resisted and defeated by those that already surrounded him. The model of Edward V's household and how it was brought down therefore presented a variety of lessons for how the Tudor regime should prepare for the future.

There had probably already been an adjustment in the balance of personnel surrounding Arthur when Lambert Simnel's conspiracy broke at the start of 1487.[8] The impersonation of a living Yorkist prince, Edward, Earl of Warwick, by an organ maker's son from Oxford was not the most difficult thing to disprove, and Warwick was brought out of the Tower to demonstrate the falsity of the plot. More worrying, however, was the adherence of various Edwardian and Ricardian Yorkists to the deeper aim of deposing the Tudor king. Richard III's nephew John, Earl of Lincoln had assembled like-minded friends. Their allegiance was stirred up and encouraged from Flanders by Lincoln's aunt Margaret of York, the sister of Richard III and Edward IV. In what was clearly an attempt to duplicate the circumstances of Henry's foreign-sponsored invasion and victory in August 1485, Margaret arranged for continental mercenaries to join a military uprising against Henry VII. Although those immediately involved in the conspiracy were of low rank or had an unbending loyalty to Richard III's legacy, more influential figures were soon drawn in as an invading army was prepared in Ireland. By focusing on lingering and healthy Yorkist support there, the plotters were able to build an invasion force of several thousand. The force landed on the Cumberland coast of Morecambe bay at the start of June and began a march towards the estates in Yorkshire where Richard III was still a fondly remembered good lord. King Henry had to respond. The combined might of the earls of Oxford, Derby and Shrewsbury, plus Jasper Tudor and Sir Rhys ap Thomas, quickly gave shape to a very powerful royal army. The clash with invaders and rebels at the Battle of Stoke in June 1487 was the decisive battlefield victory of Henry's reign. He outwitted an attempt to reproduce his own unlikely route to power. The royal army attracted enough support to confirm that belief in Tudor kingship was growing. Once the battle was won, the way was clear for Henry to accelerate his dominance.

Defeat of the rebellion built the king's intolerance of dissenters. Queen Elizabeth Woodville fell spectacularly from the inner circle of the new regime at this time. As a godmother to Arthur and mother of Henry VII's wife, she was one of the few who would have had relatively free access to the infant prince. There is no indication that she had anything to do with her sister-in-law's plotting. But she was too close to people who were challenging the new royal family, and within days she forfeited her lands and entered Bermondsey abbey as a pensioner. Whatever other lessons were drawn from the Simnel episode, it is clear that the king learned much about the commitment of the aristocracy to the Tudor crown. His thinking on how Arthur's service developed was coloured by this fact. When the time came for Arthur to move to Ludlow there was no automatic right for the region's nobles to get involved, as they had done during Edward IV's reign. Victory at the Battle of Stoke allowed Henry VII to break free of the threat of externally sponsored invaders. He could also throw a spotlight on some of the realm's insiders who had not been too sure about where their loyalty should lie. Many more bonds were issued that obliged the guilty and those under suspicion to pledge their allegiance under threat of heavy cash fines if they defaulted.[9] Henry was not yet out of the woods regarding certainty over the nation's fidelity, but in 1488 he was more confident that his plans for the future could have a longer range. Part of the shift in thinking that occurred balanced this slightly more secure picture against a nagging requirement to use the opportunity to safeguard the Tudor crown, Prince Arthur's inheritance, more comprehensively.

Henry VII was following Edward IV's lead in reaching out to those who had opposed him on the battlefield, although any hand of friendship was often balanced by tools such as bonds that would make people weigh up the consequences before dabbling in disloyalty. It was in the king's interests to try to unite the political class so that rancour and resentment were quickly eliminated through a bringing together of former opponents in a new purpose. This was not a meaningless gesture. Henry showed an enormous degree of trust in placing in the care of others the child that was most precious and critical to the hopes for the future of his regime. The king's action was not without insurance measures: it was, of course, backed up by all kinds of lightly mentioned threats and barely noticed hints of how great his displeasure and sanction would be if any aspect of Arthur's care fell below what was expected.[10] The king did not have to be heavy-handed with his intimidation. By 1493, evidence of how Henry VII dealt with disloyalty had already given the political and administrative classes much to think about. Many of them had become ensnared in bonds and recognizances as guarantors of suspects' behaviour. There were enough people involved in the households of Ludlow and Tickenhill who could be relied upon to keep the royal council and King Henry informed about how Arthur's life was unfolding. The tougher job for the king was finding enough posts for people on the outer edges of his goodwill, so that he could be seen as inclusive in a way that reflected the make-up of his regime while at the same time constructing in Arthur's service a core of long-standing allies with good hearing, sharp eyes and tight lips whom he knew would stand and fall alongside the regime if Henry's national control began to weaken. If the danger to the regime reached those levels then Arthur was probably safer in a smaller household setup, where faces were familiar and reliable, than in the 500-strong royal household with more opportunity for human error and infiltration. King Henry's confidence in the families that controlled Arthur was not blind faith but it incorporated a stunning piece of positive reinforcement. There had to be a balance between York and Lancaster if Arthur Tudor was to blossom as the focus for all new loyalties.

The appointments to Arthur's Ludlow household underline the influence that Margaret Beaufort had in orchestrating the upbringing of Henry VII's heir within this carefully controlled framework. Arthur's early household had a Yorkist flavour and connection, but once he had departed Farnham it was the network of Margaret Beaufort's servants, friends, dependents and relatives who had responsibility for Arthur's development. Sir Richard Pole was typical of men who delivered in multiple ways. Pole's mother was Lady Margaret's half-sister Edith St John. He would come to wield enormous power in north Wales and the Marches, filling the administrative shoes of both William Stanley and Jasper Tudor, Duke of Bedford after they died in 1495. His deep connection to the Tudor family can still be seen in the rood screen at Aberconwy church, which bears the English and Spanish badges of Roses and Pomegranates.[11] Pole had ancestry that linked him to the princes of Powys in north Wales, but his father and grandfather had emerged from the Cheshire gentry community that would have been very familiar to Margaret Beaufort's husband, Thomas Stanley, Earl of Derby. The efforts of the king and his mother to extend the dilution of previously divided loyalties also continued through the arrangement of Pole's marriage. Towards the end of 1487, he became the husband of Margaret Plantagenet, daughter of George, Duke of Clarence, brother of Richard III and Edward IV. The nearest figure to a governor for Arthur was Sir Henry Vernon. His role suggests a stronger private connection to the prince's wellbeing than some of the other administrative posts. One such was occupied by John Arundel. He was named as Arthur's chancellor at the end of June 1493.[12] He probably oversaw the governing institutions over which Arthur presided as Prince of Wales and Earl of Chester. At that stage of his career he was dean of Exeter and a canon of Windsor, so an association to Peter Courtenay was his most obvious route into royal service. Arundel also became close to the president of the prince's Council in the Marches, Bishop William Smith of Coventry and Lichfield, and later Lincoln. Smith was associated with the prince's council from 1493, about the same time that Arundel appeared.

Arthur's Appearance[13]

The known portraits of Prince Arthur show a tall boy, possibly in his early teenage years. He has auburn hair and pale skin and a long, flat, angular face. He has a slim and wiry build and is dressed very richly with intricate pieces of jewellery in his hat and around his neck. His father, Henry VII, was also known for these physical characteristics, and the prince also shares the hooded and bagged eyes of his grandmother Margaret Beaufort. A quick correlation of these features makes it tempting (but dangerous) to suggest that Arthur therefore was blessed with the same kind of personality ascribed to his father and to his Beaufort relatives – serious, focussed, dogged, suspicious and calculating. Arthur's brother Henry, on the other hand, in near-contemporary pictures, has the round, slightly chubby appearance of his mother, Elizabeth of York, and her father Edward IV. A painted terracotta bust by Guido Mazzoni from the Royal Collection is thought by some experts to represent a laughing Prince Henry aged about seven, from the period 1498–9. The unproven association of this work with Henry has made enough of a connection for later writers to link imagery and personality. It is all too easy to use identifiable images of people from the past to begin to reconstruct what their personalities might have been like. The works above, when addressed together, instantly separate the character of the two princes and tend to confirm our beliefs about written descriptions of their personalities. Prince Henry was full of life, carefree and impulsive; Arthur was cold, detached and careworn. Written comments and notes often help to qualify such descriptions but they might also only compound what we have taken from visual evidence. The ambassador to Milan in September 1497 described Arthur as taller than his age might suggest, with striking grace and beauty. The prince's conversations in Latin were also noticeably impressive.[14] That brief summary suggests that Arthur's education was working very effectively.

It provides some basis for analysing the known contemporary and later representations of the prince.

Arthur would have been seen by thousands of people during the course of his wedding ceremonies and celebrations. Henry VII ensured that Arthur looked magnificent alongside his bride but, unfortunately for us, neglected to capture any images of the event. Near-contemporary representations of Arthur are found in the Magnificat window at Great Malvern Priory, completed between 1499 and 1502; in an illumination depicting Henry VII's family at prayer in a book of ordinances presented as part of a petition to establish a London gild in 1503; and in an altar-panel painting showing the Tudor family beneath an image of St George and the Dragon. All of these images are stylised. They are representative or symbolic depictions of the prince. While they show Arthur in appropriate dress, the portrayal of the prince's features varies so much that they cannot be relied upon as attempts at likenesses. Expert analysis of the faces in the panel painting show that they have been overpainted at a later date. Without a sculpted tomb effigy, and barring any new discoveries of images created in Arthur's lifetime, we have to rely upon artworks created later in the sixteenth century as the best evidence of what Arthur looked like.

All other known portraits of Arthur were made after his death. Many copies might have been made for the royal collection to fill the galleries of Henry VIII's new building projects.[15] Pictures of the prince now surviving at Hever Castle and in the Royal Collection show similarities in the settings, the facial appearance and the framing with other surviving pictures of his father Henry VII and his grandmother Queen Elizabeth Woodville. In the first of these portraits, Arthur is depicted in his very early teenage years. He is dressed richly and is usually seen holding a white gillyflower in his right hand. This flower (a white carnation), was a symbol of virginity associated with betrothal and marriage. That symbolism makes it likely that an original painting was made as part of the proxy marriage ceremonies for Arthur and Catherine in 1497 or 1499. The Royal Collection portrait is of Arthur in a red hat with a brooch image of St John the Baptist. He is shown as a little older and with a slightly fuller face. The physical development of the sitter might suggest that the original picture was painted nearer to the wedding ceremony, perhaps even at the same time as the set given to the Spanish delegation when they departed London in November 1501.[16] It is also a copy, probably made in the first decade of Henry VIII's reign, of a lost original. If the original picture was the same one that was the basis of the other portraits, then this one been altered by the copying artist to take account of changes in fashion and the tragic end of Arthur's life. Looking back from 1518, it would not have made much sense to depict Arthur as the pure bridegroom. He was dead and King Henry VIII had married his widow. But there is nothing in these copies to indicate or suggest that Arthur was sickly, infirm or anything other than a robust and quite tough teenager. Since there are no other reliable images of Arthur, these portraits cannot reveal much about the sitter. Nevertheless, they present a striking backdrop to his story that emerges more fully from the written record.

4

THE POWER OF THE PRINCE

Arthur and the Mortimers

As soon as Henry, Earl of Richmond won the Battle of Bosworth and was transformed into King Henry VII he started a new phase of his battle for people's hearts and minds. He had already mustered all of his powers of persuasion in pulling together a group of unconnected die-hard rebels and evacuees as part of his conspiracy against Richard III. Once he was king, to endure and ensure the survival of the Tudor monarchy he had to spread his message of legitimacy even more widely across England and Wales. His claim to national leadership had to be clear and backed by strong bonds of loyalty; factors that were deficient among his backers, brought together with the sole aim of deposing Richard III. Henry would need knowledge, persuasion and the ability to take methods used by his predecessors and adapt them. When Queen Elizabeth presented him with a healthy baby boy he was free to finalise and lock into place his thoughts and preparations that had been built upon the dynastic and geographical links that his new son could absorb and carry into the future.

Arthur's transition into the leader of Marcher society did involve a clever reinterpretation of regional history that put the new prince at the centre of an old story. The area that became most important to Prince Arthur was the region in the Welsh Marches linking Worcester, Bewdley, Ludlow, Weobley and Leominster. Along with Shrewsbury to the north, Wigmore to the west and Hereford to the south, this was the centre of power for the Prince of Wales, and the area that his Council in the Marches dominated as representative of the more distant Westminster government. In setting up Arthur's seat of power here, Henry VII was consciously merging several strands of political influence.

Those people that surrounded and served Arthur in the late 1490s knew that this region had been the heart of the lordship of the earldom of March. The last living earl had been the young Edward V before his father died and he disappeared. Once Edward was believed to be dead, Arthur's mother, Queen Elizabeth, became the last heir of the Yorkist kings and therefore the most prominent living descendant of the Mortimers as earls of March. Arthur was being linked to that earldom and the Mortimer family as a direct expression of his mother's lineage and what it represented. The earldom had for many years been a critical part of the House of York's power. Mortimer blood was also a factor in building a Yorkist claim to the throne. Elizabeth's grandfather Richard, 3rd Duke of York had been a product of the marriage of Anne Mortimer and Richard, Earl of Cambridge, one of Edward III's grandsons. Anne was the sister of the last Mortimer Earl of March – Edmund Mortimer, who had died in 1425. Richard, Duke of York had inherited the Mortimer estates and the dormant Mortimer claim to the crown through dual descent from Edward III. It was Edward IV that brought this fusion of rights and entitlements together when he became king in March 1461.

Edward consciously proclaimed this aspect of his genealogy when, in the parliament of 1461, he annulled the attainder of Richard, Earl of Cambridge (who had been beheaded in 1415 for his part in the Southampton Plot against Henry V). Anne Mortimer herself was also a direct descendant of Edward III's second surviving son, Lionel, Duke of Clarence. Lionel's only daughter, Philippa, had married Edmund Mortimer, 3rd Earl of March and was Anne's grandmother. It was this dual ancestry to Edward III that led to Roger Mortimer being proclaimed in parliament as Richard II's heir in 1385. His death in Ireland in 1398 allowed the Lancastrian claim of Henry of Bolingbroke, Duke of Lancaster to build momentum. Henry's seizure of the crown in 1399 led to the opposition of the Mortimer family group to the Lancastrian kings. It was also a longer-term factor in maintaining belief in the royal rights of Richard, Duke of York during the 1450s. When Edward IV decided to locate the household of his eldest son in the Welsh Marches he was reconnecting the dynastic roots of the Yorkist crown with its regional and royal origins in the legitimate but sidelined rights of the Mortimer family.

Another strand of Henry VII's thinking related to the Arthurian connection that had been explicitly employed by the crown in the early years of his reign. This link has usually been assumed to have been part of a general promotion of the king's ancestry to compensate for his complex connections to the English royal line and his unclear right to the crown. Henry made much of his descent from Brutus and his links to Cadwaladr ap Cadwallon, the last king of all Britain (according to Geoffrey of Monmouth). In itself, this appeal indicated that Henry was deeply aware that previous kings of England had promoted legend and romance as they built support and justified their policies. Edward I, for example, had used Geoffrey of Monmouth's vision of Britain as part of his justification for overlordship of Scotland in the 1290s. Evidence suggests that Henry VII had an understanding that the exploration of his legendary ancestors would resonate with his subjects. For Prince Arthur to be seriously considered as the fulfilment of the prophecy of King Arthur's return to lead Britons in a new and glorious age, the king's subjects were expected to know the significance of the story. They were probably helped out in their recollections by the representation of parts of King Arthur's story in the pageantry that accompanied many ceremonial events in which the royal family was involved. When Prince Arthur visited Coventry in 1497 he was greeted by a pageant that featured King Arthur and the other eight of the Nine Worthies, in which the legendary King of Britain made a speech of welcome. This entertainment carried an important and repeated message about the legitimacy of the place of Henry VII's family in the long line of England's rulers. It is possible, however, that there was a more specific justification for Henry VII's use of the legends of early Britain, namely Prince Arthur's inheritance of Mortimer power and his presence in the borderlands of England and Wales.

The Mortimer family had shown considerable interest in the Arthurian stories as part of their genealogy.[1] The legendary figures Cadwaladr, Brutus and Arthur were viewed as ancestors and not mythological predecessors. When the Mortimers married into the family line of Llewelyn ap Iorwerth in 1228 they absorbed the descent of the princes of Wales growing from Cadwaladr. A genealogical roll of the Mortimer family provides some valuable evidence of how Arthurian tradition was heavily promoted by family members as they developed their relationship with King Edward I in the 1270s and during the English war with Prince Llewelyn ap Gruffydd before 1282. Later Plantagenet kings allowed the Mortimers to build up vice-regal power along the border from their castles and estates at Wigmore, Ludlow, Cleobury and Chirk. Even after the treason and execution of Roger Mortimer, 1st Earl of March in 1330, the family were able to recover their influence in the Marcher lands. Many of the key events of King Arthur's tale became associated with the physical features and remains found on Mortimer possessions – or at least a connection was claimed by the earls of March. The reinvention of the Arthurian myth moved closer to the centre of crown power during the fourteenth century, to the point where Roger Mortimer, 4th Earl of March was, by 1398, a short step away from becoming king.

Set-piece events during the century, such as spectacular round table tournaments in imitation of King Arthur's court at Camelot, benefitted the Crown as they emphasised the king's lineal proximity to the great leaders of historic Britain. The lords of the Anglo-Welsh border, with their strong direct ancestry to ancient and independent British rulers, also sent a clear message that their personal power was deep and strong, and was offered to the late medieval English crown in alliance and not through subjugation. That was one of the main reasons why the Marcher lords and the justiciars of north and south Wales continued to have such semi-independent potency into the fifteenth century. Even after Edward I's conquest of Wales and Henry IV's defeat of Owain Glyndŵr a century later, the annexation of Wales by England was never seriously contemplated. The English Crown's authority was exercised by deputies from within the regional communities that knew the people, landscape and history of the March. They were the king's intermediaries and were agents whose relationship with the Westminster government and court was essential to the achievement of aspirations of national security and stable rule.

Henry VII's interest in ancient British stories was a prop to the extension of his royal authority generally, and that of the Marcher lords in particular. It fitted with his grand scheme to revive an older form of lordship for his son in order to create a foundation of loyalty for Arthur's future kingship. King Henry's prominent use of the red dragon standard associated with Cadwaladr – still one of the most identifiable of Tudor images – tapped right into this familiar Welsh and British heritage. Prince Arthur had the good fortune to inherit the Mortimer connection to King Arthur, and a claim to descent from the Welsh princes through his father Edmund Tudor. With the birth of his male heir, Henry VII could pass on this part of his own Welsh ancestry alongside his queen's Mortimer inheritance.

The fifteenth century had been one of hostility between the Mortimers (and those that inherited their estates) and the Lancastrian royalty. When Edward IV had been Earl of March, his drive to depose Henry VI in 1460–61 was partly based on his reputed command of the Welshmen of the borders. As early as 1452, when he was only aged ten, the muster of some of his father's supporters in defiance of the king at Dartford generated rumours that young Edward was about to march on London at the head of a Welsh army. The early battles of the Wars of the Roses, at Blore Heath and Ludford Bridge in the autumn of 1459, were fought as attempts to damage the ability of the Yorkist forces to draw on the resources of the March. A century of opposition to the legitimacy of Lancastrian rule by the Mortimer/York group presented Henry VII with some major problems once he intended that his son should take on the mantle of Earl of March at the same time as he, the king, was obviously identified as the last heir of Lancaster. Had backing for Edward V been maintained at the top of the Yorkist regime in April 1483, Henry Tudor would have remained a potential enemy to this group and an ineffectual claimant to the crown. Looking forward from mid-April 1483, the veterans of the household of Edward, Prince of Wales would have expected to be working hard to support the Duke of Gloucester's protectorate for the underage King Edward V. Although Richard III shared the descent of his father and brothers back to the origins of the Yorkist family, the nature of his accession in destroying Edward V's kingship had undone any chance that Richard could rely upon the support of the network that had developed around the prince in the Welsh Marches. Richard had declared that all of the children of King Edward and Elizabeth Woodville were illegitimate but he was unable to persuade a large tranche of Yorkist servants that it was true. Their allegiance was transferred to Princess Elizabeth, who retained her status as Edward IV's last heir. When Arthur was born he acquired this right, as well as the blood ties of his mother's Mortimer ancestry. The connection was a powerful aid to how the power of the new king was identified and projected. Henry VII was careful to include the imagery and heraldry of this descent in the iconography associated with Arthur, since it was a reminder to observers that he embodied a unity of claims to the crown and could call upon a range of former loyalties as a result.

Naturally, King Henry was very careful in the way that he navigated these issues in the definition of his own royal rights. He was helped by some key factors in his favour. Only the Tudor campaign had a realistic (if improbable) chance of restoring Yorkist landholders to everything so hastily abandoned after the failed rebellion of October 1483. Henry's public announcement at the end of 1483 of his intention to marry Elizabeth was the product of negotiation and agreement between the Yorkist and Tudor elements of the alliance against Richard III. Once the Yorkists had agreed to transfer their backing to Henry, the expectation of a male heir meant that he could map and exploit Elizabeth's genealogical connections to kings with undisputed royal rights and glories, both real and legendary. Henry's need to graft his own family on to the strongest branches of the English royal tree was clear. His personal descent in the male line soon entered the ranks of more obscure north Welsh landholders, whereas Elizabeth's ancestry had a more direct link to earlier medieval English kings and border lords. Henry's appeal for the loyalty of Yorkist lords and gentry therefore magnified their importance in the early years of Tudor power.

In November 1493, Arthur was formally granted the lands and rights of the earldom of March during the king's pleasure. He was not expressly given the title, which had already been in Crown hands for thirty-two years, but this was an absorption of Marcher power into the new regional force that Arthur was to embody.[2] Once he held the power and estates of the earldom of March, Arthur acquired the real and the mythical associations of the earldom into his personal lordship. His arrival as a new border figurehead offered Arthur the potential to build a very strong and stable structure of lordship in the communities of the Marcher region. Since it distilled his personal power into a more potent form, immediate acceptance of Arthur's inheritance of the March was as important as a boost to Arthur's royal presence as was his national status as Prince of Wales after 1489 or earlier title of Duke of Cornwall. As he grew into his role, Arthur would develop this network and nurture the service of families connected with the earldom of March and the Yorkist Prince of Wales without the need to labour his relationship to the legendary power of King Arthur.

The Struggle for Influence

At the end of 1485, the threat posed by opponents biding their time in Richard III's northern power base was the most immediately pressing problem for Henry VII. Unfortunately, he could not simultaneously relax his efforts to promote his kingship and make the presence of the regime felt elsewhere. In the areas where encouragement was offered by the loyalties of those who had already declared their allegiance to the new regime, the king moved swiftly to establish his allies. Henry VII could not afford to be seen to be undermining, manipulating or threatening the old Yorkist and Mortimer networks. Nationally, Henry had little choice but to rely upon the acceptance of his general pardon of October 1485, and the willingness of people to disengage from the cycle of conflict and throw their energies into making the new king's reign a stable success. In the Marcher areas, recognising and unpicking dynastic and political issues from more routine but no less dangerous border lawlessness was a particularly tricky challenge. It could not be done from Westminster or by inserting lords and gentry from distant parts of the county. Henry's own time in the Herbert household at Raglan and Weobley would have made it clear that border lordship required local experience, connection and respect.

It is not known when the top levels of the Tudor regime decided that Prince Arthur would come to live on the Welsh Marches, but within a year of his birth powerful figures began to shift and manoeuvre in expectation of the changes that would be necessary to support his time as a child-prince in Shropshire, Herefordshire and Worcestershire. It was obvious that all that was valuable, desirable and useful about Edward V's time as prince would be duplicated by Henry VII. There were differences, however, in how the new king filtered what was important to him. The choice of officials and the curriculum of education and training required would come to reflect the Tudor king's concerns over the sustainability of support for the prince and its constancy in the face of stress and threat from enemies of the new regime. Announcing that Arthur would follow in the footsteps of Edward V certainly led directly to the identification of loyalists to fill posts. It also required contingencies to deal with other figures who had been important while Edward V was on the border and that now wanted to slide back into their posts of responsibility and proximity around the Tudor Prince of Wales. Times had moved on but the sense of entitlement running through the ranks of regional gentry was an issue that Henry VII had to address.

Some of the first restrictive bonds for allegiance and good behaviour issued in Henry VII's reign concerned suspects from this region. Individual disloyalty might account for some of this. Other incidents were linked to the decline in control and leadership across the border following the death of the Duke of Buckingham in November 1483 and the repercussions of the Tudor seizure of the crown. The restoration of Jasper Tudor emphasised that the most important figures in the regime were to take regional responsibility for upholding Henry VII's power. Jasper had been away for a long time and reintegration could not be achieved overnight. His reinstatement occurred in south Wales, with the earldom of Pembroke and lordship of Glamorgan in his hands by March 1486. The grant of the lordship of Monmouth gave Jasper a strong role at the southern end of the March, but even then his seniority with the king and the wider responsibilities he carried throughout Wales meant that he governed through deputies. Further north, the dilution of Stafford influence and the Crown's need to appoint stewards did provide an opportunity for some jostling for position among the gentry until the pattern of overlordship was fully worked out. The initial absence of a dominant figure might have been a factor in the attack on the Stafford Castle at Brecon by Sir Thomas Vaughan in 1486, for example, which Sir Rhys ap Thomas, as steward, suppressed. By the following spring there is evidence that the Crown was becoming more concerned and more involved. In May 1487 several men from Elfael in the Marches, both English and Welsh, were summoned before the king and his council at Westminster for violently occupying a piece of land in Elfael and for using force and arson against their opponents.[3]

The most worrying demonstration of why a royal presence was required on the Marches came with another eruption of violence in June 1487. That month, a riot occurred in Leominster that had serious implications for the future power of the nine-month-old Prince of Wales. Two of the region's senior gentry, Sir Thomas Cornewall and Sir Richard Croft, were already contesting rights to the manor of Brymfield.[4] Regime change expanded the points at which they clashed, most notably in a direct confrontation for dominance of the area around the town of Leominster. Cornewall was in his late teens and probably a ward of the 4th Earl of Shrewsbury. He was also an ally of the king's chamberlain, Sir William Stanley, and so might have felt he had powerful backers. Croft, too, had influential friends. As treasurer of Henry VII's household he could mobilise high-ranking colleagues. The regional connections of both men and their families had brought them close to the Prince of Wales in the 1470s. Edward V's demise had suddenly cut off all of their influence and that of many other borderers. Future prospects, steadily built up after Edward's physical arrival at Ludlow in 1476, were also frozen. The birth of Prince Arthur, however, immediately reactivated their hopes of direct connection to the prince's service. This was all the more exciting once it was clear from the set-up at Farnham that Henry VII's boy would follow the pattern of education established for Edward V.

In June 1487, with Henry VII's kingship hanging in the balance as he faced an invasion and rebellion, Sir Thomas Cornewall entered Leominster with over 150 men and broke into the priory.[5] Not knowing what was going on, the monks fled to their dormitory where they hid until the riot ended. Cornewall's men felled a large tree and smashed the wall of the prior's gaol and released two men who were locked in the stocks. Both were Sir William Stanley's liveried servants. One of them had been arrested by Sir Richard Croft's man Thomas Acton for murder, and the other for fighting. In the market square of the town, in full view of the residents, Cornewall's men smashed the prisoners' fetters. A short while after these events, Cornewall's brother-in-law Sir Richard Corbett returned to the town with 100 men and threatened the prior and brethren of the priory. In the later legal record, the two knights, who were both justices of the peace, were alleged to have already started to retain the tenants of the priory and had been supplying livery clothes and distributing heraldic badges in the town. The removal of the priory's labour force quickly threatened the income and livelihood of the monks. The prior brought a case before the king's council asking for a Crown investigation into the riot. He wished that the perpetrators should be bound to keep the peace and that Cornewall be forbidden from retaining the tenants of the priory. The prior did not allege that Cornewall was illegally building a private army based on his tenants, but he implied that lawlessness was not far away unless the king did something about the situation.

Sir Thomas Cornewall's answer did not deny that he had released the men from the gaol. He argued that they had been wrongfully imprisoned by Sir Richard Croft out of malice towards Cornewall. As a JP, Cornewall had taken a bond from friends of the men to ensure that they would appear at the next quarter sessions. The bailiff of the gaol had nevertheless refused to release them, contrary to Cornewall's application of the law. He therefore recruited a group of willing helpers to enforce his legal decision and take the men from the gaol by direct action. Finding the gates closed against him, Cornewall improvised a solution to see that the men were freed. He denied that he had engaged in granting his livery to the prior's tenants for anything other than his recruitment for the king's army at the Battle of Stoke on 16 June 1487. He also apologised for frightening the monks with the methods employed to free Stanley's men. The depth of Cornwall and Croft's enmity for each other is shown by counter-accusations that each had lain in wait, rioted and plotted murder against the other. Cornewall and Corbett accused Croft of illegally compelling men from Leominster to become his retainers and of blocking the legitimate influence of the king's chamberlain, Sir William Stanley. The ugly mutual dislike between Stanley and Croft in their joint service within the king's household was being projected on to the regions through willing agents like Cornewall. This was something that Croft would not tolerate, and he responded to defend his position.

Croft was steward of Leominster – it was parcel of the earldom of March – but he was absent fighting at Stoke with the royal household troops. On his way home, he alleged that Cornewall ambushed him with over 100 men. Cornewall was accused of sending his son-in-law, Christopher Throgmorton of Harefield in Gloucestershire with various criminals, outlaws and sanctuary men from the lands beyond Wigmore, to kill Sir Richard Croft and his servants. The counter-accusation of Cornewall and Corbett was that Croft assembled many felons and outlaws from Radnor in the earldom of March with the intention of killing Sir Thomas Cornwall in his house at Burford. They were even alleged to have murdered Corbett's tenant in the church at Ruther during Mass. Croft maintained these murderers by giving them his livery. Cornewall was a burgess and tenant of Leominster and any gathering of men was done as part of the musters for the king's army at Stoke. Cornwall and Corbett also alleged that on 1 June 1487 they had left Herefordshire to join with Sir William Stanley and meet up with the king's army to fight the rebel force of John, Earl of Lincoln. They suggested that during this time Croft, his son Edward and his illegitimate son Thomas openly called Stanley, Cornewall and Corbett traitors. Croft got his bailiff at Kingsland to seize the goods of Cornewall and Corbett and throw their wives and children into the street.

Croft was further shown to have overreached his authority by proclaiming that he was authorised by the king to have sole licence to give livery clothes in the town of Leominster. Servants in Stanley livery had been arrested and put in prison to be bound for their good behaviour. Others from Cornewall's circle were held on suspicion of treason and left in prison on Croft's verbal authority, which he claimed had come directly from King Henry. Those who were retained by others, chiefly Cornewall, would by Croft's presumed authority also lose their land in the town held by copyhold. Croft hid the king's commission of muster from public scrutiny but claimed that it gave him the right of general array: the authority to recruit all able-bodied men for national defence. As a result, Croft assembled a small force of 1,000 men with the sole intent of destroying Corbett and Cornewall as traitors. All of this pressure had the effect of driving Cornewall's tenants in Leominster into Croft's service. Ultimately, he was accused of making the king's laws at his will. Cornewall estimated that this had caused him damages valued at 1000 marks – an outrageously high sum, but some indication of the scale of the struggle between these men.

The dispute of Sir Richard Croft and Sir Thomas Cornewall highlights all manner of issues bubbling under the surface of the community that the Prince of Wales would come to lead: competition for landed income, social superiority, political alignment, loyalty and allegiance, representation of Crown authority, inter-family quarrelling, manipulation of the middle ranks of society and the proximity of society's leaders to lawlessness and violence. Most of these themes would have been present in any county society. Attempts to manage them can be found in the business of courts and the records produced by the king's representatives throughout the country. Worrying for Henry VII was that his son would be nominally responsible for dealing with this entrenched local social structure that still bore the scars of the Wars of the Roses. Croft and Cornewall were among the six chief men of Herefordshire appointed by the Crown in 1488 to summon all lords, knights and other nobles to certify how many archers they could supply to the king's army to be sent to fight in Brittany. Corbett held similar status in Shropshire. Given that they were effectively the face of the king's authority, Henry VII had every right to expect his leading gentry to cooperate with each other in representing the Crown locally. Until Arthur was old enough to enforce this in person, the people who had to carry his responsibility were the very same people who were perpetrating much of the disruptive violence. In 1487, it would be many years before Arthur could be expected personally to take the lead in the region. He still had to learn the techniques for controlling the people who would make his rule effective. The intervening period would therefore be a crucial time in the search for stability through the establishment of an unchallengeable Crown presence.

The rough edges of Sir Richard Croft's lordship were tolerated by Henry VII because he was a regional leader whose repositioning over time had already influenced the decision-making of other members of the networks in which he operated. He had shown his commitment to the York family and the earldom of March by joining Edward, Earl of March (Edward IV) at the Battle of Ludford Bridge in October 1459. His local knowledge of border families and communities earned him the stewardship of the earldom once Edward IV was crowned. Croft combined this with the post of treasurer of the household of the Yorkist Prince of Wales from 1473. These skills were put at the disposal of the royal household, where he became treasurer under Richard III in 1484. Yet his transition into service under Tudor royalty was seamless. By 1485 he had over a decade of intimate knowledge of the administration and resources of the earldom of March. He offered a point of continuity for the personnel that moved between Westminster and Ludlow, and he became the first Tudor sheriff of Herefordshire from September 1485. In 1486 Croft stated that he had known Henry VII for over twenty years. That dates their earliest association to the period of Henry's wardship at Raglan castle in the mid-1460s. Their connection is a small glimpse of how Henry Tudor's childhood had created memories that were put to good use decades later. It also implies that the connection had been maintained during Henry's period of exile. A personal link to the king would have helped in the transition of Croft's service to the new administration. By the close of 1494, Henry VII asked him to focus all his experience upon organising Arthur's household and he surrendered his Westminster offices.

The problems that the prince's council would have to face were laid bare by the viciousness of hostilities in 1487. Common knowledge that the Council of the Marches was to be revived for the new royal heir, even before he became Prince of Wales, led to some very direct action. Once Arthur was resident, the Crown's scrutiny would become stronger in the area between Hereford and Shrewsbury than almost anywhere else in the country. Securing precedence and position before the prince arrived became a concern for many, since slack enforcement of the law would not last for long. The evidence of Sir William Stanley's servants active in the middle of the March should also make us consider that more powerful men also recognised that a longer-term advantage was there to be grasped through the exertion of some pressure while Arthur was an infant. For as long as Cornewall and Croft continued their feud they would remain a block to Prince Arthur's leadership becoming truly effective. For that reason, many more of the king's friends and Beaufort cronies than might have been envisaged eventually appeared in the service group around the prince when he first settled at Ludlow. The arrangement was a counterbalance to the local gentry, who had shown themselves to be dangerously focussed on personal squabbles. Men like Cornewall and Croft might have seen the situation differently. Whoever gained the upper hand would pull the strings within the hierarchy of the prince's council and the powerful influences that fed off it. Within the prince's direct service, the leaders of Herefordshire and Shropshire who controlled the day-to-day operation of the council and managed the resources that had been part of the earldom of March would hold effective regional power.

The dispute remained impervious to investigation by the king's councillors. As it rumbled on, so more men were drawn in to support friends or defend what they saw as their own rights. In September 1491 Sir Ralph Hakluyt and Sir Thomas Cornewall were directly competing to retain men from Leominster. Both agreed to hefty bonds of £500 in Chancery to cease trying to retain or to accept the service of anyone from the town or its liberties, and to actively deter men that wished to offer their service. Each was given a list of fifteen names. Presumably these men were their most identifiable followers. They were to be brought to Hereford Castle's gaol and remain imprisoned until the king had examined the matter directly and decided what to do with them. Both Hakluyt and Cornewall activated their connections to the prince's council to call in high-status Crown servants to act as guarantors of these conditions. Sir Richard and his son Sir Edward Croft backed Hakluyt, while Cornewall secured the support of Henry VII's old friend Sir Rhys ap Thomas and Sir Thomas Vaughan of Weobley. Hakluyt was a prominent man in his own right. From March 1490 he held an indenture with the Crown to ensure that his Marcher lordships of Clifford, Winforton and Glasbury were run as the king required – and the requirement was that it was the prince's Council in the Marches to which the Marcher lords would report. Just over a year later he was using this Crown-given power to build his own private army.

In addition to the issuing of new indentures that set out the legal responsibilities of the Marcher lords, the bonds from September 1491 are a snapshot of the action taken by the Crown against retaining and the rivalries that fuelled it. Without a dominant regional leader, the Council in the Marches might have felt uneasy about forcing a resolution against members of its own regional elite. Jasper Tudor, Duke of Bedford had the status to dominate the prince's council but was aged around sixty in 1491 and was scaling back his public role. For that reason, the involvement in these bonds of regional leaders who also had prominence around the king indicated considerable effort to resolve some of the major border problems linked to the effects of misdirected lordship. The delivery to gaol of fifteen men on each side of the dispute has the feel of a negotiated settlement brokered at Westminster and delivered through Sir Rhys or Sir Richard Croft. A concerted effort by the Crown to stabilise the relationships between gentry families and affinities in Herefordshire and Shropshire would certainly have been an essential step in preparing the region for Arthur's arrival.

Yet many of the protagonists were members of the Council of the Marches. As an institution only as effective as its constituent members were diligent, it was clear that it could not be relied upon to sort out problems in which they had a deep interest. In the spring of 1493 King Henry took the plunge and finalised arrangements for Arthur to move household from Farnham to Ludlow. In April 1493 Arthur joined his councillors on the March in a spectacularly heavyweight demonstration of legal power and the reach of the king's trusted officials. A session of the peace held at Hereford Castle on the Friday after St George's day 1493 was conducted in the presence of 'precarissimo primogenitor dicti domini regis Arthuro principe Wallie', 'the most beloved first-born son of the said king, Arthur, Prince of Wales'. Clearly too young at six years old to have had any direct input into proceedings, Arthur was assisted by a group of great national figures from the heart of Henry VII's regime: his great-uncle Jasper, Duke of Bedford; Thomas Grey, Marquis of Dorset; Thomas, Earl of Arundel; George Neville, Lord Bergavenny; Sir William Stanley; and Sir William Hussey [6]. To this body of the king's experienced counsellors can be added some of the active counsellors of the Marches who had already been holding the reins of power on behalf of Arthur, and a couple of the king's chief legal officers: Sir Richard Pole, Sir Richard Croft, Sir Henry Vernon, Sir William Uvedale, David Phillip, John Mordant, Thomas Inglefield, Roger Bodenham and William Rudhale. All sat as justices of the peace. That this was a special event was amplified by the high status of the jury that sat on this session of the peace. It included several esquires from prominent border families such as Baskerville, Lyngen, Scudamore and Monyngton. Many men used this as an opportunity to demonstrate their willingness to serve the newly arrived Prince of Wales. Despite his youth, this was another stage-managed event through which Arthur could be seen in the context of the unified group that supported and represented him. At the next quarter session, held at Hereford on Monday after the feast of St Margaret (20 July) in 1493, Arthur was not present. Proceedings were directed by Dorset, Croft, Vernon, Sir James Baskerville, Sir Thomas Cornewall and other local knights. The jury was also not quite so well packed with gentlemen and esquires – that group was the more typical core of the Herefordshire nobles and gentry that oversaw the business of quarter sessions. Business was back to normal when the bench reconvened at Michaelmas.

In April 1493, Arthur's introduction to his new seat of power was built upon the presence of some intimidating individuals. Their involvement was the equivalent of reading the riot act. Arthur's power was royal power and it was to be flouted at great risk of the full weight of the law. Jasper Tudor was as close to the centre of Tudor power as it was possible to get. His tenacious defence of his nephew's interests was pivotal in the survival of Henry, Earl of Richmond, during the bleak years of his exile in the 1470s. The Earl of Arundel was Arthur's godfather. Dorset, Stanley and Croft had all been involved in building the Marcher power of the Prince of Wales during Edward IV's reign. Any undertones of the quarrel of Stanley and Croft were crushed by the status of the king's other representatives. Sir John Mordant was another prominent lawyer. He was close to Sir Reginald Bray and was a counsellor to Margaret Beaufort. He became Prince Arthur's attorney. Sir William Hussey was the Chief Justice of the King's Bench, but was also an associate of Bray. In these two legal officers alone we can see the influence of Margaret Beaufort – with the king's acquiescence – on the shaping of Prince Arthur's future.

After the powerful initial display, whatever messages of harmony, loyalty and obedience had been proclaimed at Hereford were soon ignored. Croft and Cornewall continued to confront each other, but efforts to force a solution upon them were intensified once Arthur had taken up residence at Ludlow. On 3 July 1495 it was announced that witnesses had been examined by the prince's council in the case of *Croft* v. *Cornewall* and that both parties had been brought before the king in person a few days later in the palace of Westminster. Cornewall seems to have been the worst offender at that stage, since he was also bailed to keep the peace. For two JPs to be flouting the law that they were sworn to uphold was damaging to perceptions of Crown control of the March, even if privately Henry VII was more willing to tolerate the transgressions of these two knights as part of a bigger picture related to Arthur's arrival in the region.[7] The command that Cornewall appear personally before the king was a very serious step. It was rare for Henry VII to summon offenders before him directly. This was all the more damaging because of Cornewall's seat on the Council of the Marches and the influence that he and his friends were able to exert on its effectiveness. As an eight-year-old, Arthur was completely reliant upon the loyalty and cohesion of the people assembled to serve him. When the king heard of this kind of disruptive violence, he could not know how it might escalate. The shocking allegations of treason thrown around in 1487 stoked Henry's nervousness that private conflict could build towards dynastic unrest if left unchecked. The region of the March had been a centre for Yorkist loyalists raised against the Lancastrian crown in the late 1450s. Thirty years later, a Tudor king had to head off any recurrence of private power-building before it escalated to undermine Arthur's position and, potentially, increase his physical vulnerability. Placing his son within a hotbed of gentry violence was certainly not part of Henry VII's intentions.

As late as 1497, Cornwall was still in trouble for his disruptive behaviour. He was put under a bond of 1,000 marks in mid-December 1496 which ensured that he remained within twelve miles of London. In January following, he had to surrender himself to the Fleet prison to await a summons to appear before the king's council. That might have brought enough pressure to bear, since Cornewall's presence within the central government records tail-off after that time. He and Croft gave the appearance of harmonious mutual respect in the work they were doing on the Council of the Marches, and they both were very visible later at Arthur's funeral.

The rivalry of Croft and Cornewall gives the impression of a breakdown of order. Violence and intimidation were part of their armoury, as was the case in many English counties where regional prestige and influence were hard to give up or adapt. Petitions submitted to the royal council often made allegations that exaggerated or even invented lurid details in an effort to persuade. Successfully convincing the judges through the power of argument and evidence was what mattered and not the absolute truth of how that conflict or dispute was explained. The Crown's response through injunctions and bonds does, however, show that the problematic relationship between these two families had the potential to distract the local gentry from their focus on supporting the prince's supremacy. In 1487, that was a few years into the future. Yet despite the violent attacks and refusal to give way, both Cornewall and Croft remained loyal to Arthur and to the Crown. They and their gangs of rural riders and urban followers never posed any direct challenge to Arthur as representative of his father's power. Neither man was removed from Arthur's service. Their later connection to Arthur was reflected in the account of the prince's funeral in 1502. There were other candidates available to fill their places on the council and in Arthur's household, but Henry VII chose not to take the step of removing them. These men remained essential to the gradual expansion of the prince's control over the border region. Their family and ancestral connections made it vital that the king and his allies on Arthur's council put in the effort to force these men and their friends into a position where they considered service to the Crown before upholding their own private power. The struggle was a symptom of how Arthur's assimilation into the existing power structure caused some division and hostility as the gentry realigned their priorities, but it was never an attempt to damage the prince or his status.

The Instrument of Arthur's Power – the Council of the Marches[8]

Prince Arthur's household was the engine of his personal lordship. The hall and private chambers of Ludlow and Tickenhill were where he learned about interaction and the quiet manipulation of influence. Those rooms and the people who passed through them were his version of the king's court at Westminster, Greenwich or Richmond. This was the space in which finery and status was paraded, alliances and agreements forged, and gossip and information exchanged without formality. Arthur's household and court generated the shape and colour of the prince's authority. The projection and enforcement of that personal power was managed by the Council of the Marches. The council was an offshoot of Arthur's household, and many of the same people made both agencies tick. The few surviving late medieval records of council proceedings indicate that the prince's influence stretched along the English side of the border from Gloucestershire to Cheshire. Its form varied in different parts of the prince's empire and at different times. At some point in Henry VII's reign, the Abbot of Westminster petitioned the king for recovery of rent and the occupation of a house called Ankerchurche near Whitfield in Gloucestershire held by John Cassye, Esquire. Cassye had resisted the abbot's requests because of his local power and kinship, which was strengthened by his status as a servant of the Prince of Wales. For that very reason, the abbot wanted the king to direct resolution of the matter to the prince's council.[9] At the other end of the border, 143 miles away, Arthur was directly involved in business as soon as he was able to grasp what was going on. In August 1499, the prince personally witnessed a *quo warranto* inquest into the rights of William Troutbeck to the manor and town of Budworth in Cheshire. The prince was a few weeks short of his thirteenth birthday but still directed his officials to look especially at the bounds of the manor and how the manorial court functioned. Here, Arthur was defending his own prerogative rights as Earl of Chester. He was following his father's national lead while also taking responsibility for the resources of his personal power base.[10] Another order of his council survives for a dispute over the lordship of Usk in Gwent in March 1494. This order was made at Hereford Castle by Bishop William Smith and other members of the council at the very start of Arthur's tenure as resident lord in the Marches. Another arbitration of Sir Walter Herbert concerning a manslaughter case in Archenfield in south-west Herefordshire in December 1495 might also have been done under the authority of the prince's council. These verdicts do suggest that Arthur's administrators were active in establishing his authority long before he was able to exercise his right in person.[11]

Arthur's responsibilities as a visible independent lord were taken seriously. When the entire royal court assembled at Westminster for the festivities of Prince Henry's creation as knight of the bath and Duke of York in November 1494, they did so without Prince Arthur. He stayed at Ludlow, probably with Sir Richard Croft, who was also absent from the account of the tournament. It would have been unusual, however, had senior members of Arthur's household not had a presence at the feasts. The assembly of the nation's elite happened rarely enough and it was an important time in which to assess the state of the nation.

Sir Henry Vernon and others joined the king and would have brought back to Ludlow news, orders and information, as well as fine goods purchased from the London merchants.

The prince's jurisdiction existed above the level of established government of the English border counties built around the offices of JP and sheriff and the personal lordship of the great magnates and knights. In the Welsh counties and lordships that bordered England, the prince's presence was a unifying influence that gave access to the law and helped to integrate Marcher lordship with English administration. The prince firmly planted the authority of the Crown within the Marches and helped to bring focus in royal service in a region that had been traditionally dominated by powerful noble families. Without attentive preparation by councillors and effective training of the prince so that he became a physical presence with obvious authority, many leaders on the March might have seen the arrival of a young, weak, inexperienced and disconnected king as an excuse to reassert independent authority. When Arthur went to live in Shropshire and Worcestershire he stepped into a network that was expecting him. Simply by moving to the centre of it, Arthur activated the links in a community that had been anticipating his arrival since 1486. This action began a rapid closure of the gaps through which the influence of local lords had previously chipped away at the king's power.

Arthur's rite of passage in preparation for his reign would follow exactly that which was put in place for Edward V. The first Yorkist Prince of Wales came to Ludlow as a six-year-old child in 1476 and was there for about seven years before his father died. While Prince Edward was under the age of fourteen, a council was established to manage the estates and jurisdictions associated with him in the principality of Wales, the duchy of Cornwall and county of Chester.[12] Much earlier, however, on 21 February 1473, the prince's authority had been more clearly defined in the same region. Officers were named to oversee his education and enforce his lordship. They had responsibility to safeguard his lands, receive fealties from his feudal tenants, grant licences for church and monastic elections and appointments, present priests to church livings, grant the marriage and wardship of underage heirs, issue pardons, appoint stewards and other officers of estates in his hands, and grant letters under his great seal as long as such grants were not made for life but during pleasure or good behaviour in office. All of this activity was subject to the higher authority of the king's council at Westminster. It did, however, leave the prince, through his advisors and guardians, with enormous scope to influence the communities, networks, governance and power in the areas he controlled. The selection of the prince's representatives, servants and supporters was particularly important. Delegated or proxy power gave them enhanced influence in relation to others not admitted to the prince's household or his network of manorial stewards and other officers.

Most important to national politics was the way that Edward IV used the service network around his son to lay the basis for future Yorkist power. The prince was being trained and developed, but so too were his aristocratic servants. The private and household officers with whom the young boy would grow up were intended to be his companions, advisors and friends once he was an adult king. The local Marcher gentry gravitated towards this opportunity for advancement. To counteract over-aggressive jostling for attention, the prince's wellbeing was ensured by powerful members of Queen Elizabeth Woodville's family. Her brother Anthony, Earl Rivers was Prince Edward's governor. He discharged Edward's semi-regal powers in the borderlands. Other committed backers of Edward IV, like John Alcock, Bishop of Worcester, were rewarded with key posts. Sir William Stanley was another main beneficiary, becoming steward of the prince's household.

The king intended to integrate his son into a balanced and pre-existing power structure rather than impose a new authority to dominate a region that included some very senior families (such as the Staffords and Talbots) upon whom the king partly relied for his national military strength. Their presence around the prince provided greater support for his control of the resources and responsibilities of the earldom of March. Administrators of the earldom of Chester and Flintshire and the chamberlains of north and south Wales were to pay the monies due from their lordships directly to the prince's council. Alcock, Rivers and Queen Elizabeth Woodville were to have the keys to chests where the cash was received and paid out. Alcock, as president of the council from November 1473, had oversight of the books and documents that were the permanent record of the prince's border governance and its decisions.

The names and backgrounds of the chief personnel around the prince had changed by Arthur's time. Their function of representation and guidance was broadly the same but there was a significant difference in the balance of people and their individual status. In 1502, after he had been married, Arthur's council contained a core of ten men – many of whom had additional roles in the prince's household as well as his specialist advisors. Sir Richard Pole represented Margaret Beaufort's blood and probably her interests on the council. Her control of the wardship of the Duke of Buckingham made her a powerful figure in the borders at precisely the time that Prince Arthur entered the final phase of his training as a great lord. Pole's election as a knight of the Garter in 1499 recognised the importance of his work in preparing Prince Arthur for personal rule, and moved Pole to the heart of the Tudor establishment. Sir Henry Vernon of Tong was Arthur's governor. Through his marriage to Anne, daughter of the second Earl of Shrewsbury, Vernon represented the interests of one of the country's strongest military connections, the Talbots. He was reported to have taken Prince Arthur regularly to his residence at Haddon in Derbyshire, where there was a prince's chamber and carvings of Arthur's heraldic badges. This route to Arthur's ear was one of the few ways that the great nobles could penetrate the layers of Tudor relatives and crown-appointed loyalists surrounding the prince. Sir Richard Croft was treasurer of Arthur's household and a domineering presence around the Leominster area of Herefordshire, as has already been noted.

From 1494, the president of Arthur's Council of the Marches of Wales was William Smith, Bishop of Coventry and Lichfield. He was soon promoted to the diocese of Lincoln, but continued to spend much of his time absent from his flock, working in the border counties of England and Wales. Smith is a prime example of how the servants of the prince emerged from the small inner group around the king. Smith was from Lancashire and was part of a clique that became connected to Margaret Beaufort through her residence at Lathom House, near Ormskirk, with her husband Lord Stanley in the 1470s. His church career started in Wimborne in Dorset, where the tombs of the Beaufort family lay. Smith was a typical hard-working but unspectacular Tudor administrator. Alongside his close friend Sir Reginal Bray, Smith helped to pull the pieces of Tudor government together. One of his first Crown jobs was to look after the money coming into the chancery office from the issuing of government letters. A surviving household account from the end of 1491, just before his promotion to the bishopric of Coventry and Lichfield, shows his concern to master information about the administration of his diocese as well as a more colourful political role as a courtier.[13] But Smith was not a preaching prelate, and his talents as a Crown servant kept him away from church for much of his career. Smith ended up living near Worcester. From there his personal devotion to Prince Arthur could be brought fully to bear on the prince's education. He was the most important intermediary between Arthur, Margaret Beaufort (whose council he also headed) and the king. Yet his connections to Oxford University, where he was chancellor from

1500, gave him a natural link to other bishop-administrators like Hugh Oldham and Richard Fox – men who were vital elements in the balance of the polity that kept Henry VII in power. Smith worked tirelessly to make Arthur ready to rule. His letters indicate that this effort was stressful and exhausting and he was devastated by Prince Arthur's death.

Other councillors included Sir David Philips, Sir Peter Newton, Sir Thomas Englefield, Sir William Uvedale, John Wilson, Henry Marian and Charles Booth. Vernon and Uvedale were both knighted alongside Arthur when he was created knight of the bath and Prince of Wales at the end of November 1489. They had missed earlier opportunities for knighthood, so their investiture at the same time as the prince and their consistent close association with him in the Marches afterwards might show that Henry VII had already worked out his plans in establishing the status of those people he had identified as being suitable to guide his son. Neither Vernon nor Uvedale were natural choices for service in the border counties, since they held no lands there. It was their association with the Crown or with other important figures that secured their appointment within Prince Arthur's regional government.

If the prince's income from his private estates was meant to make him self-sufficient then it was his direction of the law that enforced his dominance as a representative of the more distant king. The council had authority to array men to pursue and arrest felons who fled into the Welsh lordships. It also spent much time in managing commissions to better punish serious crimes such as robbery, murder, destruction and oppression of the king's subjects. The border remained dangerous and the frontier between lordships was porous. The rising of Owain Glyndŵr and the waste and damage it caused to livelihoods and lordships along the border was, after the 1470s, still an event that could be recalled by later generations. The frontier areas suffered from a propensity to lawlessness without constant and active intervention by the authorities. Many communities might have been weighed down by the potential for a return to disturbance and rebellion without the strong government and a real royal presence that Prince Arthur brought. A bolstering of the authority of the prince's council did that, too. It also presented real opportunities for the prince to apply the intricacies of model kingship learned from the books of John Rede and Bernard André.

One of the most dynamic and powerful figures of the early part of Henry VII's reign who was with Arthur on his appearance at Hereford in April 1493 was Sir William Stanley; however, he was absent from the list of Arthur's chief men by 1502 because he had been executed for treason in February 1495. His case was a shining example of why Henry VII was right to build a corporate body around the governance of the prince and not to trust Arthur's upbringing to a dominant individual. It cannot be overstated how tricky the situation with the Stanley family must have been for Henry VII. They were related to the royal family through Lord Stanley's marriage to Henry's mother, and in the end had made the victory at Bosworth possible. Stanley became chamberlain of the king's household, a post of central importance to the security and magnificence of the monarch. Stanley loyalty remained a fickle thing, unsteady and driven by self-interest. Their support for Henry was balanced by selfish calculation of the wider benefits they would gain. Building power beyond its core origins in Lancashire and Cheshire was how they intended to reap the rewards of backing the Tudor cause. William Stanley had used his connection to Prince Edward in the 1470s and 1480s to strengthen his influence along the border. Although Richard III had robbed Stanley of a certain route to prominence under Edward V's rule, Arthur's arrival represented a second chance.

When Sir William Stanley's servants appeared at the centre of the conflict at Leominster in 1487, they highlighted the route his influence was taking. Stanley was working his way back into the communities that he had known during his time on the border with Edward, Prince of Wales. His presence and search for allies on the March triggered an immediate response from Sir Richard Croft as these two officers of the king's household fell out spectacularly over who might be best positioned to control the future of the prince.

The royal household roles of both men also dragged the heated emotions of this local issue back to the centre of the king's power. The royal household was meant to be the secure heart of the regime. Dangerous division between household leaders could infect other parts of the machine if not confronted. In 1485, Henry VII had been obliged to invite a range of people into his service as his personal following was not numerous enough to fulfil all of the Crown's responsibilities nationwide. This need to involve those willing to serve was secured by bonds and other measures, but it did expose King Henry to conspirators hiding behind expressions of loyalty. It also overrode his natural caution about why members of the ruling elites had pledged their allegiance to him when he was unknown and untested as a national leader. Since Prince Arthur was not yet old or prepared enough to live on the Marches as the king wanted, Henry VII might have felt that he had more time to sort out how the prince's household would be led. Greater certainty about whether the country truly backed his rule was a more pressing concern before the end of the 1480s. While the king was distracted by rebellions and the question of loyalty, Sir William Stanley began to feel that the rewards expected or promised after Bosworth were slow to arrive. He was unlikely to have been dabbling in treason in 1487, but his frustrations were shown by the aggressive expansion of influence.

A few years later, by February 1493, King Henry was convinced that Stanley was a traitor. News of the supposed reappearance of Edward IV's son Richard, Duke of York (in the person of Perkin

Warbeck) at the end of 1491 had captured William Stanley's attention. As he tried desperately to discover if the survival of a Yorkist prince was true, Stanley revealed that he was not totally committed to Henry VII. Even that level of doubt was completely unacceptable. Stanley was chamberlain of the household. He literally held the keys to the king's private chambers and organised court events and directed the staff that made them successful. Uncertainty over his loyalty must only have created panic about how vulnerable the Tudor royal family had suddenly become. If Prince Richard of York had indeed returned, then Stanley's abandonment of his allegiance to the Tudors would have to include Prince Arthur's rights and status. If Stanley and Lord Fitzwalter, head of the service side of the household, could be convinced of Warbeck's identity, then the rest of the Yorkists close to the Tudor royal family might also switch their loyalty. Had Stanley been reappointed as steward of the prince's household, or had he achieved an even stronger personal role around Arthur as part of his package of gifts and grants, then the defections from the Tudor king that Warbeck set in play could have been truly disastrous.

While his heir was underage, Henry VII needed to find a balance between keeping Arthur safe through the exclusive appointment of loyalists and preserving good government by ensuring that those who did rule on Arthur's behalf did not overextend their authority. Closeness to Prince Arthur in this respect did carry consequences. Henry VII put in place all manner of checks and balances to ensure that those surrounding the prince remained focussed and loyal. In some cases, the price of this role as mentor and guardian to the prince bred resentment. Arthur's governor, Sir Henry Vernon, was praised by the king in an undated letter for the organisation and sensible measures he had put in place to regulate Prince Arthur's household. Almost in the same breath, however, the king reminded him that he had to keep to that standard of effort and vigilance in collaboration with the other men on the prince's council. If he failed to do so, then he would be replaced in his post by another of Henry's chief officials from Westminster and be called back to serve the king instead. In his will of 28 January 1515 Vernon complained that

> where the kyng that dede is caused me to be bounden to paye £900 whereof £500 is paid. And which some in my conscyence I ought not to have payd or paye but to have restytucion of that that I have payde and so apperith by a byll assigned with thande of Edmund Dudley.[14]

In this case, Arthur's premature death probably robbed the Vernons of a significant part of their regional influence. Control of their estates had already been under pressure on the Derbyshire/Cheshire border from the Savage family. In the year that Arthur died, Vernon abducted the heiress Margaret Kebell and forced her to marry his heir, Roger (one of twenty-two children born to Henry Vernon and his wife Anne Talbot). Henry Vernon's pardon for this offence cost him the £900 noted above, and it was this fine and the related bonds that irked Vernon thirteen years later. Vernon must have worked hard to use his personal connections to secure a position of influence around the Prince of Wales – as much an investment for future patronage as an immediate cementing of his local authority. His abduction and marriage of an heiress looks like an attempt to find immediate compensation for the loss of longer-term gains that service with Arthur had been expected to bring. It was, obviously, a flagrant abuse of Vernon's position and brought a harsh reaction from the king; although it did not rob Vernon of royal favour. Edmund Dudley, in a confession of the most unreasonable financial demands that he made on behalf of Henry VII, recorded that he felt Vernon's was an excessive penalty. The fact that Vernon had paid £500 testifies to his wealth, but at the end of his life he is also rather angry that he might still be pressed by Henry VIII for the outstanding amount. Did Vernon's decision not to name Henry VII in this statement indicate a great deal of resentment that his efforts on behalf of Prince Arthur had still left him out of pocket, with the prospect of further massive payments hanging over his heir and executors?

King Henry also chased the debts owed by other of Arthur's former officers. John Waleston or Wallaston, who was cofferer of Arthur's household, was bound in September 1503 for about £300 that was still unaccounted for from his time in the prince's service.[15] He had previously been a clerk of Henry VII's kitchen before transferring to the prince's service. Waleston was an experienced administrator very well versed in the sharp practices of running a household. He had done well enough out of Arthur's service to acquire property in Ruislip, but the eagle eyes of the king and his chamber staff soon found a trail of unaccounted money. Part of the sum owed was related to official business; £57 had been allocated to him for use in the household but had not been spent and had been kept in Waleston's hands. Other parts of the debts grew from the elevation of Waleston's status that service with the prince had brought. He still owed £30 for the wardship and marriage of Peter Christmasse. Evidently it had taken the king and the treasurer of his chamber, John Heron, some time after Arthur's death to go through the records of his administration and household structure. Once the debts were identified, Henry was quite ruthless in ensuring that his son's servants did not get away with the apparent financial gains and abuse of status arising from their posts in the Ludlow or Tickenhill households.

Other evidence points to a regional division between those on the inside of Arthur's regime, and others unable to break in and enjoy the benefits of membership. In November 1502, Bishop Smith wrote to Reginald Bray about the possible transfer of two of Arthur's servants to the household of the Duke of Buckingham.

They had to make their living and needed a new post. Smith asked Bray to be a good master to John Gifford and Roland Egerton and have a quiet word with the Duke of Buckingham. Buckingham flatly refused. It would be easy to see this decision as Buckingham's payback for the way that his lands had financed the prince's household from 1486, when the duke was a ward of the king's mother. Buckingham only came of age in February 1499.[16]

Military Power

Earlier in the fifteenth century the impact of youthful heirs of the royal blood was often found in battle. Their roles partly reflected the times in which they lived. Civil war and the struggles of usurping monarchs to maintain control in their more distant dominions forced kings like Henry IV to use the status of their sons as an additional source of strength in a military struggle with internal rebels and foreign enemies. The less warlike accomplishments of many princes were often subsumed beneath more immediate demands on their military and diplomatic expertise, and also depended upon their age. To have been successful in that capacity and to have credibility as leaders, princes had to receive the kind of rounded education that all royal boys could expect in the later medieval period. Many princes displayed the opposite balance of skills to Prince Arthur. Chivalric activities were achieved at an early age. Spectacular accomplishments in arms have made it harder for modern researchers to uncover details of how rapidly their other intellectual abilities and social skills developed during their early teenage years. With Arthur, his learning is well documented but his physical accomplishments remain obscure.

As Prince of Wales, Arthur had some impressive shoes to fill. The future Henry V had a difficult relationship with his father. As an eighteen-year-old, around 1405 he was handed responsibility for leading the resistance to Owain Glyndŵr's Welsh uprising. He had already been seriously wounded as a sixteen-year-old at the Battle of Shrewsbury in July 1403. Henry had an early experience of battle in common with Edward of Lancaster (Henry VI's Prince of Wales) and with Edward IV. Prince Edward of Lancaster was killed after the Battle of Tewkesbury in May 1471 at the age of seventeen, and Edward IV, as the eighteen-year-old Earl of March (effectively prince after his father's claim to be king after Henry VI), had led troops at Mortimer's Cross in February 1461. Of course, by the time they were raising armies and inspiring men in battle these princes were considered to be adults, even if the legal age of majority remained twenty-one. Behind their precocious abilities also lay an elite education, combining the classical scholarship available at the time with knowledge of the law and long training in managing men and land.

In reality, Arthur shared all of these opportunities and abilities. His father prepared him to emulate his forebears as sons of a King of England. Our knowledge is limited by the almost non-existent opportunities that the fifteen-year-old first Tudor Prince of Wales had to demonstrate his accomplishments as a leader in war. Even as a child, Arthur's status as prince, his landholding and his control of the law as a justice made him one of the foremost military figures in early Tudor England. He would not be in a position to take up arms and be a general for many years, but a key part of his training was to make him understand how military resources were recruited and controlled on behalf of the state. Long before standing armies were part of the nation's preparation and readiness for war, the Crown relied on the nobility and gentry to muster, mobilise and lead the companies of troops that formed England's armies. The king would supply his own cavalry, archers and billmen based on the capacity of the servants of the royal household. He could also choose to license lords and knights to raise the tenants of Crown lands. When combined, the various strands of recruitment could put an army of over 30,000 men into the field, as Henry VII did when assembling an invasion of Scotland in 1497.[17]

When he became king, Arthur would be expected to behave confidently as a military leader, both as a field commander and as a campaign strategist. The nobility no doubt hoped ardently that their monarch fundamentally understood how armies were put together and deployed against the enemy. The aristocracy wanted to be led by a ruler with the skills and drive of a young Edward III, not those of a distracted, middle-aged Henry VI. Kings had to speak the language of war with competence even if they were not required to lead in the thick of the fighting. The experiences by which Henry V or Edward IV bloodied their hands at Agincourt or Tewkesbury were exceptional and borne out of military necessity. Their exploits on the battlefield did, nevertheless, accelerate a wider acceptance of their capacity to rule England. Their prowess inspired poetry and literature and strengthened cultural identity. Success in war helped to unify the nation's leaders behind the king; certainly for as long as victories kept coming, opportunities for land and ransom continued, and the national costs of war did not outweigh the benefits. Where regimes were less confident of support or security, kings tended to think that they were more useful at the back of the field. After Bosworth, for example, Henry VII was happy to let experienced tacticians like the earls of Oxford and Surrey or Lords Broke and Daubeney take the fight to the Crown's opponents. Making judgements about the right moments to hold back or to become directly involved were skills that could only come from the experience of others who had already faced such challenges.

When King Henry was in exile in Brittany and France he evidently developed some military expertise. There is no evidence of how his skills were encouraged, but he did fight and was prepared to die on the field at Bosworth. Henry was fully equipped as a king in waiting with appropriate armour, weapons and banners. We may presume that he knew how to use them, and also that he was clear about how and why the Earl of Oxford had arrayed the army against Richard III, and how he intended to counteract Richard III's manoeuvres on the battlefield. Henry fought with courage in 1485, but two years later he watched the Battle of Stoke from the tower of Newark church. By then, the king had others to put themselves on the line on his behalf. He did order new and very expensive complete sets of armour for the invasion of Scotland in 1497. It is unlikely that he would have done any fighting unless put into a desperate situation, but the intention to be a visible commander-in-chief would have been there for all to see had the full-scale invasion actually taken place. It does seem probable that Prince Arthur would have received similar encouragement from his father. Those military men with a connection to Arthur's household and to his lordship, such as Sir Richard Pole, the Earl of Shrewsbury and the Marquis of Dorset, might have been the experienced soldiers who imparted anecdotes as well as hard experience of war to the prince.

The provision of training in this way does seem likely because Prince Arthur could nominally command one of the largest forces within the kingdom. Even before he became resident at Ludlow in the spring of 1493, the men connected with the estates that Arthur would soon occupy along the Welsh border contributed an impressive number of troops to the king's campaigns. Figures like Pole joined Arthur's household because they were so highly trusted by the king and so clearly aligned with the nature of the regime that Henry VII was building. In August 1492, as part of an indentured army of small contingents to be sent to France, Sir Richard Pole brought 101 cavalrymen and almost 200 archers – as much as many earls.[18] In the far more desperate times of the 1497 Western Rising, a rebel army from the south-western counties marched largely unopposed towards London. Before it was defeated at the Battle of Blackheath on 17 June, the royal family had retreated into the Tower of London. Prince Arthur was not with them. Arthur's whereabouts are unknown during 1497, but he was most likely securely protected in Shropshire as a possible alternative source of government should the very worst have happened. The estates of the earldom of March would have generated a sizeable force in their own right, as Edward IV had demonstrated when he held that title at the start of 1461. The absence of some of Arthur's senior counsellors from the army payment lists, like Sir Richard Croft and Sir Henry Vernon, could indicate that there was a core government in the Marches ready to take the reins of power if necessary. Croft's office of steward of the lands of the earldom might have been key to the provision of a mobilised force that remained with the prince in the borderlands.

At the same time, other parts of the prince's administration were on the move. Sir Richard Pole, as Arthur's chamberlain, was leading the prince's retinue towards the musters for the king's army assembled to invade Scotland. He was paid £569 for the wages of the prince's retinue brought to fight at Blackheath. That was only one pound less than the Earl of Shrewsbury, whose army consisted of 7 men-at-arms, 19 cavalrymen and 1,161 archers. Some of Pole's force had been assembled as part of the vanguard to invade Scotland in an attempt to dislodge the pretender Perkin Warbeck from the protection of James IV. It was diverted south as soon as the south-western rebellion was known. The key men of the prince and the king in Wales, Sir Richard Pole, Sir Rhys ap Thomas and Sir Walter Herbert, between them supplied 80 per cent of the cavalry in the army's vanguard: 1,046 of 1,300 demi-lances. Both Pole and Thomas were exceptional commanders of light cavalry but Arthur's contribution of 540 archers and 8 men-at-arms also represented the highest single retinue of foot soldiers.[19] The strength of his lordship of the earldom of March and the importance of his role as resident prince in the Marches meant he could already supply a force that was indispensable to the Tudor crown.

5

THE ROYAL WEDDING OF THE CENTURY

Arrivals

The preparations for Catherine of Aragon's marriage to Arthur had lasted almost the entire lives of the two royal children. Before Catherine would be sent to England, the Spanish monarchs wanted assurances, if not guarantees, that their daughter would be under no threat and could flourish as Princess of Wales. Henry was undoubtedly more secure after the capture of Perkin Warbeck in 1497, but Ferdinand was more concerned about Yorkist nobles with royal blood. By 1499, Henry's pressure on Queen Elizabeth's relatives had produced mixed results. Edmund de la Pole had briefly fled overseas in July that year. In doing so he revealed his unease at King Henry's attempt to enforce his loyalty. By November 1499, the pretender Warbeck and the last direct male Plantagenet figurehead, Edward, Earl of Warwick (son of Edward IV's brother George, Duke of Clarence), were executed following a conviction for treason. The Spanish monarchs were awaiting that step and an assessment of its aftermath before finally agreeing to send Princess Catherine to England for her marriage. Once this had happened, Ferdinand and Isabella saw few reasons to doubt that the Tudor regime would continue to strengthen and flourish. By the time Catherine was expected in England in September 1501, the king's council had drawn up detailed guidelines and timetables for what they intended to happen. These instructions were amended and changed even after Catherine made her landfall in England, which was at Plymouth rather than Southampton as intended. The final version of the instructions also differs from what happened in practice. Comparison of the plan formalised by the king's council and what came to pass in October and November 1501 also reveals important evidence of how the dynamics of conciliar government worked, something that Arthur's Council of the Marches was also subject to.[1] The contemporary account of these events was almost certainly written by a member of the royal household who witnessed several otherwise unrecorded incidents at first hand. The text recording the princess's arrival and the accounts of the subsequent pageants of entry into London, the marriage ceremony and the spectacular tournaments, indicate a viewpoint that was physically very close to the king. The account might even have been an official record, drawn up for the royal family. Either way, its description of the sights and sounds of Catherine's arrival and wedding paints a unique and detailed picture of some of the most spectacular ceremonies planned and performed in late medieval and Tudor England.

Katherine had left Corunna in Spain on 17 August. A massive storm forced her ships back to the port of Laredo for repairs and the arrival of favourable weather. Henry VII was worried enough to send out master mariners and pilots familiar with the routes to Spain to search for the fleet. One of these captains, Stephen Brett from Devon, located the princess's ships and agreed to guide them towards England. The planned landfall had been Southampton but it was likely that Brett's piloting abilities led them into his own harbour, Plymouth, where they arrived on 2 October. Since the king had prepared a magnificent formal reception at Southampton, hasty rearrangements had to be made to dispatch some senior representatives into Devon. News took only two days to cross the 230 miles between Plymouth and Richmond. After discussion of how best to proceed, the king and council decided to send the steward of the king's household – Robert Lord Willoughby de Broke –to greet the princess with as much dignity as was possible after her delayed appearance in England over 100 miles further west than expected.

Willoughby was a very good organiser; it was his job to keep the king's domestic service running smoothly. He had excelled in the execution of the maritime part of England's invasion of Scotland in the summer of 1497. Willoughby brought with him a team of ceremonial experts and security specialists – heralds, pursuivants and sergeants-at-arms – headed by Robert Browne, Richmond King of Arms. They were to attend upon the steward and intercept the princess at Exeter. All were then to escort her to London. Another remarkably fast journey brought Willoughby to Honiton on 7 October and then to Exeter with twelve palfrey horses and a litter to join Catherine and her companions. The king's men had to wait until Tuesday 19 October before she arrived in the city, accompanied by 'all the nobles of the far south-west'. They had taken proper measures to greet her honourably and deliver her safely to the king's appointed representative. She then began a progress towards London, passing through Honiton and Crewkerne by 20 October – a journey of about twenty-one miles. Even allowing for the autumn weather and road conditions, Catherine's party moved at a fairly swift pace. On the outskirts of Crewkerne she was greeted by a collection of Dorset gentry led by the knights Amyas Paulet and Hugh Lutterell, who had been assigned to escort Catherine to Sherborne.

The princess usually stopped overnight at the abbeys and priories found along the route. The sight of a Spanish princess with her attendant nobles, officers, ladies and baggage train must have been spectacular and so unusual as to draw massive crowds – although it is possible to question just how ceremonial the progress was and how visible Catherine would have been before the final formal stages of her wedding. The herald's account of the journey gives little information on how the princess was received, but it is likely that her arrival was genuinely a cause for rejoicing and celebration. The next stages of her passage through Dorset and Wiltshire were a direct route via Shaftesbury (sixteen miles, with no travelling on Sunday 31 October), Amesbury (twenty-nine miles) and Andover (thirteen miles).

By the time the caravan reached Amesbury, the rank of the welcoming parties had increased. She was met by Thomas Howard, Earl of Surrey and Elizabeth Talbot, Duchess of Norfolk. Surrey was Lord Treasurer of England and by then was among the king's most trusted officials. The duchess was one of the senior women of the realm. The duchess's ladies included unnamed countesses accompanied by the bishops of Bath and Wells and Hereford, Lords Zouche and Dacre of the South, and Sir Robert Poyntz. William Hallibrand, fluent in the Spanish language, read out a prepared speech of welcome on behalf of the queen. At Andover the procession stayed in the Angel Inn on the High Street on the night of 3 November. The building was then relatively new, having been built by Winchester College before 1455. Her visit is still marked over 500 years later – a communal memory that must have lingered in many other places visited by Princess Catherine at that time.

Catherine's route to London was like a royal progress. A very large number of lords and gentry would have played some part in aiding her journey from one night's lodging to the next.

All of these involved in welcoming the princess to the towns, monasteries and inns on the way towards London had received their instructions from Lord Daubeney, the chamberlain of the royal household. The heralds sent into Devon when Catherine first landed required that all lords and nobles should be waiting for her upon arrival at the end of a day's travelling. They should ensure that she was lodged properly before taking their own rest. As was fitting for their rank and status, they were to keep her company on each stage of the route. She was also to be protected by a gentleman riding before her chair or carriage and two yeomen of the crown behind. Only those who were allocated a role in the entourage were to come anywhere near the princess on the road. Her honour and security were maintained by the Lord Steward, Lord Willoughby, and his men. Of particular importance was the assignment of lodging according to the scheme devised by the king's officers. None of the noble or gentry companions accompanying Catherine were to arrange their own rooms or food. Such a stipulation was sensible management of a large entourage on the road but might also have been a reflection of how the security of the king's household organisation had been deficient during his first progress in 1486. When Henry VII was at York at Easter 1486 individuals had been able to infiltrate the king's lodging chambers and make an attempt on his life. Catherine's physical wellbeing was King Henry's main responsibility towards his allies King Ferdinand and Queen Isabella. No mishaps could be allowed to arise during this early part of Catherine's time in England when she was potentially at her most vulnerable to mischief or random accident.

The speed of travel increased so that Basingstoke, Dogmersfield and Chertsey were reached on consecutive days between 4 and 7 November. The king was annoyed by the natural and human delays to the schedule he had planned. He seems to have been impatient to meet the princess and finalise the ceremonies with her and her advisors. The lack of splendour and diligence under which Catherine had been greeted in the outlying parts of the south-west of his kingdom might also have been a niggling source of embarrassment. Whatever his motive, on 4 November Henry left Richmond Palace with the intention of reaching Dogmersfield, where the Bishop of Bath and Wells (Oliver King, also king's secretary) held the house that would later become Dogmersfield Park. The king suffered his own delays and only managed to travel the twelve miles to Chertsey before night drew in. The following day, King Henry rode hard from Chertsey for a meeting with Prince Arthur at the royal hunting lodge near the village of Easthampstead by Bracknell. Given the delays that Catherine had experienced since the start of her original voyage on 17 August, Arthur's own journey from Ludlow or Bewdley must have been subject to all kinds of changes and amendments to take account of his prospective wife's late arrival in England. Although the yeomen of the crown seem to have made phenomenal efforts as messengers, covering hundreds of miles in a few days during this period, news of incidents at sea might have been very slow to reach the king's ears and then be transmitted to the Welsh border. Arthur's appearance on the roads of East Berkshire at the start of November does suggest, however, that regular communication with his household had established the same level of coordination as between Westminster and Ludlow.

Henry and his son spent time together at Dogmersfield overnight on 5 November. The next day Henry met with Catherine's advisors, headed by the Protonotary of Spain. They had been instructed by King Ferdinand to retain control over the princess at all times until the wedding was solemnised. She was also rather horrified to think that she might meet Arthur before the wedding ceremony. There might already have been a little tension between Lord Willoughby's men and the Spanish lords because of this custom. After a brief discussion with King Henry, they nevertheless agreed to the English becoming more involved in directing Catherine safely to London. To that end, a meeting was held between the king and the princess at Dogmersfield house on the afternoon of 6 November. She had arrived a few hours before the king and Prince Arthur with her party of about sixty servants, including the very senior Dom Pedro de Ayala (the ambassador), Alonzo de Fonseca, Archbishop of Santiago (effectively the archbishop of Spain), Diego de Cordoba (the Earl of Spain) and Antonio de Rojas, Bishop of Mallorca (known to the English as the bishop of Spain). She was resting in her chamber when Henry arrived. Having travelled with the express intention of making an assessment of the princess, he impatiently threatened to talk with her even if she was in bed! Catherine had little choice but to calmly receive the king. There then followed a stilted and slightly confused conversation between the forty-four-year-old king and his son's fifteen-year-old bride, conducted in English and Spanish translations with occasional Latin as a common language. During this audience it was decided that Arthur and Catherine should renew in person the wedding vows that had already been taken by proxies – the formal betrothal in August 1497 at Woodstock and a marriage ceremony at Tickenhill Place in Bewdley on 19 May 1499.

The king changed from his riding clothes. We assume that Arthur did the same, since his crimson outfit was conspicuous in its finery. Henry then spent thirty minutes giving his son another inspiring lecture before they both entered Catherine's chamber. The same multi-lingual conversation followed and the espousal ceremony was concluded. The king then headed off for his supper and allowed Arthur and Catherine to have some time together. Her Spanish minstrels played and a small dance party followed. Arthur was able to demonstrate his skill with Lady Guildford (Joan Vaux), who was married to Sir Richard Guildford, one of the king's oldest friends. Formal and personal emotions were running high between the two young people. They represented their countries and were duty bound to perform the required ceremonies without flaw or error. Catherine was aged almost sixteen and Arthur just over fourteen. By any standards they were very young to be the centre of international attention. Yet they had been born to it.

At the end of 1501, Arthur had been developing his kingly skills for eight years. He was used to the adult world of noble decision-making, negotiation, arbitration and leadership. This was the period when his preparation to rule was coming to fruition. Despite this, one can't help but imagine how nervous and excited he must have been to see his bride for the first time. They had corresponded officially and Arthur had expressed the expected sentiments and his intention to be a good and loving husband. After their meeting, however, there was more than a hint of the prince's personal delight when he wrote to Ferdinand and Isabella with news that he was immensely happy to have seen the beautiful face of his lovely bride. Catherine was indeed a striking beauty; but she must also have been a steely and highly capable politician – even during her teen years. Portraits and commentaries back up both of these judgements. Catherine had also been brought up to bear a range of responsibilities and had shown herself to be fearless in her dramatic journey to England up to this point. Henry VII surely must have been satisfied with the qualities he saw in his daughter-in-law.

Arthur departed the next day, presumably towards London in preparation for the wedding that was now imminent. Catherine continued on her planned route to Chertsey, where she stayed on the night of 7 November. Her caravan was then meant to head for Croydon and the Archbishop of Canterbury's summer residence, which was to be her base during the organisation of the final stages of the journey. Before she got too far beyond Chertsey, however, she was met near Kingston-upon-Thames by a group of peers led by the Duke of Buckingham, the Earl of Kent and Arthur's brother, the ten-year-old Henry, Duke of York. Henry met his future wife only a day after his elder brother. The account suggests that 300–400 other people were officially gathered at this rendezvous to hear the abbot of Bury St Edmunds make another lengthy Latin speech of welcome.

The council had instructed Buckingham to meet Catherine on the road across Banstead Down, between Chertsey and Croydon. It would appear that the king's decision to ride out from Richmond had forced more changes to the itinerary. Croydon was no longer suitable as a stopover point – it would introduce yet more delay – and so was replaced by Kingston. Buckingham and Lords Fitzwarren, Stourton and St Amand, as well as many of the king's senior household knights like Walter Hungerford and Edward Darell, acted under the chamberlain's amended instructions. They conducted the Spaniards directly to La Place in Lambeth. This house was the London base of the Bishop of Rochester, Richard FitzJames. Everyone else in her group, including her English conductors, had lodging elsewhere in Lambeth town.

Meanwhile, the king returned to Richmond via Windsor. He was reported to have given Queen Elizabeth a personal update on what had occurred over the previous days and how delighted he was with Princess Catherine's appearance and demeanour. With all of England's nobles converging on London along with the Spanish and the royal family, there was little time to wait at Richmond. On 10 November, the king and queen reached Paris Garden manor on the Southwark side of the river where their barges awaited to convey Henry and Elizabeth to Baynard's Castle. The grand entrance of the princess into London had long been planned as a river pageant. The foreshore provided an opportunity for thousands of citizens to catch a glimpse of the barges and boats and to see the visual imagery uniting England

and one of Europe's great powers. The delays and changes to her journey meant that some aspects of the day had to be altered. The account suggests that London was absolutely thronged with people who had travelled from the suburbs and elsewhere in the country. All lords and servants were dressed in their brightly coloured liveries with badges and tokens. The common people jostled through the streets in preparation for the wedding. Only St Paul's was large enough to accommodate the mass of subjects wishing to get close enough to see the ceremonies. The herald recording the event made a point of noting that despite the multitude, no one was injured in the crowds or by getting too close to the horses of the procession. The king set up his household at Baynard's Castle, which had recently been extensively rebuilt specifically as part of the City's backdrop for what Henry VII intended to be the wedding of the century. The house had strong associations with the House of York as the main London residence of Queen Elizabeth's father and grandfather. Might there have been some symbolism in Henry VII's redevelopment of the building as part of the redefinition of his regime through the wedding of his heir? If this is difficult to perceive then other projects to transform the venues for the wedding events were more explicit.

Pageants

On Friday 12 November Catherine breakfasted in Lambeth and proceeded with her retinue to St George's Fields below Southwark. There she was met by the Archbishop of York with many clerics and another group of aristocrats headed by Prince Henry and the Duke of Buckingham with other lords assigned to attend the princess and escort her to London. They travelled by road through Southwark to the southern end of London Bridge. Already assembled on the bridge was the first of six pageants of welcome.[2] These scenes were loaded with allegory and symbolism.

They carried the key public messages that Henry VII wished to project about the marriage alliance between England and Spain and about his own family's right to the throne. They had been in development since November 1499. A lead-in time of two years allowed for preparation of spectacular performances dripping with precise propaganda. The government of the City of London had assigned two men from the livery companies to share the preparation and implementation of a plan that was probably created within the royal household and council. The herald's account of Catherine's entry is explicit and comprehensive in its detailed recording of what took place. The author had either seen written accounts of what was to be performed or was able to incorporate his own observations into the written detail of the pageants. The content of the enactments was interrelated in a very sophisticated way and the show at each station on the journey to St Paul's extended and developed the previous performances.

The pageant on London Bridge presented the story of St Catherine and St Ursula. A two-floored and open-fronted wooden structure had St Catherine visible in the bottom storey and St Ursula on the top. Each woman playing the part carried the symbols of the saint's life: so St Catherine carried her wheel and was accompanied by many virgins, while St Ursula was accompanied with yet more virgins. Both were presented under a large image of the Trinity. The structure was decorated with garters, red roses, ostrich feather badges, portcullises and a red lion holding the arms of England. It was also painted gold and azure blue. The actress playing St Catherine had a clear role to flatter the princess's virtues while emphasising the earthly benefits that would follow from her marriage to Arthur. The characters in the pageants linked the narrative and a sequence of allusions to the principal requirements of good governance. Thus the captain of this first castle on the bridge was Policy. Catherine's journey through the other pageants would take her towards Honour.

Here, the English were championing the wedding itself but also expressing their ideas about a model marriage and its relationship to future good governance. Arthur would become king. At his side, Catherine would have a powerful role in safeguarding his wellbeing and kingly qualities through a life of virtue.

Through this first pageant, the king's council and the London corporations through whom the councillors worked tried to link Catherine to ancient Britain (Ursula being the daughter of an early Christian king in Britain) and to her own connection to the House of Lancaster (from John of Gaunt's daughter Katherine, who became Queen of Castile in 1388). In the pageant, Ursula also spoke of her own status as part of the celestial constellation Ursa Minor – adjacent to that of Arcturus as part of an arrangement of seven stars in Boötes (Arcturus being the brightest individual star in the northern sky). As Sydney Anglo has pointed out, this allusion related to the proximity of Arthur and Ursa Minor, which had been misidentified as one and the same. Just as the bright heavenly bodies were joined harmoniously, so Arthur and Catherine would be on earth. Arthur's tutor Bernard André in his *Life of Henry VII* claimed that the prince had been born when Arcturus was ascendant in the night sky and that this was one of the reasons for his given name. The prominence of the star had also diverted the attention of Christian thinkers who had developed a sophisticated biblical relationship between Arcturus and what it represented regarding the Church's teachings on virtue and grace. Associating Arthur the prince with the high point of Christian virtue demonstrated an impressive understanding of conventional spiritual teaching by whoever devised the overall theme for the welcome event.

At the far end of the bridge, in Gracechurch Street, the second pageant was cleverly built over the watercourse that ran down the middle of the road. This device was a castle and portcullis. Part of the tower was of free stone. More royal badges decorated the structure, including Tudor roses, white harts and the Beaufort portcullis. The gate of the castle was defended by a real portcullis with red roses at each joint. An even larger red rose and the royal arms supported by Henry VII's red dragon and white greyhound completed the far from subtle display of royal and family imagery. A fully armoured knight stood waiting in the gate of the castle. This was Policy. He shared the structure with other actors representing Noblesse and Virtue, who were present in tottering pinnacles, turrets and towers emerging from the main castle. Policy let onlookers know that the gates of the castle had spontaneously opened because of the presence of the light beams of the star of Spain, Hesperus, in the form of Princess Catherine. Hesperus was the evening star, the child of the dawn. The evening star could also have been seen as an interpretation of Venus (which was often visible at dusk), or even as a step towards Lucifer, the Latin name for the related morning star. The genealogies of Arthur and Venus (Catherine) were the subjects of a book by Richard Maryngton dedicated to Lord Broke in 1502. This allusion took the star's relationship to Catherine in an unwanted direction towards those associated with Lucifer's fall from heaven and those who were without virtue. So this allegory has been interpreted as a straightforward shortcut for Hisperia, or the western land of Spain. Catherine is praised for being both noble and virtuous. Her marriage to Arthur would bring these qualities to bear on his future kingship, since she would guide him towards Honour.

The princess then proceeded to Cornhill, where the next scene awaited her at the conduit. Panels were painted to look like stone and marble. A cornice in the colours of the Tudor and Trastámara royal houses was decorated with the English royal badges of roses, dragons and lions, along with the arms as in the previous scene. The pageant was dominated by a mechanical representation of the zodiac set above actors playing a group of characters associated with astronomy: Job, Boethius, the Archangel Raphael and Alphonso the Wise (Alphonso X of Castile, an ally of Henry III of England in the 1250s and patron of Iberian astronomy). The device featured a blue sphere of the moon that also showed the order and course of the planets and stars. The structure was a practical manifestation of the knowledge of astronomy and drew on earlier associations with particular stars. The focus on celestial and heavenly associations brought Arthur and Catherine closer to God and emphasised the fitness of the royal couple to rule England in the future. The philosophers and prophets demonstrated that man's knowledge of the world and heavens only came from God. These learned men were present to assure that audience that God was especially connected to those like Arthur and Catherine who had a virtuous, honourable and Christian marriage. Their noble status further strengthened the bridge between heaven and earth, while the image of the celestial wheel might also have linked the stars with St Catherine – whose martyrdom would have been known to the onlookers.

The fourth pageant continued the starry theme. At the conduit in Cheapside a structure was set up with four great heraldic beasts at each corner: red dragon, white hart with golden crown, white greyhound and red lion. At the front, another great wheel with a shield of St George at its centre. A representation of God and various angels surrounded a depiction of Prince Arthur in splendour as an ideal knight at the centre of the sun and cosmos. Other knights ascended a moving escalator-type staircase towards Arthur. By portraying Arthur as the sun, his role as defender of justice was made all the more obvious (although the precise meaning of Arthur as the sun, linking him directly to Christ, was not spotted by commentators on the pageant). This motif also praised Arthur's wisdom and belief in justice as a foundation for honourable rule.

The next scene, outside the Standard Inn in Cheapside, presented God's throne within the Temple of God. A red rose the size of a man was supported by Tudor beasts, the red dragon and white greyhound. At each corner of the structure by four pillars stood a figure representing a prophet. This structure drew attention since the figures and the tops of the pillars were covered in artificial pearls. On top of this was a representation of heaven, with an actor playing God resplendently dressed in gold, pearls and precious stones. Seven large candles in impressive candlesticks burned before the God figure (a reference back to the seven stars of Arcturus). A choir of children as angels sang as if in a church, to the wonder of those watching. God's speech at this point distilled all the other imagery to make it clear that this was a representation of Arthur as justice in dazzling spiritual armour. The characters then emphasised the power of a virtuous marriage, blessed by children. Marriage was highlighted as the route to salvation, especially as Henry VII was simultaneously praised as the most Christian king. The king and his son were directly portrayed in the display as God the Father and God the Son. The real king and queen, courtiers like King Henry's friends the earls of Oxford and Shrewsbury and also ambassadors had decided to watch the arrival of the princess from the house of the haberdasher William Geoffrey, which overlooked this pageant. As far as the king was concerned, there would have been no surprises in the content of any of the performances. The propaganda, religious imagery and linkage of the prince to a celestial hierarchy would have been approved by King Henry. His decision to watch the fifth pageant implies that he was particularly sympathetic to the messages presented there.

The final performance was at the entrance to St Paul's churchyard at the end of Cheapside. Another building of painted and gilded wood with the familiar royal badges contained figures of the seven virtues: the three theological virtues of Faith, Hope and Charity, and the four cardinal virtues of Courage, Temperance, Prudence and Justice. They were arranged on steps up to the space in which the figure of Honour waited beside empty thrones for Arthur and Catherine. Achievement of these seats could only be gained through a life lived according to the principles already laid down in the previous pageants. Virtue would literally lead to honour, since the steps of each virtue had to be climbed, one at a time, before Honour was reached. The actor playing Honour made this even more obvious when he referenced two temples built by the Roman general Claudius Marcellus in 205 BC. Named Honos and Virtus, the former could only be reached by passing through the one named after virtue.

We do not know what Arthur and Catherine made of this display. At the end of the ceremonies of welcome, the princess was presented with gold and silver vessels and plates filled with coin by the mayor, recorder, sheriffs and aldermen of London's government. She then moved swiftly through the churchyard, entered the church and made offering at St Erkenwald's tomb. That done, she headed for the bishop's palace where she was able to rest and begin preparations for the wedding ceremony and festivities to come two days later. The rest of her noble escort dispersed to their London houses, inns or lodgings. Prince Arthur made his preparations from a base at the King's Wardrobe, just to the south of St Paul's churchyard. The original plan was to house the prince at Salisbury House on Fleet Street, but the wardrobe was more convenient for a quick entry into the cathedral. Some time must have been given over on the Saturday to rehearsals within the cathedral. The clerics conducting the service and the members of the royal household involved had all had plenty of opportunity to practice their roles. Princess Catherine had barely paused long enough to take stock of her surroundings since landing at Plymouth. While the king conducted official business with the Spanish ambassadors at Baynard's Castle during Saturday 12 November it seems most likely that Catherine was given a private explanation of what the ceremony would be like and what was expected from her.

The prince might have been primed about the content of the welcome procession through London and he would at least have understood the intent behind the pageants. The visual religious, cosmological and philosophical tableaux were designed to appeal to observers at various levels of education and understanding. To some, they were purely spectacular curiosities; others would have understood something of the sophisticated meaning behind the dazzling visual displays. The Spanish entourage was well educated but could not be expected to follow the convoluted English speeches of the actors taking part. The magnificence of the show would, of course, have been impressive. There were written clues, such as placards presenting the Latin names of the characters, that would have alerted educated observers to the roles being portrayed. The general level of astronomical allegory and heraldic imagery would have been immediately obvious to many from the staging; but the subtleties were likely to have been lost on the majority of the audience.

Some of these allegorical messages would have been too obscure for a general London audience, but those educated people who mattered politically and diplomatically would have understood the intention behind the performance and the unity of the imagery proclaimed by the author of the pageants. The staging was very important as evidence of how Henry VII envisaged the development of his son's power. As his existing role in the Marches progressed and he began to absorb some of his father's national responsibilities, the key imagery of Arthur would remain in the minds of the people of London. If they remembered all of the extravagance and splendour but only a fraction of the allegorical pageantry it was important that the key motif was Arthur at the centre of a cosmological puzzle, chosen by God as the embodiment of His power through justice, salvation, vengeance and zeal. That demonstrated God's favour and placed the king, the prince and his wife in a linked celestial and earthly hierarchy. Foreign observers had much to digest from the presentation of the pageants – not least the ideas behind Tudor kingship that Henry VII articulated and what they meant for the future, once Arthur became king. The road to honourable rule for Arthur and Catherine therefore broadcast a strong message about what Henry VII envisaged for his son. Arthur had little say in how he was presented in these performances. Much of this layering was unsophisticated. The abundance of family and royal badges loaded the streets of London with images of Tudor legitimacy. Other than sending a powerful reminder about the identity of the ruling dynasty and how long it had been in power, an abundance of repeated iconography did little to demonstrate how Arthur would rule when he followed his father as king. The pageants at least provided some guiding principles on which to judge how Henry VII wished to present his son's qualities to England's new and powerful Spanish allies. Concepts such as honour, virtue and noblesse might have been so commonplace among the ruling elites that they were almost abstract and divorced from the kind of real policies that kings would be obliged to implement. But they were an aspirational basis for the prince's conduct and outlook that stood alongside the long-established bureaucracy through which late medieval English government functioned.

On the Saturday after the entry pageants, the king received the Spanish ambassador at Baynard's Castle. There, the king discharged the usual business of audiences and meetings against the backdrop of high diplomatic interchange. This formal stage of Catherine's arrival in England drew the attendance of both archbishops, plus almost all the other bishops, peers, lords, knights and lesser officers of the household. Everyone who could attend was in town for the most spectacular wedding for a generation. However, such an influx did bring a mass of hangers-on and less savoury characters. The risks to the royal family and to honoured guests were increased slightly. To counter that, and in a demonstration of power and magnificence, 300 yeomen of the Guard lined all of the corridors and passageways of this riverside house. In green-and-white damask jackets embroidered with vine branches and bearing a large red rose raised with goldsmith's work, they symbolised the extravagance Henry had thrown at the preparations for his son's wedding. Each was also a chosen man – proven archers, strong, valiant and bold. Each carried a shining new halberd and was ready to defend the king and his family. As well as offering an impressive spectacle, Henry was taking no chances with security at this crucial final stage of his grand alliance with Spain.

The king received his Spanish guests on a highly stylised throne. This elaborate chair was a seat-regal with a cloth of estate overhead and much other evidence of magnificence and majesty. Princes Arthur and Henry were with him to endure the formal diplomatic speeches and the official transfer of Catherine into the care of the English royal family. Bishop FitzJames of Rochester made a very eloquent, if 'clerkly' Latin answer to the Spanish address. While this was ongoing, the queen arranged to meet Princess Catherine for the first time. By about four o'clock, Elizabeth's master of horse brought Catherine from the Bishop's Palace in a litter. The king and other courtiers soon joined them for a less formal reception in Baynard's Castle. The event lasted for many hours with dancing and other 'disports', before Catherine was escorted back home by torchlight. At some point during the evening the king and queen slipped quietly from Baynard's Castle to Lord Bergavenny's house and then to St Paul's to rehearse their own role for the day of the wedding.

Ceremonies

Sunday was the day of the wedding ceremony itself – the culmination of over a decade of discussion and negotiation between England and Spain. The cathedral staff had all the plate, gold, jewels and relics put out on display. The choir was decorated with many hanging arras tapestries with scenes from the Bible, from classical stories and from military history. Lord Daubeney had been charged to supply and arrange the display of the tapestries around the walls eight feet from the floor. He might even have brought the fine pieces from Calais that the king had commissioned from Pascal Grenier of Tournai in northern France. Priests wore new and very expensive matching vestments and made ready for a massive spectacle. Within the nave a raised wooden platform had been built. As was the case at Arthur's christening, this construction was a stage and walkway up to 700 feet long that allowed the packed congregation to view the ceremony. The focus of everyone's attention, however, was the princess as she made her entrance. At the end nearest the altar it was made circular with six steps all around. This arrangement served to keep the happy couple and those involved in the ceremony free of the press of the crowd and better able to undertake the services and move freely about the nave. The wood was covered in red say cloth, fastened with gilded nails and would have been a familiar sight to courtiers and churchmen used to such set-piece ceremonial.

The accounts of the works involved in preparing this space for the marriage ceremony, and for other repairs and upgrades at the royal palaces and venues for the wedding celebrations, indicate that almost two years' worth of planning went into reconfiguring the public and private spaces to be used around London. At St Paul's, over 4,300 feet of plank board was used to build the raised platform. Other joinery works repaired joists, rails and tables and transformed many other rooms in the Bishop of London's palace in preparation for Princess Catherine's brief stay. A crucial construction was the closet with lattice windows from which the king and queen would watch the marriage ceremony without offering any distraction to their son and his bride.

A small furnace and forge had been set up on site to make nails, cast lead and produce other ironwork for the bishop's palace and the church. A boiling and scalding house also allowed craftsmen to work other materials to be used as decoration. Many of the chambers received a refresh of paint and replacement window glass. Much of the finer work consisted of new sculptures. John Moore, Richard Codnam and others were paid for almost four weeks spent carving dragons, leopards and lions.[3]

On Sunday 14 November Arthur was brought from the Wardrobe to the south door of St Paul's between nine and ten o'clock in the morning. He made his obedience and walked through the church to a room in the palace that had been set aside for him to change into his wedding outfit of white satin. Catherine was to enter the cathedral by the west door upon the arm of Arthur's ten-year-old brother Prince Henry, which must have been a charming sight, since Henry was already learning how to turn heads and ingratiate himself with powerful women. Almost eight years later, on 11 June 1509, in a subdued ceremony at Greenwich Palace, Henry would stand next to Catherine as her second husband. During this first, more lavish, ceremony, however, the princess walked at the head of a large escort of nobles, ladies and Spaniards from her chambers in the bishop's palace. From the moment of her emergence until she entered the cathedral, the king's trumpeters and other minstrels blew fanfares and anthems. The queen's sister, Cecily, the widowed Viscountess Welles, carried Catherine's train. As the crowd within the cathedral were awaiting the entrance of the prince and princess there was a sermon of announcement and welcome based around Simeon's prayer from the Gospel of St Luke (2:26).[4] It merged the scriptural message of Simeon's joy when he recognised the infant Jesus with the gladness felt by all people present at the marriage of Arthur and Catherine; this was a high day of celebration worthy of long remembrance. The connection also continued some of the imagery linking Arthur to God the Son presented during Catherine's pageants of welcome. Although some of the 'rudes and unlearyd' persons in the church might not have understood much of this, they would have grasped the scale of the visual spectacle. The aristocratic company chosen to attend upon and to assist in the ceremonies would also have been the subject of much attention from the congregation. The earls of Oxford and Shrewsbury were again prominent. Oxford, as Great Chamberlain of England, was responsible for organising the ceremony and its related events.

Various lords, knights and gentlemen then processed in pairs to escort Catherine, 'this beautiful princess', and her ladies to her place by the altar at which the ceremony would be completed. These courtiers had been chosen for their fair appearance, magnificent clothes, chains of office and splendid jewels. Henry had already spent the enormous sum of £14,000 on jewels from France to be used in the wedding. Some of them may have been distributed as gifts to increase the general splendour of the courtiers involved at this point in proceedings. The material cost would have been outweighed by the value of advertising the wealth, sophistication and stability of the nation to which Catherine was wedding herself. She was dressed in white satin. The couple must have been dazzling as the light caught their exquisite clothes. Their gowns were finished with gold, pearls and precious stones. Catherine wore on her head a coif of white silk bordered with gold. The coif was a béguin hood, made popular by Anne, Duchess of Brittany and Queen of France. It was a close-fitting hood with an outer band onto which pearls and other jewels would be fixed. This part of her dress also served as a veil, since it fell to her waist. The dress seems to have been full, with large sleeves and many pleats. The princess and her ladies wore hoops on the outside of their skirts to increase the volume. This *'verdugeo'* style was a recent Spanish fashion, which was then spreading to Italy and France.

When Catherine reached the step of the platform by the altar, she was greeted by Henry Deane, Archbishop of Canterbury with eighteen other bishops and abbots in their ceremonial vestments and regalia. At that point members of the king's council publicly read and proclaimed the marriage agreements and accords between England and Spain that had been formalised over the preceding years of negotiation. Importantly, the speech began with details of the marriage portion that King Ferdinand had agreed to pay (200,000 crowns). King Henry then ensured that the princess received the letters patent recording the estates that were offered to her as part of her dower. These financial arrangements satisfied the representatives of both rulers. The Spanish were particularly concerned to ensure that as Princess of Wales Catherine was certain of an income and status that reflected her international standing. Henry VII was conscious that this could have been a sticking point in cementing the marriage alliance. Publicly transferring into her hands the letters before the marriage was solemnized was an appropriate acknowledgement that Catherine would be well provided for during her life in England while she remained Princess of Wales. Once she became consort and queen to King Arthur then her position at the highest level of English society would be more solidly assured and underpinned. The formal ritual and court ceremonial that had been developed under Margaret Beaufort's guidance were intended to separate and preserve the Tudor royal family's superiority over the rest of the aristocracy. Catherine and her children with Arthur would become the most important agents in extending and embedding the place of Henry VII's family within the history of the English monarchy.

The marriage ceremony then commenced, overseen by the archbishop and assisted by the other senior clerics. Despite its setting, the service was traditional and followed all of the conventions of the period. The report suggests that it lasted over an hour, with the entire event from the arrival of the princess taking about two hours altogether. King Henry and Queen Elizabeth must have positioned themselves very early in the day within the specially built closet from which they could see and hear all of what took place without themselves being observed. They remained out of sight as the noble company began to move down the church for a glorious Mass of the Trinity, led by the Archbishop of Canterbury. They did so to the sound of the king's trumpeters. The newly married couple walked hand in hand along the raised platform up to the high altar. As they reached the door of the choir they turned and showed themselves to the mass of the people all the way down the body of the church. The herald's account strongly suggests that he was there in person when it was recorded that wherever Arthur and Catherine looked at that moment, all they could see were faces – some even crammed high up into the windowsills and roof vaults. As the prince and princess began to move off, the crowd spontaneously began to shout in celebration; some for King Henry and others for Prince Arthur.

The Mass was heard with well-rehearsed music from the organ and choir 'moost pleasure and excellently'. Refreshments were taken before the nobles and the princess were led back to the bishop's palace by Prince Henry and Diego de Cordoba, Count of Cabra, known to the English as the Earl of Spain (one of Catherine's chief advisors, whose wife was also one of her leading ladies). As they came out of the west door of the church another pageant was already underway. This device might have been one of the more popular ones since it was an endlessly running wine fountain in the form of an imitation mountain, complete with visible rocks, trees, herbs, amber, coral and chunks of metal ore. Great trees were placed on the summit. Some bore flowers of gold and others oranges or red roses, one of which was topped with a white greyhound. Other trees presented the familiar figures of red dragons and white harts. Three more unusual displays depicted variation upon the three Christian worthies of the Nine Worthies of chivalric ideal. Charlemagne, the King of France, was imposed on the picture of the hart, with a silver ball in his hand. A figure of Arthur as the legendary King Arthur was on another of the trees, sword in hand. A king of Spain, possibly Alphonso X of Castile, was shown elsewhere, again holding a silver ball. He replaced the usual worthy, the ruler of Jerusalem after the First Crusade, Godfrey de Bouillon. Placing Arthur in this company confirmed his position as a valiant and ideal chivalric figure. The French, Spanish and English connections reminded the watching aristocracy that the English royal family already merged these three lines of descent. The other heraldic symbols and the fruit continued the symbolic excess.

The flow of wine had been started before the ceremony got underway and it did not run out. The small gate that let people in to fill their cups must have been heavily used. The fountain had been intended as a basic diversion for the crowds of London's common people; a way for them to join in the celebrations without getting too close to any of the more important figures. At some point in the planning process, however, it was decided to make the fountain into a more elaborate piece of imagery. The theme had been devised by Henry's friends Reginald Bray and Charles Somerset. Constructing it had cost of over £100. It was a visual pun on the king's earldom of Richmond, his 'rich mount', and it remained a favourite symbol of the king during the rest of his reign. Richmond was also the new name for the rebuilt palace of Sheen, which had partly burned down at Christmas 1497. The building was made to Henry's exacting standards in the style of recent new palaces on the Continent. That, too, became one of his favourite residences. So this element of the pageant must have brought happiness to the king and drunken joy to the people (even if the London authorities complained at the extra cost).

1. The Welsh Marches looking towards the Malvern Hills from Clee Hill, between Bewdley and Ludlow. Field boundaries and the shape of the farming landscape have changed over the past five hundred years, but this land has the same rolling green view as it did when the teenage Prince Arthur rode across it in the 1490s. (Author's collection)

2. The gatehouse of Ludlow Castle, with chambers for the justices of assize added in the sixteenth century. Started in the 1280s, the structure was developed until the early fourteenth century. Improvements continued over the years, ensuring that the castle was not only safe and strong but also comfortable for a king-in-waiting and his court. Royal chambers and a hall were used by Arthur and his Council of the Marches. (Author's collection)

3 & 4. Two prints of Ludlow Castle. This was the where Arthur brought his young new bride in December 1501 to start their married life. (Author's collection)

5. The circular chapel at Ludlow Castle with the late medieval residential building range in the background. (Author's collection)

6. The remains of Prince Arthur's chamber and personal rooms at Ludlow Castle. (Author's collection)

7. The internal wall of the domestic building and hall at Ludlow Castle. Many of the fireplaces are still intact, showing the upper levels where the guest rooms and the royal apartments were located. This served both as Arthur's home and as the central hub of his ruling power. (Author's collection)

Above left: 8. Print of St Laurence Church, Ludlow. (Author's collection)

Above right: 9. The 135-foot-tall tower of St Laurence Church, Ludlow, the 'Cathedral of the Marches'. The church was a key part of the relationship between the prince's household in Ludlow Castle and the town government. It was extensively rebuilt and expanded in Edward IV's reign. (Author's collection)

10. The view down over the town of Ludlow showing the proximity of Ludlow Castle and St Laurence Church. (Author's collection)

Right: 11 Almost as soon as Arthur died his remains were embalmed. An important initial part of this process was to remove the internal organs. It is telling that once the young prince realised he was dying he requested that his heart be buried in Ludlow, his home. Prince Arthur's heart and organs are interred in a lead box beneath the floor of St Laurence Church. (Author's collection)

Below: 12. Detail of the misericords in St Laurence Church. The three ostrich feathers had been a heraldic symbol of the royal family since the fourteenth century when it was used by Edward of Woodstock, the Black Prince. Arthur's use of the badge marked the start of its regular use by the Prince of Wales. (Author's collection)

Bottom: 13. Detail of the misericords in St Laurence Church. White Hart and greyhounds. The white hart was a symbol of Roger Mortimer, Earl of March and by Arthur's maternal grandfather, Edward IV as Earl of March. Arthur inherited the lands and power of the earl in 1493. (Author's collection)

Top: 14. Detail of the misericords in St Laurence Church showing the griffin. (Author's collection)

Above: 15. Detail of the misericords in St Laurence Church. The creation of the Tudor rose was symbolic of the joining of the two sides of the fifteenth-century conflict for the crown. The white Yorkist rose was bound with the red Lancastrian rose to create the familiar double rose. (Author's collection)

Above left: 16. The window in St Laurence Church commemorating the earls of March. (Author's collection)

Above right: 17. Nineteenth-century glass in St Laurence Church commemorating the earls of March. The lower right-hand panel shows Prince Arthur. (Author's collection)

18. The first Yorkist and the first Tudor princes of Wales, shown together in the large west window of Ludlow church. Both boys had a deep influence on English royal politics between 1470 and 1547, even though they died as teenagers. (Author's collection)

Above: 19. Leominster Priory Church, the scene of a riot in 1487 that revealed some of the tensions between the border families of whom Arthur became lord. (Author's collection)

Below left: 20. The Magnificat Window of the Priory Church, Malvern. (Author's collection)

Below right: 21. One of the few contemporary images of Prince Arthur, form the Mignificat Window of the Priory Church at Malvern. The window was built between 1499 and April 1502, probably by Henry VII's loyal knights Reginald Bray, John Savage and Thomas Lovell. The window depicts Arthur with other members of his family in prayer to the Virgin Mary. (Author's collection)

Above: 22. Worcester Cathedral. After days in formal procession from Ludlow and Bewdley, the mourners in Arthur's funeral cortege reached Worcester Cathedral. This was to be the final resting place of the first Tudor Prince. It was here that the emotional service took place and where Arthur rests today. Sir Griffith ap Rhys took a leading role in the proceedings and requested that he be buried here too, near his friend Arthur. (Author's collection)

Right: 23. The tomb of Prince Arthur. The Chantry Chapel in Worcester Cathedral. Much of the damage inflicted on the statues and symbols in the cathedral was carried out under Arthur's young nephew Edward VI during the upheavals of the church in the early 1550s. (Author's collection)

Above: 24. Arthur's heraldic arms as Prince of Wales on a small shield or escutcheon on his tomb chest in Worcester Cathedral. (Author's collection)

Left: 25. Arthur's Chantry Chapel, Worcester Cathedral. (Author's collection)

26. The badge of the Order of the Garter on Arthur's tomb. (Author's collection)

Above right: 27. The falcon and fetterlock badge of Richard Plantagenet, 3rd Duke of York (d. 1460), with roses on Arthur's chantry chapel at Worcester. This emblem was first used by Edmund of Langley, son of Edward III and 1st Duke of York. Duke Richard's version displayed the lock open. He was Earl of March and Arthur's maternal great-grandfather. The sheaf of arrows was a personal badge of Princess Catherine. (Author's collection)

Below right: 28. The royal arms of Prince Arthur and Princess Catherine on Arthur's tomb. (Author's collection)

29. The tomb of Sir Richard Croft (d. 1509), in Croft Church near Leominster. Croft was steward of the lands of the earldom of March and also steward of the household to Prince Arthur. He was one of the key officers that supported the prince's education at Ludlow. (Author's collection)

30. Tickenhill Place, Bewdley. By 1499, Henry VII had rebuilt this comfortable house of the earls of March as a less austere home for Prince Arthur and Princess Catherine. (Author's collection)

31. Rainbow over Ludlow Castle. (Author's collection)

Above left: 32. Henry VII and Henry VIII, cartoon by Holbein. (Courtesy of Elizabeth Norton)

Above right: 33. Elizabeth of York. (Courtesy of Amy Licence)

Above left: 34. Margaret Beaufort.
(Courtesy of Elizabeth Norton)

Above right: 35. Elizabeth Woodville.
(Courtesy of the Amberley Archive)

Left: 36. Catherine of Aragon. (Courtesy
of Ripon Cathedral)

Top right: 37. Mary Tudor, detail from a group portrait of Henry VIII and his family painted in about 1545. (Courtesy of Jonathan Reeve JR997b66fp40)

Below right: 38. Anthony, Earl Rivers presenting a book to Edward IV, attended by his court, Queen Elizabeth and Prince Edward (Edward V). Richard of Gloucester is also depicted, the only other figure to be in royal robes and wearing a coronet. (Courtesy of Jonathan Reeve JR1580b4p582)

Bottom: 39. Whitehall Palace. (Courtesy of Jonathan Reeve JR1884b46fp192)

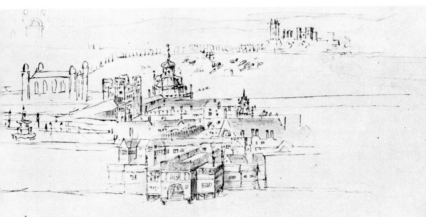

Above: 40. Old St Paul's with the spire that was lost in 1561. (Courtesy of Jonathan Reeve JR715b46fp28)

Left: 41. Margaret Tudor in a sketch thought to be drawn from life. Found in the *Recueil d'Arras*. (Courtesy of Jonathan Reeve JR982b20p837)

Once the aristocratic guests re-entered the palace to enjoy the wedding breakfast, they stepped into a magnificently decorated chamber. It was hung with the most delicate and expensive tapestries. Gold plate shone dazzlingly as it was stacked on cupboards along the walls, which must have groaned under the weight of the vessels and dishes. Some of the joinery work on the palace rooms might even have made new cabinets in which to display the king's precious goldsmith's work. The richness of the surroundings emphasised that England had a sophisticated and wealthy monarchy. This was part of Arthur's inheritance. At the very beginning of the Spanish colonial exploitation of their new American lands, Henry VII was doing his best to show that England was a worthy and dynamic ally; certainly no damp northern backwater. At the banquet that followed, Catherine was honoured with a separate table, where she sat in estate with the Bishop of Mallorca, Antonio de Rojas.

All the most honoured guests were served by lords and knights that day. King Henry's household cooks also made a good show of their culinary skills as they devised elaborate dishes of the most delicate and curious meats and fish from throughout England. The spices and wines and the subtleties of the table decorations were also designed to impress. The meal was comprised of three courses, with each course containing in turn, twelve, fifteen and eighteen dishes. The banquet was an opportunity to put on show the wealth of the country and also its sophistication. The nobility of England and Spain was intermingled at the other tables below Catherine, so that the magnificence of the day could be re-emphasised and the astonishment of the foreigners noted. All diners were surrounded by more displays of silver and gilt plates and dishes. What was particularly impressive to some of the observers that left accounts was that even as the banquet was served on or in golden plates, jewel-encrusted goblets and silver jugs, the items mounted on the cupboards were left untouched. In other words, as the *Great Chronicle of London* suggested, the king's wealth was so great that he could leave a display worth about £12,000 in place merely as decoration and still deliver a state banquet on a massive scale on another set of gilded tableware. The plate in this one room was worth the same as a third of the value of a normal national taxation. This was where much of Henry VII's fabled wealth went, into hard gold and bullion.

Beddings

The banquet continued until nearly 5 p.m. and many of the plates were given as gifts afterwards – more evidence of the king's largesse. As the meal was drawing to a close, the Earl of Oxford, in his role as Lord Great Chamberlain, was sent by the king to begin the preparations for the wedding night bed rituals for both the princess and Prince Arthur. The chamber and bed were to be prepared for their 'reste and ease', although at the age of fifteen and sixteen they might have had something a little more active in mind. It took about three hours for the bedchamber to be made ready. Oxford then went off to inspect things for himself. He tested each side of the bed before expressing his pleasure at the state of readiness.

Catherine was dressed and 'reverently leied and reposed' in the bed, while Arthur stayed up late with his friends and other nobles, engaged in disports, dancing, pleasure and mirth (of a wholly honourable nature, of course). The wedding-night ritual for people of noble blood consisted of a blessing of their chamber and the marriage bed and the saying of prayers by the bishops over the couple as they lay in bed. Their involvement was an extension of the wedding service. This stage of the rite invoked God's blessing for the procreation of children. As is evidenced from the statements of those still alive at the end of the 1520s, there was also a more boisterous and informal ritual that marked

Arthur's passage from boyhood to manhood: he was carried to his chamber door with much carousing and singing by friends and other nobles who had been drinking and celebrating for several hours.

At least three of the witnesses interviewed at the end of June 1529 as part of the evidence-gathering for Henry VIII's divorce proceedings were present when Arthur emerged from his bedchamber on the morning after his first night as a married man. Sir Anthony Willoughby was one of them. He had been a servant and companion of Prince Arthur for five years before 1502. His father, Robert Lord Willoughby (steward of Henry VII's household), had pulled a few strings to enable Anthony to be involved in the wedding-night customs. Arthur's other young friends were waiting for him the next day, including Griffth ap Rhys and Maurice St John. When Arthur came out from his chamber he called Willoughby over with the words, 'Willoughby, bring me a cup of ale, for I have been this night in the midst of Spain'; then to all of the others present, 'masters, it is good pastime to have a wife'.[5] Willoughby assumed that Arthur was telling the truth of the previous night's intimacies. He also said that he believed they had lain together as man and wife at Ludlow until the beginning of Lent in 1502. Another unnamed witness reported hearing from Maurice St John the news of these same words being spoken at the chamber door. It is possible that this was a well-rehearsed line, designed to impress, or that it was simply very memorable in the circumstances of the happy marriage. That same witness also corroborated the information that the prince began to go into physical decline after Shrovetide in 1502. Thomas, Viscount Rochford (who was then Sir Thomas Boleyn) was at the wedding ceremonies but not at court the following morning. He nevertheless heard reports of Arthur's witty quip to his chamber servants in the morning as he arose after his first night as a married man.

Anthony Poyntz, who had served Arthur when he was still an infant, echoed this sentiment and the statements of others; as did Robert Radcliffe, 2nd Lord Fitzwalter who, as a ward of the king and son of the attainted former steward of the household, moved to the king's service after Arthur died. Fitzwalter was another of the rowdy group that had carried Arthur to his marriage bed. Sir William Thomas was a groom of the prince's privy chamber. He recalled escorting Arthur many times to Catherine's door and collecting him again in the morning. Catherine's tutor and confessor, Alessandro Geraldini, also believed that that level of contact between the newlyweds would have led to a consummation of the marriage, although it is unclear if he was drawing on private knowledge received in confession. The Marquis of Dorset was another of the courtiers who had delivered Arthur to his waiting wife on the evening of their wedding day. Catherine was seen to be waiting for Arthur under the bedclothes. The 'good and sanguine' complexion that the prince showed the next day was enough to convince Dorset that the marriage had been consummated.

Mary Blount, Countess of Essex and Agnes Tilney, widow of Thomas Howard, Earl of Surrey, chief mourner at Arthur's funeral, offered an insightful female perspective. Mary was certain that Arthur and Catherine had shared a bed many times after their wedding night. Agnes went a little further. She had prepared the bedchamber that the newlyweds would share, and had been one of the last to see them lying together on the night of the wedding. She then retired to sleep in a nearby chamber in the Bishop of London's palace. As one of the senior women of the realm, Agnes would have been one of the English ladies that worked hard on the king's behalf to make the Spanish delegation comfortable in London over the subsequent days. In contradiction of this, Catherine's older governess or chaperone, her duenna Dona Elvira, had been reluctant to let the young couple spend too much time indulging their teenage sexual energies. Clearly, that was expected once they were married. Henry VII, too, had at first been wary of allowing them to live fully as man and wife – preferring to send Prince Arthur back to the Welsh Marches alone, while his wife remained in the royal household. The king was persuaded by Geraldini and the princess herself that the couple were so besotted with each other that separating them would be a cruelty that might also displease her parents in Spain. Arthur had already written to Ferdinand and Isabella after his marriage. He expressed the joy he felt at seeing the face of his sweet bride. She was a most agreeable companion to him and he would do his best to be a good husband. The expectations inherent in late medieval marriage meant that the royal family anticipated the begetting of children soon after the couple were lawfully wedded; just as his father and mother had done after their wedding.

Teenage male boasting and swaggering about sex were probably little different in 1501 to what they are now. Arthur was in the company of familiar servants and was relaying exactly the news of a successful consummation of his marriage (albeit a bit crudely) that his friends, servants and above all his father and Princess Catherine's father would have hoped and expected to hear quickly. Even if Arthur was inflating the truth of his sexual success, he still had to report that he had done his duty as a husband. Everything else being normal, his wife was unlikely to reveal any problems or difficulties at that early stage of their marriage: both would have believed that time was on their side.

From the pageants to the spectacular ceremony in St Paul's and then the luxurious wedding banquet, London had turned Arthur's marriage into the most spectacular state occasion England had witnessed for decades. Yet it is important to remember that at its heart were two teenagers who had only just met but who were now joined in marriage. The strain and expectation to perform on the lavish public stage but also in private might have affected

Arthur and Catherine a little, but they had both been bred to remain calm when at the centre of attention. Young as they were, being a focus of the gaze of thousands of onlookers might not have been as daunting as the close personal contact they were now free to enjoy. There was no real training for dealing with such intimate social situations. The prince might be advised by people he knew who had already been married, but the personal experience of meeting his future wife and then sharing a bed with her can only have been a revelation to the young prince. One of the disadvantages resulting from Prince Arthur's residence in the small town of Ludlow was that he would not have met many young women of noble rank. Unlike his younger brother Henry, who was surrounded by women in the royal household and court, the social side of Arthur's upbringing had a more limiting horizon. If, as Queen Catherine later claimed, the marriage was not consummated on the wedding night, then shyness related to the awkwardness of their first intimate time alone together was a far more likely cause than any physical ailment afflicting the prince.

Catherine might also have found the previous three months to have been a tiring whirlwind. As already mentioned, the wedding and bedding ceremonies had gone ahead at the end of a very long period of discussion, negotiation and planning. Based upon Catherine's original itinerary, the ceremony could have been delayed by about six weeks. The Spanish had been expected to arrive in England towards the end of August. The wedding might originally have been planned for around Michaelmas (25 September), and not mid-November when the weather would have been more changeable and cold. More likely still, the princess would have had a far more leisurely journey to London from her intended landfall of Southampton, and a longer period in which to acclimatise to the capital and the royal spaces in which she would spend time before the ceremony. After the delayed landing at Plymouth the Spanish entourage made a very swift journey towards London. There was very little time for the princess to rest or to contemplate how her life was changing very rapidly – she was only sixteen, after all. If anything was likely to have ruined Arthur's plans for his wedding night, it was the exhaustion of his new wife.

The following morning, Arthur emerged flush-faced and full of jokes and quips. His demeanour was exactly what many had hoped to see. He convinced the majority of onlookers that he had done his very best to start his married life in the expected manner. This must have been great news for King Henry. The full part that Arthur had played in the build-up to the wedding and the apparent ease with which he had embraced the ceremony and the daunting wedding night itself would have made Henry proud as a father and as a king. On the Monday after the ceremony, the noble people of the court were feeling the after-effects of the celebrations. Within the palace there were no early risers since King Henry had given the morning off to as many servants as he could spare. Catherine remained in her own privy chamber with her ladies. Only the Earl of Oxford sought access as he brought her a gift on behalf of the king. That day, Margaret Beaufort and her husband, Thomas Stanley, Earl of Derby had arranged dinner and supper for the Spanish aristocrats at Coldharbour House, close to the Wardrobe, and at nearby Derby House. In the evening, the king gave notice that he expected everyone to be at St Paul's at 9 a.m. the following morning for a service of thanksgiving. Arthur met his father at Baynard's Castle and headed a procession of over 500 nobles, lords and knights, both Spanish and English, into the cathedral once again. Princess Catherine was already waiting secretly in the closet from which the king and queen had watched the marriage service. The king was able to meet and talk with the princess before they joined Arthur and the other lords as they were rowed in a pageant of forty barges upriver to Westminster.

Tournaments

The ceremonies continued to come thick and fast, but Prince Arthur is not described as having much of a formal role in them. In the afternoon, preparations began for the ceremony to create fifty-eight new knights of the Bath. King Henry selected five of them to receive his personal explanatory speech of the virtues of knighthood, but it was the Earl of Oxford, rather than the prince, who prepared the rest for their night of vigil and the ritual purifying bath that would come the next day. The ceremony followed the laws of arms meticulously, demonstrating to the Spanish and other observers another dimension to the Tudor regime's legitimacy and understanding of chivalric culture and practice. The king dubbed all the knights in the great chamber of Westminster Palace, but the autumn rains fell to such an extent that the new knights could not ride to the door of the hall, as Arthur had done in 1489. Addressing any disappointment at the reduced spectacle or pageantry, the king created an additional eighteen more knights that day. The new knights soon had a chance to become involved in the type of activity that their new rank required of them (even if, at first, they were to observe and not join in).

A major part of the expenses for works had been spent on improving Westminster Palace and its grounds as a venue for the tournament that was to be held on Thursday 18 November. Almost £60 had been spent by Sir Richard Guildford in creating a space in front of the hall and in preparing a sanded and gravelled tiltyard. Guildford had been connected with Margaret Beaufort since the 1470s and had served Henry Tudor in organising the military campaign towards Bosworth. His reward was to become master of the ordnance and chief organiser of many of the regime's martial activities, even building new fighting ships for the Crown. After 1494 he was also comptroller of the household and was given the task of organising this most spectacular of tournaments.

The palace itself was another building that had undergone a major refurbishment ahead of the ceremonies; at a cost of almost £200. Many chambers had joinery repairs and new window glass. Westminster Hall seems to have had a completely new set of Tudor royal badges on a massive scale. By the east door six statues of royal beasts were made. The arch of the north door was remade to include portcullises, *fleurs-de-lys*, roses and stars newly made of metal. Two lions, each one supported by four angels, held up a great red rose with an imperial crown.[6] The most interesting addition was glass work on the windows of the north side of the Hall. Guy of Warwick was depicted fighting the Danish giant Colbrand. This imagery had a partial link to Arthur's birth at Winchester and more generally, to the resistance of invaders and a vision of a unified England. In the stories of the origin of Britain, the Trojan Brutus was responsible for wiping out the giants that lived there before his arrival. Guy of Warwick's story was almost completely fictional, but was woven into the history of the Beauchamp earls of Warwick in the early fifteenth century. One of Guy's most famous feats was the defeat of the Dun Cow on Dunsmore Heath between Coventry and Rugby. The Dun Cow banner was one of three brought to London from the battlefield by Henry VII in September 1485 (the others being the flag of St George and the king's own red dragon standard). Its association with Henry puzzled historians for some time until it was connected to a possibly crucial role at Bosworth for the remnants of the Neville affinity of Warwick the Kingmaker or the city of Coventry.[7] Since Richard of Gloucester attracted the service of many of the followers of the Kingmaker during the 1470s the vanquishing of the cow by Guy might also have been an allusion to Richard III's defeat. Either way, the link was obscure in 1485 and its prominent revival in the preparations for Arthur's wedding still more unusual. Henry might simply have seen his own victory over Richard III in the same terms as Guy's heroic battle with Colbrand. By the time of Arthur's marriage chroniclers like John Rous and Robert Fabyan had established Guy's story as historical fact from the eighth century. Guy's epic fight with Colbrand at Winchester to help save King Æthelstan from Vikings raiding into Wessex became his most famous exploit. Guy's connection to Wallingford, one of Arthur's duchy of Cornwall castles and the name of his pursuivant, would also have been well known at the time from versions of the story produced by the king's printers Richard Pynson and Wynkyn de Worde.[8] The space created for the wedding tournament was therefore charged with sophisticated imagery that celebrated the connections of Prince Arthur and his family to England's ancient stories. It was also the venue for the most eagerly awaited part of the entire wedding festivities – the tournament.

Tournaments were the only competitive participation sport that obsessed the ruling elite in medieval England.[9] The main entertainment was provided by mounted and armoured men, separated by a long fence (a tilt), charging towards each other with the intention of scoring points by striking opponents with blunted lances on different parts of specialist armour reinforced to protect from blows to the upper body. Maximum scores and the greatest glory would be achieved by striking the head or in unhorsing opponents. Variations included jousting in groups on horseback without the barrier, with sharp lances or in ordinary combat armour; a far more dangerous test of skill. A new fashion just arriving in England was fighting on foot with tournament swords or poleaxes, separated by a barrier. Henry VII's reign previously had offered various spectacles as part of state ceremonies, such as the tournament held at the creation of Prince Henry as a Knight of the Bath and Duke of York in 1495. Just as Arthur's wedding ceremony and feast were meant to take pageantry and spectacle to a new level, so too were the jousts intended to display the fighting prowess of the men at the pinnacle of England's knightly class. The organisation of the fighting was passed completely over to the experienced hands of the comptroller of the household and the sergeant of the armoury. This tournament was likely to be so popular that access for the honest and common people was limited, but it was not a closed event, since broadcasting the king's magnificence to all the population of Westminster and London had an important role in proving the fitness to rule of Henry VII's family. Many of the 'rudes', the lowest part of the population, were prevented by barriers and fencing from wandering too near to the action. The design of the stage allowed the royal family to walk through Westminster Hall and to take their seats without being seen (or exposed to the rain). Those courtiers that were too old, too young or poorly skilled in arms to take part sat near the royal party. The Spanish dignitaries would have joined the king and queen there. It was very important that the best seats did not look into the sun, since that would have impaired the enjoyment of the event. Other stands had been built for the mayor, officials and members of the companies of London. The stands meant for those lower down the social scale would be south-facing, and would have looked into the sun, had it been shining that day.

Near the Water Gate into the palace, a Tree of Chivalry had been planted, surrounded by a picket fence on which were fixed the small shields of all the combatants challenging for prizes. The Duke of Buckingham had been given licence to issue the challenge. His document was posted outside the gates of Westminster Palace, on London Bridge and outside the Standard Inn on Cheapside in the City. Buckingham excelled himself in the sumptuousness of his appearance, the quality of his horse and armour and even the fine construction of his pavilion, which was in green and white silk.

The prince and princess were honoured by these jousts. In many cases, certainly Buckingham's, the participants were showing themselves to the king and queen and exaggerating their loyalty through the incorporation of Tudor imagery and heraldry on their clothing. The king was particularly pleased to see that Buckingham had gone to such trouble to impress. He had already suffered some shrinking of his power in the border counties and would be the man that Arthur's lordship pressurised most directly in the Marches. Three more pageants of a castle, a ship and a mountain appeared during this first day. Three days of jousting and feasting followed. The new Marquis of Dorset, head of the list of defenders, rode directly against Buckingham. Since the relationship of Dorset's father with the king had been inconsistent, the 2nd marquis had a perfect opportunity to impress the court. It might also be significant that Buckingham and Dorset were directly contesting for precedence in front of the king and Prince Arthur. Both lords were in the process of making up ground towards a full recovery of the king's affection for their families. Showing off their magnificence, loyalty and skill at arms before the prince also made a pitch for a chance to rebuild relationships in the Marcher lands. The jousts were another important piece of courtly one-upmanship. But it is significant that by 1501 this power game was more frequently resolved at court, through debate, discussion and proper use of the law than it had been at the start of the reign. In 1487 Sir Richard Croft and Sir Thomas Cornewall took matters into their own hands when their dispute became a confrontational tussle of strength around Leominster. Fourteen years of regional government under Arthur's Council of the Marches had spread the message, even to very senior nobles, that points had to be scored and issues resolved in very different ways.

Arthur did not take part in the jousts and there is no indication that he wished to test his fighting skills against the other knights and lords. The events were being held in his honour and it would have seemed strange for him to enter the field. Arthur's life based in the Marches must have meant that he was not at all well known to the members of the king's court. Those aristocrats close to the king would have been aware of how he was being prepared to take over the throne and the methods that Henry was employing in order to bring this about. There was a risk inherent in becoming involved in jousts. Arthur's education and training had proceeded exactly as the king wished. He had survived childhood health risks; he had escaped plots and conspiracies and avoided entanglement in the rebellions that had forced royal armies onto the battlefield; his time in the Marches had forced him to learn the skills of social interaction, arbitration and forceful decision-making where necessary. Henry VII had provided his son with a focus on mastering the mechanics of government rather than learning to rule from the saddle or the field camp as England's warrior kings like Henry V had done. We don't know if he was keen to ride with his friends in the tournament and demonstrate his skill at arms. No doubt parts of the audience would have liked to have seen the Prince of Wales do just that. He was not often seen in the capital. Riding out as a chivalric leader, even in some stage-managed part of proceedings, was a way to make an immediate impression on the audience. It could also have backfired. Pretence might have easily been seen through and done more damage than good to Arthur's reputation. With so much investment in the prince's development already in place, there was far more to lose by getting involved than staying aloof on the sidelines. Also, who would want to ride out against the Prince of Wales and risk harming him? The king's displeasure would surely have been too much to bear for anyone unlucky or hot-headed enough to injure Arthur.

King Henry had shown no real interest in putting on his armour once he had left the Bosworth battlefield behind him. It was likely that Arthur absorbed something of the same way of thinking about what the king's role should be. His attitude shared some elements of the conscious plan to elevate the inner royal family above everyone else in the ranks of the aristocracy, which Margaret Beaufort oversaw. To make that even more obvious it was not necessary for the king or his heir to gallop around the tiltyard in competition with recently created knights. What is telling is that Henry, Duke of York took the opposite view. He probably had little recollection of sitting in the stand for the tournament in his honour when he was created Duke of York in 1495.[10] Sir Robert Curzon, the earls of Essex and Suffolk, Sir Edward Borough and Sir Thomas Brandon stood out that day. By the time jousts were held in 1506, for the unexpected visit of Philip of Burgundy, Prince Henry was already becoming addicted to a sport that tested all of his physical qualities. When he was slightly older, the joust and the tournament were some of Henry's strongest passions and he took part regularly. This interest only got deeper once he became king in 1509.[11]

Despite being physically closer to the king, Prince Henry did not follow Arthur in taking inspiration from his father's example. Henry VIII was quite happy to take risks. He wanted to emulate Henry V and Edward IV and win fame through the revival of dormant claims to England's lost French territories and celebration of the military exploits that would be needed to win them back. Henry V had proved that the king's energy and drive could ensure successful simultaneous leadership in war and in management of government. Young as he was before 1515, on taking the throne Henry VIII began to delegate the less glamourous administrative duties of kingship. The type of business that his father only divested himself of when he was ageing, ill and worn out, was being passed by Henry VIII to Thomas Wolsey within a few years of the accession. Had Arthur been the second Tudor king, it is much more likely that he would have had a ruling style similar to that of his father. His whole upbringing was engineered to bring about a seamless transfer of power between generations. A key difference between Arthur and Henry is evidenced here.

6

A SUDDEN END

Illness and Death

The Monday after the wedding jousts, the Spaniards took their leave of Westminster. They left with many letters and reports for Spain and gifts from King Henry, including paintings and books. Descriptions of the marriage ceremony and proof that it had taken place were also important parts of their baggage. The Archbishop of Spain travelled to Southampton while others of the party left via Dover to Calais. All members of the Spanish party had the king's letters patent of safe conduct through England to their embarkation point. Princess Catherine, now of Wales and Spain, retained with her a great number of ladies, officers and servants to wait on her for comfort and solace. Since Arthur and Catherine would be departing for Ludlow as soon as reasonable courtesy allowed, the presence of familiar faces as household servants and companions was of some comfort but also of real practical value. As the earlier meetings between Catherine and the king had demonstrated, her inability to speak fluent French or English made communication difficult. Conversational Latin was also likely to have been something of a struggle between Arthur and Catherine, since neither would have learned that language for everyday speech and their knowledge was based on the different forms of the language used in Spain and England. Surviving letters from Arthur to Catherine and her parents indicate his polished but rather formal skill in Latin.[1] The compiler of the account of the ceremonies makes it clear that Catherine was very upset and pensive to be left without some of her familiar guardians. Her inability to communicate naturally was an even larger factor in her feelings of irritation and isolation.

King Henry seems to have been aware that this was likely to happen after the hectic, draining journey and ceremonies of the previous month. Whether he was advised by Arthur or the queen or saw the situation for himself, the king's solution was to invite Catherine and her ladies to the library at Westminster Palace to look through his collection of books in the company of many English ladies. As a further surprise, he also arranged for a jeweller to be waiting for them. The king had already purchased a range of rings, jewels and other goldsmith's work of 'moost goodly fashion' – of exquisite quality and high status. The princess chose the one she liked best. Then the Spanish companions were allowed to select their own items. Only then did the English ladies get to pick something from what remained. The report suggests that this activity was enough of an immediate distraction to begin to change Catherine's heaviness of heart. It also began the process of integration between the princess and her English servants.

Arthur would have seen the importance of achieving this transition as quickly as possible. Very shortly after this event designed to build common bonds around a discussion of jewellery, something that fascinated all medieval people, the newly married couple planned to depart to the Welsh Marches to take up the direct rule of prince's estates in the region and elsewhere. Arthur's previous training at Ludlow had made him very familiar with what was required to rule as a good lord should. In all probability, Henry VII would have taken good advantage of having his eldest son by his side for over a month to offer some direct advice on how kings must rule (and maybe how husbands should behave). What was most immediately important, however, was that the balance of Arthur's household was harmonious. He had been used to a stable, male-dominated environment. After his marriage, Arthur immediately had to accommodate an influx of women into his life; and a group of Spanish women, too. The clash of expectations and experiences as the royal travelling party arrived at Ludlow in mid-December 1501 must have produced one of the most memorable sights ever seen in that community. It is not difficult to imagine just how unusual and stressful this process might have been for fifteen-year-old Arthur. It was his brother Henry who had been educated in the company of women. At the age of ten Henry had already shown an impressive smoothness and charm during Arthur's wedding celebrations. Arthur, on the other hand, had been thrown directly into an education suitable for a future ruler. He had diligently matched his talents with exceptional effort to acquire the knowledge and skills that any European ruler would have been proud of at the start of the sixteenth century. The cost of learning to govern within the training ground of the March was that Arthur might have missed out on some of the smoother social skills available at his father's court. Commentaries like the *Great Chronicle of London*, when describing him receiving a gift of gilt basins after his formal entry into the city in October 1498, picked up on his stiffness and formality. His words of thanks were recorded verbatim in the text, but in their conventional politeness illuminate nothing about the prince himself.[2] That type of snapshot is unfair to Arthur, since very little personality could be confidently lifted from a few lines of description.

He had only just met his wife. They were both young, but had been brought up fully aware of the expectations of a semi-public life. They were also both highly educated. Although the language barrier would have been difficult at first, intellectually they were better equipped than most to overcome any awkwardness that grew from suddenly being thrown together. Arthur and Catherine had known since the age of three or four that their destiny was to be married. Surviving letters in Latin from Arthur to Catherine suggest his determination to do everything possible to welcome his bride and to love her as well as he could when she eventually arrived in England. The more time they were able to spend together, the easier their marriage would become. Many factors were in favour of them establishing a happy life, but a harmonious relationship would take time to build. That said, the start of married life probably had a strong element of unavoidable disappointment. After less than two months in England, Princess Catherine and her attendants had to leave their brief but dazzling glimpse of London life, ceremony and culture behind and head into the rural borderlands of the West Midlands. The whirlwind of her time since landing at Plymouth had come to a halt by the middle of December 1501 as she began her residence in Shropshire. Faced with the prospect of building a new life in the massive and isolated castle of Ludlow, one of the country's oldest stone fortresses, it would not be unreasonable to assume that Catherine's pining, unease and nervousness returned. A slow journey into the hilly Anglo-Welsh border country at the start of winter probably gave the prince and his wife some time to reflect on how their lives together would move forward. For the Spanish, it was surely a rather harsh introduction to what England was truly like beyond the walls of the City of London.

Ludlow Castle had undergone substantial improvements to host the Council of the Marches once it was revived in Edward IV's reign. Apartments and buildings were further developed and repurposed once Prince Arthur's residence there began to be planned. A residential block known as the Tudor lodgings replaced an earlier structure. It contained private chambers used by Arthur that were probably modelled on the rooms of the king's palaces at Westminster and Greenwich. There is also evidence that windows were replaced in other repair work that suggests some determination to maintain the residential parts of the medieval castle in a way that was appropriate as a home for the prince and his wife. The floors of these lodging blocks are now lost, but features such as fireplaces do survive that help to identify the function and layout of the spaces. Although the fabric of the castle remained imposing, and reflected its former status as a major strongpoint and assembly point for English campaigns in Wales, by the last quarter of the fifteenth century it had an extensive domestic and administrative role that demanded appropriate accommodation. For that reason, Ludlow Castle was no longer the austere fortress that it had been in the early fourteenth century.

Nevertheless, the impact of a winter journey across country to a small town in the Marches prompted redevelopment of other buildings that would be at the disposal of Arthur and Catherine. Tickenhill Place at Bewdley on the River Severn in Worcestershire had been virtually rebuilt before 1499. It had first been constructed for the use of Richard, 3rd Duke of York as a more modern residence for the Earl of March than Wigmore or Ludlow castles. Tickenhill had been the location for the second proxy marriage of Arthur and Catherine in May 1499 (with the Spanish ambassador de Puebla standing in for the princess). The works on the house had probably been completed by that time. Making de Puebla travel to the border with Wales that spring was clearly part of the process of highlighting the preparations that had been made for the princess's arrival and the establishment of good order and appropriate welcome in the locality where she would live as Princess of Wales. A location for the proxy ceremony at Westminster or any other of the king's south-eastern residences would have served, had Henry VII not had deeper motives. Spring in the Marches would have shown off the country to its best advantage. The ambassador could form his own views on the people among whom the princess would move, and the esteem in which Prince Arthur was already held. De Puebla would already know Sir Richard Croft, Sir Richard Pole and Dr William Smith from the time they had spent in the king's household and at court. It is safe to say that as representative of his king and queen, he had a particular interest in exploring and examining where Princess Catherine would begin her marriage. The range of his concerns would have covered everything from domestic arrangements to the quality of the men of the prince's council and the stability of the area in which Catherine was to live. All of this knowledge gathered in 1499 was intended to reassure the Spanish monarchs before their daughter was dispatched for England. It did mean that there were few surprises to hinder the young couple from settling into border life. For that reason, the type of disputes and disorder conspicuous before the end of the 1480s had to be seen to be contained, if not crushed. The state of the border in 1501 was far calmer than it had been in the first four years of Henry VII's reign. It would have been a surprise if the efforts of the Crown and the willingness of the gentry to ingratiate themselves with growing royal power had not produced results.

Arthur and Catherine spent only about four months as husband and wife in Ludlow. The feast of Christmas there would have been the first event over which they presided as Prince and Princess of Wales. It is not known when they left London or how they journeyed to Shropshire. Since the feasts of Christmas, New Year (even though the calendar year did not change until 25 March) and Twelfth Night were celebrated within the period before the record of Arthur's involvement in the Maundy Thursday ceremonies, there were opportunities for the prince's court and the councillors of the Marches to interact. Arthur's return to Ludlow as a married man with his wife beside him was a cause for celebration. Feasts, festivals and entertainments supplied plenty of scope for the renewal of old relationships and the building of new ones. The early spring of 1502 was surely one of the most joyous times of Arthur's life. It was possibly a high-point for King Henry. He was drawing up plans to deal with his latest rebel, the Earl of Suffolk, but even worries about another Yorkist claimant might not yet have diminished the shine from the success of his alliance with Spain and the ceremonies that cemented it. Whatever spectacles unfolded are hidden from us by a lack of evidence, however, and the first indication that they had reached Ludlow was the notification of Arthur's illness and death at the start of April.

Detail about the cause of Arthur's decease is imprecise. This results partly from the vagueness of medical knowledge available at the time and the fact that the information comes from commentators on the social side of courtly life and not from within the medical circles that attended the prince when he became ill. The author of the best source, the record of Princess Catherine's arrival, was not at Ludlow and had not had a chance to talk in detail to those that had seen the prince during his very rapid decline. It is in the record of the king's reaction to the news of his son's death that we get a deeper sense that this record was written by an eyewitness. It does also supply impressive detail on how much Arthur was loved by his parents.

The prince died on Saturday 2 April 1502 at Ludlow, between six and seven o'clock in the evening. His chamberlain, Sir Richard Pole, assembled Arthur's council and drafted letters to the king and court, then at Greenwich Palace. A rider managed to reach the king within two days – as impressive a feat as the transmission of the news of Catherine's landfall from Plymouth to Richmond in October 1501. As was normal, Henry VII's councillors received the letters first and, armed with the dreadful news, sent for the king's confessor, an observant friar.[3] The councillors asked the confessor to give the news to the king, in expectation that he would need much personal and spiritual comforting. On the Tuesday following Arthur's death, 5 April, the king was awoken earlier than usual and the confessor asked everyone else to leave the chamber. After introducing the most painful subject with the Latin phrase, 'If we have received good things by the hand of God, why should we not receive evil?',[4] he then broke the news that Arthur had died. Henry immediately sent for the queen so that they 'wolde take the peynfull sorowes togyders'. The writer of the account must have been on hand within the household, since he heard Queen Elizabeth's words of support to her husband. The arrival of an express rider from Ludlow would certainly have drawn attention as the household staff of Greenwich Palace rose as part of their daily routine of service to the king and queen. Elizabeth was recorded as explaining how the realm remained safe in King Henry's hands and how although he had been an only child he was preferred by God into the estate that he now enjoyed. Their other children, Prince Henry and princesses Margaret and Mary, were healthy and preserved by God, and both she and the king were young enough to have more children, if it were God's will that it should be so. She then comforted the king and was thanked for her loving words. When she returned to her own chamber, however, she was overcome with emotion:

> [the] natural and moderly remebraunce of that great losse smote hir so sorrowful in the hert that those that were abought her were fayn to send for the Kyng to comforte her.[5]

The king then came 'of true, gentill and feithfull love' without being informed of his wife's distress. It was his turn to offer words to alleviate her pain as they both struggled for enough composure to give thanks for their son's life.

This evidence offers one of the few instances of everyday human emotion apparent in descriptions of the life of Henry VII and Queen Elizabeth. These powerful hints of heartfelt feelings and humanity in the personality of the king are important reminders of just how incomplete is the evidence used by modern scholars to judge personal characteristics. The king is often identified as cold and remote, but this is to judge him on evidence of how he governed and defended his throne. Those type of records would seldom reveal anything substantial on the private nature of a monarch that lived over 500 years ago. If we do see a little more warmth and concern in Henry's actions, then it is natural to think that some of those traits would have been passed on to his son – especially in the period of intensive contact that father and son experienced in October and November 1501.

Royal children were seldom brought up in close proximity to their parents, and were particularly remote from their fathers. For Henry and Elizabeth, the difficulty of sending their first child into the care of other people, miles from wherever they spent time, was surely one of the more harrowing decisions of their lives. At the time that decision was made by Henry VII and his wife, the regime was continually beset by plotters and enemies intent on pulling Henry VII from the throne. King Henry saw Arthur's departure as essential to the sustainability of his family's ongoing rule. By separating the king and his heir, Henry was following a recent tradition among English rulers. In the circumstances of his accession, however, it was more of a risk since the loyal core of Tudor friends and allies was so small. The regime's opponents were already seeking to make traitors of those Yorkists that had lent Henry VII their military power and service since 1485.

In those circumstances, less focussed or determined monarchs might have kept their children close until major threats had been faced or hidden enemies flushed out. The decision to send Arthur away to Farnham and then to the Welsh March at the age of six has deepened the view of the king as a rather cold and calculating personality. There is enough evidence of guilt in Queen Elizabeth's reaction to Arthur's death to reveal that she was not so certain that he should have spent so much of his youth in full-time training to be king.

The loss of children was more common in the past and across all levels of society. The king and queen had already buried two children: Princess Elizabeth in September 1495, aged just over three; and Prince Edmund, Duke of Somerset in June 1500, aged sixteen months. Catherine of Aragon had already experienced a similar loss. Her brother Prince Juan had died at the age of nineteen in 1497. We might therefore think that people at all levels of late medieval society were somehow prepared for or expectant of the death of some of their offspring or siblings. Mortality usually struck in infancy or youth, so the early death of two children was more familiar if no less difficult to deal with. Although the expenses of the burial of Prince Edmund, for example, were large, there is no record of how his loss was borne by the royal family. With Prince Arthur, there is a far greater sense of shock and distress beyond the fact that we have eyewitness evidence of how the king and queen reacted to the news. Arthur had navigated the perils of childhood illness. The evidence of medical attendants offering service at Farnham indicates that he was well looked after. It does not suggest that he was any more sickly than other aristocratic children. He had lived for most of each year since the end of 1493 in the area of the country in which he was to die. There is no record of any major illness within Arthur's court and household at other times. Indeed, Ludlow seems to have been known for its clean air, at least before 1502.

Research into mortality records from the parishes of Herefordshire at the beginning of the sixteenth century reveals just how unlucky Arthur was. Analysis of wills proved at the consistory court of the Bishop of Hereford for 1501–03 suggests a higher than average rate of death.[6] The year 1502 had the third-highest mortality of the fifteenth century, with the deaneries of Ludlow and Leominster suffering more than other areas, and November 1502 was the peak period. Descriptive details for fatal diseases are often frustratingly vague, but it is possible that increasing rates of death in the built-up areas within a rural county might indicate some kind of infectious epidemic, transmissible by people in close proximity.[7] An increase in local probate administrations during this period has also been taken by some writers as evidence of more intestate deaths, since those struck down suddenly were less likely to have had time to make a will. Young people with property might have been more unprepared in this way, which also points to a sudden outbreak of indiscriminate disease to which everyone was vulnerable. The account of Arthur's funeral ceremony at Worcester certainly implies that all those that could attend, did, 'savyng those of the cite because of the siknes that then reigned emonges thyem'.[8]

When Arthur arrived back in his border domain at the end of 1501 his entourage included a large number of Spanish attendants, servants and companions of the queen. The Spanish company had been in England for only three months. All of them were newly exposed to the country's germs and diseases. Were they more likely than their English fellows to be susceptible to any routine outbreak of illness or more serious epidemic, and is this reflected in any records? If the changed dynamic of the court at Ludlow provided an easier route for sickness to strike at the heart of the household, then it is not difficult to understand how the prince might have succumbed in 1502 when he had survived earlier instances of illness. No historian has suggested that the insertion of a Spanish community into a small border town brought with it new strains of disease in a similar way to the previously unseen sweating sickness that arrived in London with Henry VII's victorious army at the end of August 1485. The acceleration and spread of any disease, however, could have been aided by the susceptibility of a newly arrived population with little natural immunity to what they were exposed to in a wet autumn and winter on the Anglo-Welsh border. So the Spanish network at Ludlow might have been a factor to be considered. At the start of the reign, it was only when the troops of the invading Tudor army reached the capital that a pattern of deaths was linked to foreigners (particularly Frenchmen) carrying a disease that had not been evident in England before. Commentators and chronicles are silent on whether Leicester, as the first billeting location for Tudor's army after the battle, saw any noticeable difference in mortality at that exact time. In 1501, the transmission of a new form of infection would have been evident at a much earlier stage of the princess's journey or in the felling of large numbers of citizens or courtiers involved in or witnesses to the marriage and ceremonials of November 1501. Arthur was probably simply very unlucky to be at Ludlow in the spring of 1502 during a period of particularly virulent sickness.

The prince was struck down a matter of days after he had performed ceremonies as part of Maundy Thursday celebrations on 24 March. If the eulogistic tone of the account can be wholly believed, Arthur had slotted directly back in to border life after the feast of Christmas 1501. By the time Easter approached, however, there

> grue and increased uppon his body, whethir it were by surfett or by cause natural, a lamentable ... and moost petiful disease and sikenes, that with so sore and great violens hedde batilled and driven in the singler parties of him inward.[9]

The description has been taken to show the rapid development of symptoms. But it also goes on to describe the disease as being so violent that it had battled and driven the singular parts of him inward. What is to be made of that particular description? It is certainly vivid and specific. Does this refer to some obvious affliction of his sexual organs, and literally to the growth of a visible tumour? Or might the report mean to describe the onset of an internal flux not unlike dysentery or other gastric illness brought on by a surfeit – overindulgence resulting in a serious imbalance of the humours of the body?[10]

It appears that the writer of the account of Arthur's marriage, death and funeral was probably a herald based in the king's distant household, maybe even John Wrythe, Garter King of Arms himself. His son Thomas was Arthur's pursuivant, Wallingford. He would have had access to information and vantage points that few others did. That might account for some of the personal and intimate details recorded. Nevertheless, he had no more accurate information to hand on the cause of Arthur's death than this. His report goes on to record that the deadly corruption completely vanquished and overcame the prince's 'pure and friendfull blood' before any medical help could have an impact on his condition. The prince's 'lively spirits' were mortified and he prepared for death. No other record of Arthur's symptoms exists. Writers have nevertheless been forthright in offering various alternative diseases as the cause of his death. Some have interpreted the phrase 'driving of his singular parts inwards' as evidence of testicular cancer, although that conclusion might be a stretch of the imprecise wording of the evidence in a very specific direction.[11] A tumour or disease of his testicles might have prevented Arthur from making his wife pregnant in their few months of married life together, despite his best efforts. As John Guy has suggested,[12] that type of medical condition could also have made it painful for Arthur to engage in sex or could have seriously impaired his sexual function. That might then account for the reputed exaggerated bragging over his performance in the bedroom on his wedding night and subsequently.

At the divorce hearing of Henry VIII and Catherine in 1529, many of the statements from men and women who were quite aged by then show that they thought Catherine to be two or three years older than Arthur. The implication was that she might have been a little more worldly-wise and confident than her husband. Thomas Boleyn, Viscount Rochford even added that he had heard from some of the Spaniards accompanying the princess, and on occasion even from Catherine herself, that she was older than sixteen at the time of her wedding. The lords and knights associated with Henry VII's household were much more certain of Arthur's age. They remembered seeing the book of the household that recorded the exact date of the royal children's birth. Some had also been present at his birth and christening and recalled events with great clarity. The slight age gap of at least a year might have been enough to make Arthur self-conscious on his wedding night, but he is likely to have become a little bolder over the next five months of married life. A winter on the Welsh Marches in 1501–02 would not have been filled with an overabundance of pastimes and activities beyond those of warm halls and welcoming houses. Travel would have happened only when necessary. The muddy conditions at Arthur's funeral in April 1502 suggest that winter was not a time of year to be outdoors between Ludlow and Bewdley. A presumption might then be that Arthur and Catherine spent a great deal of time in each other's company.

Whether by cover-up, by selective withholding of information or simply because it was not true, no mention was made in the spring of 1502 or earlier that Arthur had suffered from any serious physical condition, or that his health had been a cause for concern. He had travelled swiftly from Ludlow once Catherine's delayed arrival in England was known, and conducted himself with appropriate dignity at his wedding ceremony and the related tournaments and other festivities. Had Arthur carried a painful condition after puberty, for example, then some symptoms might have been apparent to people other than Catherine within his household at Ludlow or Tickenhill. The absence of other information on the prince's married life in the Marches does make it unlikely that such commentary from within his closed circle would have survived anyway. But since Arthur was so seldom a visitor to Westminster and London, evidence of any debilitating ailment would have been difficult to hide from the London chroniclers and the massive public scrutiny during the royal wedding of November 1501.

Henry VII had built many policies, initiatives and strategies upon the basis of England's new alliance to King Ferdinand and Queen Isabella. He would have plotted aspects of the future political power of his family as rulers of an important European state upon the success of this marriage. The overwhelmingly lavish setting for the wedding confirms that the king intended to impress all observers with England's readiness to sit at the high table of European diplomacy. That political background made it highly likely that the king and his council would have done their utmost to keep from the Spanish anything that undermined Arthur's fitness as a husband for Princess Catherine. Once the marriage took place, however, it was more likely that some hints of concern about the Prince of Wales, had they existed, might have surfaced within ambassadorial and personal communication with Spain. That modern researchers have picked up no such evidence probably confirms that Arthur had no obvious illness at the start of his married life.

His public appearances at the start of the Easter festivities in 1502 indicate that Arthur remained healthy, and there is no indication in surviving sources that he suffered any wasting or rapid weight loss in his final weeks. A contrasting example is Edward VI. His health in May and June 1553 fluctuated between complete incapacity and relatively stable health. On some days he was prostrate and coughing blood while on others he had recovered enough to move between palaces and walk in their gardens. Edward's final public appearance at a window of Greenwich Palace on 1 July, a week before his death, however, shocked onlookers. The king's emaciated and weak condition indicated a very rapid debility, which was widely reported. In 1502, Arthur seems to have been gripped by a violent illness that took him from his normal active self to death within a few days. His decline and decease were so sudden that it is mistaken to link his capabilities in the marriage bed (or lack thereof) with the cause of his death. That is not to say that Arthur did not have a problem in consummating his marriage and then had the great misfortune to die of an unrelated respiratory disease. We simply do not have enough clarity in the surviving evidence to be able to see past the scant contemporary information, and the much larger body of hearsay and circumstantial evidence dragged into the public domain as part of Henry VIII's Great Matter.

Other causes suggested for Prince Arthur's death include tuberculosis and the sweating sickness. Bacterial tuberculosis probably killed Arthur's father in April 1509 after he was stricken for many years with recurring throat infections. As already noted, the disease also caused the death of Arthur's nephew Edward VI in July 1553 (also aged fifteen); although another form of lung infection or pneumonia might have been his final ailment. Prominent in the symptoms of this disease were chronic coughing, high fever, sweating and rapid weight loss – all of which Edward VI displayed. Arthur did not. The disease was also spread through respiratory droplets in the air as sufferers coughed or sneezed. It made those in close proximity to victims very likely to become infected. For that reason, Arthur's body servants and household officers would almost certainly have been exposed had he suffered from the advanced stages of tuberculosis in 1502. There would have been many additional deaths among those connected to Arthur's household if this disease had become widespread in Ludlow. The victim's cough would also have been very obvious. Commentators on Henry VII's illnesses frequently reported on the throat infections and coughs – quinsy and tissic – that the king complained of each spring during the final decade of his reign. Had Arthur shared these symptoms then he surely could not have hidden them during his wedding celebrations and they would have appeared in the reports of his death.

A sudden epidemic in which Arthur was one of a number of victims still seems the most likely explanation for his shocking death – with the sweating sickness the cause cited in antiquarian and more recent sources. The *sudor anglicus*, or English Sweat, as it was known, was a new kind of disease that had symptoms different to the plague or fevers already familiar in England at the end of the fifteenth century. It was also a short-lived epidemic. Outbreaks arrived in the summer of 1485 and it was never again recorded in England after 1551. It was a highly contagious disease which could devastate groups of the population quickly. The sickness ravaged the leaders of London's political community in September 1485, as Henry VII's reign had an ill-omened beginning. The sweating sickness was marked by its very rapid progress once first symptoms arose. Coldness and shivering led quickly to headache and limb pains. A feverish stage then ensued after a few hours. The hot sweats for which the disease was named became rapid and extreme at this point. Chest pains accompanied a descent into delirium and collapse or exhausted prostration. Death came at the end of that stage. The course of the victim's decline might have taken only a few hours. It was particularly virulent during the summer months when warm weather led observers to blame inadequate sanitation and water supply for its transmission between people. If that were a principal cause, then population centres would have been more prone to large-scale outbreaks.

It is also unclear if the prince's household suffered many other deaths at that time. All of the chief officers in the prince's service survived this period of infection, but there is some suggestion that Princess Catherine was quite ill at the same time as her husband. That would not be surprising if the disease that killed him was a form of the sweating sickness which would have been passed through close physical contact and the transmission of infection in bodily fluids. She certainly did not attend his funeral, although a chair had been prepared for her; but whether this was due to her own illness or court protocol is uncertain. If Catherine shared some of her husband's symptoms when few others in the royal household did, then it suggests that she and her husband had spent considerable time in each other's company – to the point that their proximity contributed directly to a fatal illness striking down Arthur in 1502 when it might have spared him in previous years.

Arthur's Funeral

Arthur had a close connection to Ludlow. More than anywhere else it was his home. His attachment was revealed by a request to bury his heart in the St Mary Magdalene chapel within the castle. A plaque survived in the chancel of the chapel in 1684 that recorded the details of Arthur's death (but not its cause). The memorial included a record that his bowels were buried there very soon after his death. This must have been a personal decision of the prince as his end approached, and suggests that he had time to think about some of his affairs. The account of the prince's burial states that very quickly after death, his corpse was disembowelled, embalmed and dressed with as many sweet spices as could be obtained in the town in the early spring. Although it was usual to prepare the body for burial with a swift dignity, Arthur's household staff might have worked more quickly if he was believed to have died of a contagious disease, or if there was a fear of a spreading epidemic within Ludlow.

As part of the embalming process, the removal of Arthur's internal organs was reputedly done so well that a sealed lead chest was not required for the corpse. When a later Lord President of the Council in the Marches, Sir Henry Sidney, died in May 1586, he willed that his heart (i.e. internal organs) be taken to Ludlow and buried in the castle chapel. That process took about three days to accomplish even though Sidney died at Worcester, thirty miles away. In 1502, Arthur passed away in the castle and so his body might have been prepared almost immediately – especially if the sweating sickness was still raging within the town. A wooden coffin contained the body, which was tightly wrapped in its waxed sere cloth sheet. His organs were sealed in a lead box, which was found in the chapel in 1721 when it was removed. It was returned about twenty years later but was subsequently lost later in the eighteenth century during works at the castle.

Arthur's funeral plans were probably being formed as it became clear that he would not recover from his illness. His close connection to the border region was almost certainly behind the decision to inter him in Worcester Cathedral. Before then, however, Arthur's body would lie at Ludlow Castle as part of a home-town funeral ceremony. The prince's coffin was covered with a tight-fitting black cloth onto which was sewn a white cross. It was positioned in what was probably the presence chamber of the household suite of rooms within the domestic range of the castle. The western part of this block was traditionally known as 'Prince Arthur's Chamber'. It was probably in this space that his coffin was placed under a table covered with a rich cloth of gold. A large cross was set up over it and four great candlesticks were positioned around the body and left burning continually. Up to eighty people that had received alms from the prince on Maundy Thursday sat guarding the coffin in rotation, holding torches that burned night and day until St George's Day, 23 April – which was three weeks after Arthur's death.

Although there was time for members of the royal family to travel to Ludlow from Greenwich, neither the king nor the queen attended the funeral ceremonies for their son. That was a difficult decision. Knowledge of the extent of the sweating sickness would have been a factor, too, since it would have been dangerous to the future of the entire regime for the whole of the royal family to make a long journey to a town suffering under an epidemic. Leaving Arthur as the sole focus of the funeral ceremonies emphasised his status as an independent lord in his own country. A funeral away from the capital did make it easier to reduce the horrific impact of the death of the regime's heir. There would be no procession to Westminster Abbey or monument to remind the king's subjects that Henry VII was suddenly a lot less secure on the throne. Since someone had to represent the king, the principal mourner was Thomas Howard, Earl of Surrey. By that stage of the reign, Surrey was one of the king's most loyal courtiers and able administrators. His rehabilitation after fighting against Henry, Earl of Richmond at Bosworth had come to symbolise what was possible in Tudor royal service if subjects were willing to work hard on the king's terms and possessed the abilities or resources that he valued.

Those attending the funeral received cloth for the making of robes for the funeral. The Earl of Surrey as chief mourner and Treasurer of England signed off the bills. The largest group were the lords, knights, gentlemen and yeomen of the prince's household. They were treated as a distinct group under the president of the council, William Smith, Bishop of Lincoln, and based on the check roll of the household. They received 843 yards of cloth. There was also a more modest allowance of thirty yards for the Spanish ladies that represented Princess Catherine. Assuming that all the servants of the various lords received the same type of material, it is possible to calculate the approximate size of this officially supported attendance list. Differences in the degrees of rank were reflected in the numbers of servants accompanying each lord and not in the type of mourning cloth they were given. So the earls of Shrewsbury and Kent each brought ten servants, while barons like Lord Grey of Ruthin and Lord Dudley were given cloth for six followers. A rough-and-ready average of about four yards of cloth per person equates to just over 200 people connected directly to the Council of the Marches and the prince's household. Their number was boosted by a slightly smaller number of knights, esquires, gentlemen and yeomen of the border counties under the control of the Council of the Marches. As a group they took 699 yards of cloth – all of which had been brought from London in five cartloads by a team headed by Laurence Gower.

The planned delay was essential for messengers to be sent across the region and to the king in London. Preparations for the funeral had to be made. A window of weeks rather than days allowed the ceremonies to the planned appropriately, mourners to gather, precedence and protocol to be established and even enabled other sick people some opportunity to recover in time to attend. A calming presence was 'the lady Darcy' attending upon the Princess of Wales. She was almost certainly Elizabeth Darcy, the retired manager of Arthur's old nursery and his infant household at Farnham. Although much had happened to the prince since he had left her care, by the time that the unwelcome funeral took place it was still only eight years since the king's son had moved permanently to the Marches. Her attendance speaks strongly of the bond that she had formed with Arthur and the esteem in which she was held. The crucial supplies of mourning cloth could be ordered or dispatched from the king's

Wardrobe. Six carts were even brought back into service from the dungeon of the Tower of London. These and other wagons brought packets of black cloth to Ludlow before returning – a round trip of twenty days. The cloth then had to be made into mourning gowns and hoods for all people that would attend. Other goods were brought from Bewdley to Worcester by river. Some essential items had to be sourced more quickly. 500 torches or 1,520 pounds of pure wax were supplied by Elizabeth Peke. Another merchant, Thomas Billey of Worcester, delivered wax sufficient to make hundreds of tapers for the hearse and to burn at the graveside until a month had passed. Chandlers, carpenters, sawyers, painters worked constantly over the days between Arthur's death and the time scheduled for the funeral. Their raw materials had to be supplied. These also included all string, rope, ironwork to bear the weight of the banners and torches; wood, ladles and cauldrons for melting wax; nails, buckram and other backing cloth. The urgency of the task was suggested by the hiring of moulds for castings for the decoration of the hearse. Gold and silver leaf and coloured paint were obtained from other traders at Worcester. The extent of the purchasing power of the prince's and king's households must have put severe pressure on local suppliers. It was inevitable that some specialist and high-value goods and personnel would be obtained in London.

Henry VII's painters, John Fligh, Thomas Grene and John Serle, had time to paint and dispatch the four holy banners that would accompany Arthur's corpse – the Trinity, the Patible Cross, a banner of Our Lady and one of St George. They also completed banners of the king's and queen's arms, and the arms of the king and queen of Spain. Serle was responsible for eleven long streamers or bannerells that proclaimed the prince's titles and encapsulated a little of the hopes that Arthur had represented for the Tudor regime. They were the arms of the prince, of Wales, of Cornwall, of Chester, of Cadwallader, of Wales quartered, of Brutus, of Ireland, Normandy, Guyenne and Ponthieu. Another bannerell was made of Princess Catherine's arms – all fringed with silk. The banners and streamers were a mixture of conventional royal heraldic imagery and the traditional, ancient and mythical symbolism that had been a constant part of the main events of Arthur's life; his christening, creation as Prince of Wales, and marriage. The inclusion of Cadwallader and Brutus showed that Henry VII remained consistent in attaching his family to the heroic kings and original founders of Britain. The Welsh arms confirmed that Arthur carried forward Henry Tudor's claim upon Welsh loyalties, while the representation of Irish arms and those of the French duchies also suggest wider imperial ambitions. The French lands, especially, had been out of English control for two generations by 1502. The king had supported Breton independence in the late 1480s and had attempted a French invasion in 1492. The army assembled against Scotland in 1497 was also large enough to have occupied parts of the country after achieving the defeat of James IV and a conquest of territory – although the prospects of a long-term English presence in Scotland were unlikely, given the cost and knowledge of the difficulties faced by the English in the early fourteenth century. English attention towards France did resurface quickly at the start of Henry VIII's reign in a direct extension of the policies put in place by English diplomatic activity during the final few years of his father's reign. Might that be enough to suggest that Prince Arthur was expected to have taken up the cause of recovering the French territory to which the English kings had the strongest claim? Awareness of these rights would have emerged from his education and the king seems certain to have wanted to ensure that his eldest son could bear the weight of expectation that something would be done to revive English ambitions in Normandy, especially.

130 smaller pencil banners were also made. They were fixed to blue staves and displayed the prince's ostrich feather badge and diverse other (unnamed) royal symbols. Two more specific standards are recorded in the accounts. One was a cross of St George with a white hart wrought in silver with a crown of gold. The other bore a cross of St George powdered with ostrich feathers and fringed with silk. The banner of the hart was a significant inclusion, since it linked Arthur to both Edward V and the Mortimers (via Richard II, whose badge this was, but who had also made Roger Mortimer, 4th Earl of March his heir in 1387). Edward IV's son had inherited the claim to the throne of the Mortimers and the hart was incorporated into some of the representations of his arms. Its later inclusion in Prince Arthur's imagery was another reminder to the community of the borders that he, too, had shared this ancestry through his mother who had acquired the Mortimer right once Edward V was presumed to be dead.

This same team of workmen acted quickly to line and strengthen the banners with buckram. The absence of the direct royal family from the funeral service meant that it was as much an exercise in projecting Tudor identity and power as it was a family commemoration. Much of the black cloth and black silk had to be made and then sent from London and then assembled for the ceremonies in Ludlow; as did the finer white damask and white cloth of gold for the crosses and black velvet for the coffin and the hearse on which it would travel. Variously sized valances – thin woven cloth sheets – were prepared for it. At least one large valence included the image of Arthur's motto *Ich Dein* in gold with the badge of silver ostrich feathers. Another specialist painter, John Gayne, produced a great image of Christ on a cloth of majesty, sitting upon a rainbow with the evangelists and diverse religious writings. The painters also prepared escutcheons – small wooden shields – bearing images of Arthur's heraldic beasts, coronels, garters, crowns and the prince's motto with ostrich feathers. Some very expensive craftwork went into preparing the personal trappings of Prince Arthur's coffin and hearse. A carved wooden crowned lion and shield were gilded with fine gold; two yards of the precious cloth of gold tissue covered a hat and powdered mantles lined with white sarcenet cloth; the mantles also had tappets of silk interwoven with Venice gold. The hearse cloth was attached by nails covered in white cloth of gold. The king's armourer Vincent Tutelar made a helm, while other German or Dutch workmen of the armoury – Glawde Rambusson and Maryn Garet – gilded it and made a sword and gilt axe in matching style. Although Arthur was too young to have performed any feats of arms, the traditional trappings reflected the training he had been given and the sentiment expressed in the ritual of his creation as Prince of Wales in 1489. Eighteen yards of silver ribbon was worked in order to bear the richly embroidered coat of arms that would be offered at the tomb in Worcester. A banner and trapper for Arthur's horse were also prepared and embroidered under the guidance of John Fligh.

On 23 April, the chamber was emptied of people and the coffin was moved to the hall of the castle where it was put on trestles in preparation for a funeral procession through the town of Ludlow to the parish church of St Laurence. Four yeomen of Arthur's chamber approached with a black cloth of gold decorated with a white cross, which was tied tightly around the coffin. Of the three bishops that undertook the religious ceremonies, William Smith of Lincoln and John Arundell of Coventry and Lichfield, had been members of the prince's household and council, and had known him since infancy. Bishop Edmund Audley of Salisbury had recently been translated from Hereford. With Worcester occupied by the absentee Luccan Silvestro di Gigli, Audley represented the senior regional clergy. He was also close to the king, being named as one of the executors in Henry VII's will of

1509. The bishops cast incense around the coffin and sprinkled it with Holy Water. Officers of the prince's household then picked it up. These pallbearers might be considered as Arthur's inner circle of administrators, but not his personal friends; they included steward of the household Sir Richard Croft, controller of the household Sir William Uvedale, Sir John Mortimer, Sir Walter Baskerville, Sir John Harley, Sir Thomas Cornewall, Sir Walter de la Bere and Sir Thomas Englefield.

The chief mourner, Thomas Howard, Earl of Surrey, presented himself in a suitably impressive manner. Once the prince's cortege began to move, it was the earl that walked directly behind the coffin, dressed in a long loose jacket of black, covered with a mantle and wearing a mourning hood over his head. Surrey's prominence and the roles of other lords like Lord Gerald FitzGerald and Robert Radcliffe[13] emphasised rehabilitation through service to the Tudor royal family.

Surrey was followed closely in the procession by the earls of Shrewsbury and Kent, in black jackets and hoods only, and then by lords Grey of Ruthin, Dudley, Grey of Powys and Sir Richard Pole, Arthur's chamberlain. The sons of other lords were also present, and they might be identified as a group that Arthur had spent time with. When Arthur's body was carried from the hall of the castle towards the hearse or 'chaire', it was brought out under a canopy of purple damask decorated with flowers and lined with buckram. The canopy was supported by four of the prince's friends, Anthony Willoughby, Edward Howard, Robert Radcliffe and John St John,[14] who steadied it over the coffin with black staffs drawing string mingled with purple silk and thread of Venice gold. The hearse was expensively fitted with black cloth and drawn by six horses with expensive black trappers. It was then led in precession through Ludlow. Sir Gruffydd ap Rhys was selected for the key role of bearing Arthur's standard before the hearse. He received much attention from the craftsmen to ensure that his saddle was adapted with a socket for the standard's staff, and that he had enough twine to bear the banner comfortably. His role in the funeral ceremonies at Ludlow and Worcester tends to confirm the view of many historians that Sir Gruffydd was one of Arthur's closest friends.

The procession was a key first stage in making the prince's funeral an inclusive public event. It brought together Arthur's friends, the secular and monastic religious community of Ludlow, the king's knights, heralds, and members of Princess Catherine's Spanish household. Forming the main body of the cortege were eighty poor people in mourning robes of black. Each carried a burning torch to complement those that were already lit around the town. The funeral ceremonies at Ludlow and Worcester emphasised the importance of lights in late medieval ceremonies. Candles and torches had a defence against evil but were a key part of perpetuating the memory of the deceased. Involving the poor in the provision of light and in the receipt of doles or alms was an act of mercy. Their prayers for the dead were essential acts in assisting the soul's journey through purgatory. Arthur's funeral was conventional in its reference to Christ as the light of the world. The scale of it, however, was something that had rarely been seen in the border counties. In the parish church the coffin was laid in the choir. Stalls had been set up for the mourners and once the church was full (with many more outside), the funeral Mass began. The dirige was started by a herald proclaiming the purpose of the service. William Smith then sang vespers for the dead – *placebo Domino in regione vivorum* – and was joined by the bishops of Salisbury and Coventry and Lichfield in reading three lessons. After the service the coffin remained in the church while the chief officers and mourners retired to the castle. A vigil over the corpse was held all night.

On the next day, 24 April, three funereal Masses were performed. Bishop Arundell sang the Mass of Our Lady, accompanied by the child-choir at St Laurence and the church organs. The next Mass, of the Trinity, was led by the Bishop of Salisbury, unaccompanied. A requiem Mass came third, sung by William Smith. The bishops received offerings of gold, led by the Earl of Surrey and all the other mourners from earls and lords to the Spanish ambassador Don Pedro de Ayala and the high and low bailiffs of Ludlow with the aldermen and councillors of the town. Arthur's confessor and almoner, John Edenham, delivered the sermon on the theme 'blessed are the dead that die in the Lord'.[15] Alms of 4*d* (a groat) were then doled to each poor man and woman in attendance; the eighty people already noted as torchbearers. Another mass was led by Richard Lye, Abbot of Shrewsbury with the help of the unnamed abbot of Bordesley. Further masses were sung on the next day, before the procession left Ludlow on a journey by foot to Bewdley.

25 April was recorded as being a foul, cold, windy and rainy day. Although fine black velvet cloth of gold covered, wrapped or shielded everything on the hearse, the casket itself had to be protected from the elements by another waxed black cloth. Naturally, the passage of hundreds of people also turned the roads to mud. The emotionally draining journey also became physically exhausting. The cortege passed through many parishes on its route towards the River Severn, probably including Withypool, Cleobury Mortimer and Rock before reaching Bewdley. The Earl of Surrey gave a golden noble coin worth 6*s* to each church or place of worship that rang bells as the hearse passed. On this journey, Arthur's body was accompanied by the main group of lords, clerics, heralds and 120 torchbearers from Ludlow, all in mourning gowns and hoods. Twenty-four of the torches were kept lit, which must have been a struggle in the horrible weather. When the company did reach Bewdley four labourers were paid to work through the night to clean the horses, their trappings and probably the wheels of the hearse.

It is likely that Arthur's body rested that night in the chapel of his own house, Tickenhill Place. Another Mass was said over the coffin the following day before it was prepared for the short passage to Worcester. From Bewdley, Sir Richard Croft and Sir William Uvedale, as steward and controller of the household, rode ahead directly to Worcester to see to the organisation of the interment ceremonies in the cathedral. They closed the gates of the city so that everything could be prepared without distraction. The procession followed more slowly. The members of the orders of friars of the city met the corpse at the north gate and censed the coffin as it passed. 120 new torches were supplied and fresh draught horses brought to lead the hearse through the city streets. All of the burgesses and common people lined the way until the lords leading the cortege met the vicar general of the Bishop of Worcester at the churchyard. He had with him all of the staff and children of the cathedral. At the entrance to the cathedral close, the coffin was taken from the hearse and carried by its same supporters and under its canopy into the church. The three bishops that had performed ceremonial masses at Ludlow were on hand in their rich clothes to bless the coffin once again.

Arthur's body was moved through to the chancel, lit by almost 400 candles in massive candelabra. The abbots and priors of all the regional houses were also present with very many of the monks from each abbey or priory. With well over a thousand people more-or-less formally involved, and much of the rest of the city brought to a halt by the spectacle, the funeral must have been a magnificent sight – outdoing even the funeral for King John in October 1216, which had taken place during a period of civil war. The services and ceremony at Worcester were on a grander scale. The account reports that 1068 lights brightened the church, the standards on display, and the dirge and nine lessons that were read by bishops, abbots and priors in attendance. That day's services were ended with the Magnificat and Benedictus in the Lady Chapel and more censing of the coffin.

The following day saw the most solemn and emotional part of the entire funeral period. The body was watched all night by many of the senior figures involved. By eight o'clock in the morning the congregation reassembled for Masses of Our Lady, the Trinity and Requiem which were sung again by the three bishops and with the Earl of Surrey's offering as at Ludlow. During the Requiem the offerings began to be made. All mourners offered the Mass penny. Then two heralds brought forward the rich embroidered coat of arms to the earls of Shrewsbury and Kent. Lords Grey of Ruthin and Dudley received the shield from the heralds, Lord Grey of Powis the sword, pommel forwards, Sir Richard Pole the helm and Lord John Grey the crest. Then a group of Arthur's household officers escorted the Man of Arms into the middle of the choir. This was Lord Gerald FitzGerald, son of the 8th Earl of Kildare. He rode the prince's courser and wore Arthur's full armour or harness. The horse was fully equipped with a trapper embroidered with the prince's arms and Lord Gerald carried the prince's poleaxe, head downwards. He was received by the Abbot of Tewkesbury, who had read the gospel at the requiem Mass. The horse itself was an offering which was received by Croft and Uvedale. This amazing moment was recreated during the 2002 commemorative re-enactment of the funeral.[16]

As the time approached to lay the body in the grave, the intensity of singing and prayers increased. At that point there seems to have been an eruption of weeping and crying from the congregation – as people realised, finally, that Arthur was dead. What had been a well-defined future for the people connected with the prince, his household and power, suddenly had become less certain. The account says that 'he had hard heart that wept not'.[17] Convention was that the chief mourners then made direct offerings to the corpse. Lord Grey of Powis came forward into the choir with a pall made of cloth of gold tissue. It was the first pall cloth to be laid on the coffin by two of the heralds. Another was offered by Grey of Ruthin, while each of the three earls present were given three more pall cloths by the gentlemen ushers of Arthur's chamber. The palls were all laid in a cross-formation over the coffin. The sermon was read by a learned doctor, possibly Charles Booth, a member of the Council, or John Edenham once more. Another dole of alms of a groat was commenced. During the reading of St John's Gospel, Sir Gruffydd ap Rhys passed the prince's standard to the cathedral clergy as an offering. More anthems were sung by the whole congregation as the prelates gathered to cense the coffin. At each repetition of *Kyrie Eleysion* (Lord have Mercy) one of the heralds cried 'for Prince Arthur's soul and the souls of all Christian souls, Pater Noster'. That was an invocation of the Lord's Prayer as the pall cloths were removed from the coffin and the gentlemen of Arthur's household took it up again. It was carried to the small chapel at the south end of the altar. With much weeping and lamentation, it was laid in the ground. The bishop of Lincoln, William Smith, started to say the prayers but could barely speak his words for crying. He placed a cross on the coffin in the grave and was the first to cast holy water and earth onto it. Arthur's own herald, Wallingford, took off his coat of arms and laid it on the coffin. The chief officers of the household, with Croft and Uvedale leading, then demonstrated the end of their personal service with the prince by breaking their batons of office and casting the pieces around Arthur's casket. All of the gentlemen ushers did likewise. Those present formed a piteous sight as human emotion threatened to overtake the regulated form of the service. The lavish scale of the ceremony and the formal stages of mourning required to bury a royal heir were still dependent upon the human beings involved being able to fulfil their roles. Since the clergy leading the service were as close to the prince as anyone else present in the cathedral, shared grief must have put a strain on completion of the ceremony. Part of the sadness undoubtedly stemmed from a sense of what was now lost to the region and to England's future. The service ended with a massive banquet and a call for those with claims for money owed by the prince's household to present them to the financial officers before the end of the day. After that, the household would be disbanded.

7

FRIENDS AND FAMILY POLITICS

The suddenness of Arthur's death and funeral was a massive shock to the border region. The devastating emotional blow felt by his servants and officials is apparent in the accounts of the ceremonies. Those events also reveal patterns of other networks that were beginning to form around the Prince of Wales. The most interesting one is a group that was probably made up of Arthur's friends. Related to the prince's personal affinity of companions were the nobles on the edges of the household and Marcher administration. Their involvement in the ceremonies suggests something of the family and political dynamics that might have been evolving around Arthur's court. Their presence at Arthur's funeral offers an indication of which noble families and kinship networks Henry VII had already started to trust around his teenage son. There could be no accident in the movement of these people towards the centre of Prince Arthur's power. Henry VII would not have tolerated any manipulation or influence that he had not encouraged. So when taken alongside the people known to have been in Arthur's personal service and present on the Council of the Marches, the attendance list at the prince's funeral might represent the bare bones of Henry VII's outline for King Arthur's royal household.

We cannot know if Arthur was a lonely boy. It does not seem likely that the heir of the kingdom would have been without hangers-on and companions. It is more important to question whether any of them were his close friends. Without details of visitors or entertainments at Ludlow or Tickenhill, his life on the Marches does appear austere and focussed on learning the business of government. During Arthur's lifetime there is very little evidence that enables us to say how his daily life progressed. It would be a mistake, however, to be led too far by the poor survival of letters or accounts. It was not in Henry VII's interests to have an heir who did not possess the social sophistication needed to perform at court or manage a household. Arthur had to live up to expectations that English and Welsh subjects already had of what kings should be like. King Henry was probably aware that a comparison would be made with his own ruling style. Distant as he was from London, it was vital that Arthur should come to the throne ready to fulfil all hopes for a second Tudor king with an ancient name to live up to. There were several large centres of population nearby and many lords had estates within a day's ride of the prince's main houses. The River Severn was navigable and delivery of luxury goods from ports such as Bristol to Worcester and beyond was relatively easy. Supplies of materials were on hand to make Arthur's funeral spectacularly impressive,[1] so there is no reason to doubt that their availability also improved his quality of life to something approaching the standard any prince might have expected around London. Hunting in Wyre Forest north of Bewdley would have been excellent. Deer were sent from there to re-stock the king's park at Richmond later in the reign. Arthur would have lived like a great regional lord. He was no prisoner at Ludlow and he did travel widely.[2]

One of his closest friends seems to have been Gruffydd ap Rhys ap Thomas, the son of Sir Rhys ap Thomas. Gruffydd was about eight years older than Arthur. He too was in training for a prominent role in the service of the Tudor crown – this time as successor to his father's dominance of Wales following the death of Jasper, Duke of Bedford in 1495. Gruffydd probably travelled to Ludlow with Arthur and Catherine in November of that year. Other youngsters like Anthony Willoughby and Maurice and John St John only appear in the historical record at this stage of their lives in association with each other and with Prince Arthur. The parents of all of these young men were committed to the bone in their support for Henry VII's crown. Their friendship guaranteed that a continuation of the close personal bond between the Tudor king and his friends in adversity, forged before 1485, would continue into the sixteenth century. In other cases, a connection to the prince was seen as beneficial for sons of aristocrats who were royal wards.

The role of Gerald FitzGerald, son of the 8th Earl of Kildare, as the Man of Arms at the funeral was significant. He was a ward of the king as surety for his father's good behaviour as Lord Deputy in Ireland. He was also the same age as Arthur. His part in the funeral suggests a particular closeness to Arthur and a familiarity with his household at Ludlow. The king would have been shrewd to use the environments of the royal household and the prince's own small network to build the foundations of a new crown affinity. Binding in friendship the heir to the English crown and the son of the natural leader of the Anglo-Irish political community was an astute move by Henry VII. It does suggest that the king's power was developed and projected in subtle ways and with long-term strategic goals in mind. Ireland had given the Tudor crown much anxiety during the first fifteen years of the reign. Taking steps to ensure that the next generation of political leaders had a personal understanding decreased the chances that unfamiliarity and miscommunication would have an adverse effect on the unfolding of Anglo-Irish relations during the early sixteenth century. Lord Gerald later married Elizabeth Grey, sister of the 2nd Marquis of Dorset. John, Lord Grey of Powis was another Crown ward in this same circle of Arthur's friends. John was also born at the same time as Arthur. Since his guardian was Margaret Beaufort he came to Arthur's service with the highest Tudor credentials. His status would have been built consistently while he was side by side with Arthur, and his presence around the Ludlow household shows us what type of ally the king envisaged at the centre of the next reign.

These family and marriage connections between the group of young men that were linked to Prince Arthur are most likely to have been formed during the 1490s when many of the crown's wards from within the senior peerage, with the conspicuous exception of the Duke of Buckingham, were being educated alongside the prince. Henry VII would have seen the sense in building the future of the Tudor regime upon the personal allegiance of a small group connected directly to Prince Arthur. A sufficient number of the Henry VII's personal servants would also transfer their loyalty readily. In combination, the hope was that Arthur would inherit the crown at the head of a broad network that would provide him with a stable national platform, a range of experienced officials and a more intimate foundation of support to underpin his personal rule.

In some cases, the king's lingering suspicion of the older generation of Yorkist nobles actually provided the route for their children to form direct links with Arthur as part of a process of reintegration. Part of the restraint placed on the 1st Marquis of Dorset by Henry VII was the requirement that his son become a ward of the crown in 1492 to guarantee his father's good behaviour during the invasion of France. Once at court it was far easier for young Thomas Grey to ingratiate himself with the king and the royal family. In doing so he probably helped to secure the king's favourable opinion of his father, the 1st marquis. The court connection might have aided the introductions that brought young Thomas's first marriage to Margaret Beaufort's cousin Eleanor St John.

Young noblemen who were in royal wardship would normally have resided within the king's household around London. It was there that the most direct influence could be exerted upon the formation of their loyalty. Yet if Arthur was to be a successful king he needed to carry with him the devotion of a core group of lords, friends and servants when he made the transition from his princely household into his royal inheritance. Henry VII would have been all-too aware of the difficulties faced by a new monarch in trying to create and keep allegiance from uncertain or disrupted beginnings. By the close of 1501, Prince Arthur's intellectual education and development as a leader ensured that he possessed elements of all the regal bearing that Henry VII had lacked before he defeated Richard III. At the age of fifteen, Arthur's skills were not fully formed. He clearly had yet to experience the pressure of military leadership, of maintaining national income, stimulating trade and commerce, or of managing the crown's interaction with the representatives of the realm in Parliament. But aside from mechanical responsibilities that could be learned or delegated, Arthur was in the process of building experience in working with and alongside the type of people that ran the country for any regime – the peers and gentry and their networks of lesser urban and rural followers. The members of the Council of the Marches had been an effective regional governing body before Arthur joined them at Ludlow in April 1493. As he worked with them and learned from their experience over the following nine years, Arthur became a teenage lord with as much intensive royal training behind him as any previous Prince of Wales.

The prince's personal network of friends would have been closely involved in the running of his teenage household, but are not likely to appear in the records of the Council of the Marches (unfortunately the only agency for which even fragmentary documents survive). The account of the funeral reveals their main purpose, which was to form a tight-knit core of support to give strength to the foundation of King Arthur's rule. All medieval kings needed companions for those rare quiet periods away from the demands of running the country. The patterns of a similar network had been set out for Henry, Earl of Richmond in the household of his mother Margaret Beaufort and Lord Stanley at Woking in the 1470s. It was here that men like Reginald Bray, Hugh Oldham and Richard Guildford first began to develop their service to the group that would create a credible conspiracy to put Henry Tudor on the throne. Henry's absence overseas during this decade and more makes it far more difficult to see this as his personal affinity, but at some stage real friendship with men like Guildford and Bray emerged. Once Henry was king, he could call upon the known organisational skills of his allies without any concerns over their loyalty. Henry VII and his mother encouraged repetition of this link between friendship and key responsibility around Prince Arthur as he grew into his role.

Another, more surprising route to Henry VII's affection and therefore to Arthur's circle were the links between the Marcher gentry and Henry VII's childhood. These associations with Prince Arthur give a strong impression of Henry VII's lasting sense of connection with the gentry of the borders. The impression of Henry VII given by many studies is that he would have had little room for such sentiment or warmth. Yet there was a fondness for a very small number of people associated with Henry's own period of wardship. That might explain why the king encouraged the process of Crown wardship as a means to extend and strengthen loyalty among his followers. When he returned as king those that had known him in the 1460s must have faced difficult decisions about how to exploit Henry's remembrance of former associations, had they been good, or to hope he had an imperfect memory, if their past contained things that they wished would remain forgotten.

Alongside Thomas Howard, Earl of Surrey, the earls of Shrewsbury and Kent were part of the very small group of the king's trusted long-standing allies. All evidently believed strongly in Henry VII's kingship. They had turned out many times with large numbers of troops to defend the Tudor crown from rebels and to support Henry's foreign expeditions. They were dependable men who time and again had proved their loyalty. Both combined prominent roles in court ceremonial with reliable representation of the crown in the regions where their estates were concentrated. George Talbot, 4th Earl of Shrewsbury was born in Shropshire, but had developed his estates in South Yorkshire and Derbyshire. His connection to Prince Arthur -apart from his obvious investment in the regime - developed through his aunt Anne's earlier marriage to Sir Henry Vernon, controller of Arthur's household and the prince's guardian. Vernon's estate at Tong was next-door to the Talbot manor of Shifnal, where the earl was born in 1468. Shrewsbury had a regular presence at the formal events of Arthur's life so it is reasonable to assume that he might have had frequent unrecorded contact with the prince at other times, especially as Arthur seems to have been quite widely travelled in the northern Midlands and Cheshire. It is also possible that Shrewsbury was more involved as a supporter of Arthur's council and lordship during the minority of Edward Stafford, Duke of Buckingham before 1499.

Buckingham's absence from Arthur's funeral ceremonies is as telling as the presence of many other nobles. The Stafford family were traditionally great lords across the Anglo-Welsh border. Margaret Beaufort, as Buckingham's guardian during his minority, regularly used the income from his estates to fund Arthur's household. Once he was of age, Buckingham was happy to display himself in the spectacle of Arthur's marriage ceremonies and tournaments in November 1501. He had also been the chief mourner at the funeral of Arthur's brother Edmund in 1500. Two years later he was less willing or able to attend the funeral of Arthur himself. Giving Buckingham too prominent a role could only invite discussion of his royal connections, which was a short step away from questions about the succession of the crown. Unlike other aristocratic male wards of the Tudor family that had been born in the early-mid-1480s, Buckingham seems to have had little personal connection to or affection for the Prince of Wales. Buckingham was about fifteen years old when Arthur was moved from Farnham to Ludlow. On the cusp of manhood, he probably realised that the prince would begin to supplant his own family's power on the border. More immediately, Buckingham might have resented the draining of his landed income during his minority to pay for Prince Arthur's upkeep. The duke retained a haughty belief in his own royal ancestry and the rights that he felt were associated with it. It was probably also apparent to Buckingham that the immense power his father had built up and briefly enjoyed before his summary execution in November 1483 was being deliberately diluted in preparation for the regional dominance of Prince Arthur. With Sir William Stanley and Jasper Tudor, Duke of Bedford, occupying the major justiciarships of north and south Wales, there appeared to be little room for Buckingham to slot back into a traditional Stafford powerbase. Stanley's execution might have offered Buckingham some hope, but Jasper Tudor proved implacable. When Jasper died on 21 December 1495, he did so at Buckingham's main residence of Thornbury in Gloucestershire, where he had lived for the last few years of his life. Duke Jasper had married Buckingham's mother within three months of Bosworth. And although the marriage was childless, he came to control many of the Stafford lands in right of his wife. Margaret Beaufort's physical guardianship of the underage Duke of Buckingham must have left Stafford languishing under the impression that the Tudor family intended to constrain his personal power and undermine his family's resources.

Arthur's death cast Buckingham's power in an altogether more dangerous light. His father had received from Richard III a staggering amount of power along the March and beyond the region. Almost everything that Arthur's Council of the Marches controlled had been in the hands of Buckingham's father, Henry, before the autumn of 1483.³ Once Arthur was dead, it was inevitable that Edward Stafford would investigate how much of this inheritance he had a chance of recovering. His presence as chief mourner at the prince's funeral might have encouraged him to think that the crown acknowledged his regional precedence. That was something Henry VII was not keen to inspire within a family that had quickly transformed its loyalty to Richard III into rebellion when the flow of rewards dried up in 1483. More importantly, it might also have boosted the Stafford family's belief in its own royal ancestry and right. Tudor control of Edward Stafford's wardship had been partly an exercise in deflating the family's royal ambitions and in building a consistent awareness of the loyalty they owed to the new king. As Earl of Richmond, King Henry would have learned of the Duke of Buckingham's attempt to hijack the pro-Tudor rebellion in the autumn of 1483 to put himself at the head of the list of alternatives to Richard III. Buckingham's capture and execution by King Richard had removed the problem of Stafford subservience from Henry VII's list of important initial tasks. The minority of his son offered a longer-term opportunity to build Prince Arthur's personal influence within the rejuvenated power of the Council of the

Marches. Buckingham would have to learn to engage with this new structure if he was to recover any portion of the authority that his father had enjoyed.

After Arthur's untimely death, the king was certainly not going to provide an invitation for the old nobility to flex its muscles at a time of weakness and uncertainty for the ruling house. When Buckingham became old enough to enter his estates, the king had already decided to inflate the value of the fine that he had to pay to receive control of his lands. That was another reminder that Stafford power grew only from the king's goodwill. Had Arthur lived, it would also have to be measured against Prince Arthur's dominant position. It took until 1504 for the duke and the Crown to come to a formal agreement over how the king was to be represented in several of the Marcher lordships placed under Buckingham's control. The expanding influence of Prince Edward's Marcher council had sparked the ire of Henry Stafford in the 1470s to the point where he was happy to support the Duke of Gloucester's seizure of the throne for the rich pickings that came his way. The mutual distrust between the Crown and the Duke of Buckingham continued into Henry VIII's reign. It brought the possibility that Edward Stafford might have thought about behaving like his father had done if Arthur had lived for a further decade as prince. The duke was obliged to build a particular type of relationship with the Tudor royal family and its government. It was based on the same diet that many other lords and senior commoners were familiar with: power devolved on the king's terms with dormant threats laid against financial security and future influence.

The presence at Arthur's funeral of George Grey, 2nd Earl of Kent is less obviously explained. His commitment to Henry VII was clear. The increase in income from his estates through prudent management was something that might have endeared him even more to his king. He was certainly one of the wealthier peers and, like Shrewsbury, had been involved in the previous ceremonials of Arthur's life. Yet his estates were in Bedfordshire, Northamptonshire and Buckinghamshire. His links to Arthur therefore grew from his marriages and careful cultivation of the connections that they brought. His first wife was Anne Woodville, sister of Edward IV's queen Elizabeth, and one of the many children of Richard Woodville, 1st Earl Rivers and Jacquetta de St Pol that had dominated the noble marriage market and political scene during the late 1460s and 1470s. The Earl of Kent's first wife was therefore one of the aunts of Henry VII's queen, Elizabeth of York. He shared this relationship with Jasper Tudor, who, as was mentioned above, married another of the queen's sisters, Catherine, the Duchess of Buckingham.[4]

After George Grey's first wife Anne Woodville died in July 1489, his second marriage provided the kind of personal connection that deepened his direct links to the king. In 1490 he married Catherine Herbert, daughter of William Herbert, Earl of Pembroke and Anne Devereux; the guardians of Henry Tudor when he was their ward during the 1460s. With Countess Anne's death in 1486, the king's remaining links to his own childhood were through the children with whom he had grown up. Catherine was born in 1464 and Henry would have known her until she reached the age of five or six. Her elder sister Maud was ten years older than King Henry, but had been proposed as his wife as part of negotiations to bring the Earl of Richmond back to England in the 1470s. She went on to marry Henry Percy, 4th Earl of Northumberland. If we can accept that Henry VII was as well-disposed towards all of Anne Devereux's surviving female children as he was to William Herbert, 2nd Earl of Pembroke and his brother Sir Walter Herbert, then some of that royal attentiveness must surely have rubbed off on their husbands. George Grey's ties to the queen and her half-brother the Marquis of Dorset placed him in a primary position to benefit from

Henry VII's affection for Anne Devereux. His service at Arthur's funeral, therefore, might have been warranted by his personal relationships with the higher levels of the royal family rather than his connection to Prince Arthur. Catherine Herbert's sister, Anne, was the mother of another of Margaret Beaufort's wards and friends of Arthur, John, Lord Grey of Powis.

Another branch of the Grey family had already entered the orbit of the prince. In 1493, Thomas Grey, 1st Marquis of Dorset's connection with Prince Arthur can be seen at the prince's very first recorded public act in the Marches, at the Hereford sessions of the peace in April 1493. Although he had no concentration of estates in the Marches, Dorset made a determined effort to attach himself to Arthur. Dorset had reached his mid-forties by the time Prince Arthur was taking up his responsibilities at Ludlow. He had at first been mistrusted by the king for his attempt to abandon Henry and return to Richard III's favour before Bosworth, and he was one of those left as a hostage for Tudor's war loans negotiated in France. Dorset also survived the suspicion surrounding his mother's loyalty in 1487. His presence around the prince remained strong during the 1490s until his death in August 1501. His efforts to rebuild his relationship with the king through support for Prince Arthur ensured that his son Thomas, 2nd Marquis of Dorset (born in 1477), had a far better chance of forming a friendship with Prince Arthur. But it was actually a brother of the 2nd Marquis, John, Lord Grey, who had an equally high-profile role at the prince's funeral in April 1502. This Groby branch of the Grey family had been one of the most important groups around Edward V when he was Prince of Wales. They were destined for enormous power had Edward lived. To have recovered some of this influence within the circle of the Tudor Prince of Wales during the 1490s was a major achievement. A crucial factor might have been Dorset's half-blood relationship to Henry VII's queen, one of his closest relatives. At the time that Arthur was preparing for marriage, the king's own trusted friends were beginning to die off or diminish in effectiveness. Rejuvenation of the royal affinity was required by 1500, and the emerging leadership of Prince Arthur was the obvious way to achieve this.

Modern readers might find these marriage ties intricate and convoluted but they would have been very clear within the ruling elite of Henry VII's reign. A king so acutely aware of his own bloodline would have been fully familiar with the alliances, links and opportunities that aristocratic genealogy brought to the politics of his reign. Yet the impact might have been diluted slightly by the fact that the noble and gentry elites had been intermarrying for generations – by 1500 almost all peers, lords and knightly families were cousins in some degree. The important thing about the small group that appeared at Arthur's funeral was that it can be identified as a group that was linked through wardship with the Crown, attendance at Arthur's court and education alongside him. There must have been a common bond for that particular cross section of lords to have made the journey to Ludlow in April 1502 as a particular act of respect to Prince Arthur. That in itself suggests that they possessed a stronger connection to the prince's life than others that were not there.

Henry VII's regime was continually trying to rebalance the basis upon which its authority and security existed. This was a slow process. Sustaining confidence in the key people trusted to project King Henry's influence required the focussed attention of the king and the most trusted few of his inner circle. Sanctioning marriage alliances and then cultivating the relationships that developed was one aspect of this. Margaret Beaufort's half-blood family were already widely connected through marriage to the leaders of society during the reigns of the Yorkist kings Edward IV and Richard III. It would be wrong, therefore, to think of the Tudor family as being an isolated group with no links to the existing aristocracy. Henry VII's possession of the throne and his control over the crown as an institutional power carried great weight; regardless of knowledge or discussion of his personal right to be king. The longer he reigned, the more likely it was that challengers would diminish in number and effectiveness. When, in the 1490s, the masterminds behind Perkin Warbeck's conspiracy tried to prise open the links of allegiance that kept Henry VII in power, these former members of the Yorkist elite were a clear focus for their efforts to stir up rebellion. Their lack of converts within the higher levels of early Tudor society suggests that Henry VII had already achieved considerable success in stabilising support behind his kingship. He had put much effort into building loyalty through threat and financial penalty – achieving fidelity less through love than by extracting acknowledgement that he had a right to rule and was competent enough to lead the nation.

Prince Arthur's status was, on the one hand, tied inexorably to the survival of his father. Only for as long as Henry VII was around to develop servants through the government and household institutions on the March would Arthur be guaranteed to have the best training. On the other hand, the prince's identity and his personal lordship had been developed to be independent from the apparatus of the Westminster government. Had Henry VII been defeated and killed at the Battle of Blackheath in June 1497, or silently murdered in a palace coup before 1499, then Arthur's survival would have been in doubt. His entire upbringing had been structured to enable him to rule after just such an eventuality. Until he was married, the Spanish were unlikely to offer any support for a Tudor recovery of the throne. Arthur would have been solely responsible for organising any effort to press his own rights to the throne. His separation from the rest of his family was meant to provide a means by which he could start to achieve this. Arthur had a degree of autonomy that could have made him a rallying point for those that intended to offer the same kind of stubborn resistance to any incoming regime that Jasper Tudor had been able to manage in the early 1460s. Arthur had independent sources of income and the ability to raise troops that would be led by able commanders such as Sir Rhys ap Thomas and Sir Richard Pole. To be more assured of offering a personal presence as a leader, Arthur probably had to be considered older. Any struggle was likely to be dominated by military clashes. However, reluctant he was, the prince would have to lead and inspire as his father had after the autumn of 1483. More direct motivation came from the teenage Edward, Earl of March, who swept out of the Welsh Marches at the head of his own army following the death of his father Richard, Duke of York at the Battle of Wakefield in December 1460.

Arthur had been educated as a scholar, as a political leader and as a self-sufficient administrator. Henry VII's intention in creating precisely the kind of learning environment that Ludlow offered was surely to instil in the prince the range of skills needed to build successful kingship and the confidence to approach his task with the support of a dedicated affinity. It was certainly a long-term strategy to allow his heir to exist as a satellite king in all but name. From his experience in the year that Arthur was born, 1486, King Henry was realistic enough to realise that the threats he was likely to face would be severe and persistent. Foreign sponsors and hidden English enemies would emerge when they felt confident of damaging the Tudor king in a most effective way. Keeping Arthur close enough would have offered him the greater protection of the regime's powerful infrastructure centred on the castles and palaces near London. But such a decision would have exposed Arthur to the same risks as the king and the rest of the Tudor family, severely diminishing the chances that an able and active leader could maintain the family's royal claims in the event of a dynastic disaster such as that which overtook the Lancastrian royal family in May 1471.

The opportunities for placement and advancement attached to Arthur's service were more straightforward: barring accident or rebellion, he would be the next king. Those who served him, advised him or befriended him in his border home would reap the rewards of their intimacy with the prince once he came to rule. Henry VII was very aware of this. It was partly a desire to allow Arthur the chance to build an independent network of reliable and experienced loyalists that prompted the king to give his son a semi-independent role in a region with a distinct identity. For Arthur to be a success required the building and honing of the skills of royal leadership. The formation of a network of followers around the prince was inevitable. The challenge was in finding a balance to ensure that Arthur was not unduly influenced or dominated during the years in which he learned what was expected of him. The high-ranking heavyweight entourage that probably brought Arthur from Farnham to Ludlow descended on the March with the intention of demonstrating unequivocally that Arthur's power was an extension of the king's authority.

The future shape of Arthur's royal household was the one great opportunity for ambitious nobles to position themselves in order to gain a social advantage from the inevitable change of monarch. In 1500, when the wedding plans for Arthur and Catherine began to take shape, there was no expectation that Henry VII was nearing the end of his life. At the age of forty-three he was already older than Edward IV and Richard III had been when they had died, but his health was probably improved by the stability brought to his kingship by the final end of Perkin Warbeck's plot. Henry's periodic illnesses were to become more disabling in the first decade of the sixteenth century. The concern for the senior nobles, however, was that the king had established from the start of the reign a clear policy on promotions into the peerage and upwards mobility within the aristocracy. There was not much hope that even a spectacular track record of loyalty and support for the Crown would result in elevation, as Sir William Stanley's career had shown.

The condemnation for treason of Stanley and Fitzwalter from his own royal household only strengthened Henry VII's dilemma about Prince Arthur. He urgently had to choose. Did he delegate power to a cross-section of the nobility and senior gentry, giving opponents a direct means to threaten the king and his family? Or did he exclude all but the people he trusted most? The latter would secure the inner reaches of the regime but would lead to over-reliance on a small section of experienced individuals. Resentment at the exclusion of those on the outside of this arrangement and the regime's perceived lack of inclusivity might then drive some subjects towards Henry's enemies. The king erred on the side of caution. He had hoped to place himself in a dominant position by gathering into his hands much of the desirable patronage, lands and opportunities that the wealthy classes might desire. Vacant peerage titles were absorbed by the Crown and not re-granted. There was also a high proportion of senior noblemen who were underage for large parts of the reign. The king's reluctance to trust others beyond his established allies further restricted the opportunities for advancement. These limitations combined most effectively against the Yorkist nobility. And the dangers of mishandling the tone of relationships with powerful men was starkly demonstrated in July 1499 when the queen's first cousin Edmund de la Pole, Earl of Suffolk, withdrew his allegiance and fled to the protection of his aunt Margaret, dowager Duchess of Burgundy. Suspicions about the remaining Yorkists resurfaced, even though it was probably the pressure exerted by the king to constrain potential disloyalty that had pushed figures like Suffolk into opposition.

So just as Henry VII seemed more secure after the ending of Warbeck's conspiracy, another threatened to appear in its place almost immediately. Henry dispatched some of his councillors to persuade Suffolk to return to England. This he did, but only to fall under the king's provocative and unsubtle attempts to restrict his independence even further. By August 1501, he fled once again. This time he took his brother Richard to the protection of Maximilian, Archduke of Austria and ruler of the Low Countries. Suffolk then began to press for recognition as a legitimate Yorkist prince and rightful replacement for Henry VII. And although he was ultimately a pawn of Maximilian's very broad foreign policy, Suffolk was an uncomfortable and expensive distraction for Henry until he was handed over in April 1506 after lengthy negotiations and massive English bribes.

Henry VII evidently had some difficulty in gauging how his relationships with individual nobles were developing. A backdrop of recurring dynastic conspiracy helped to block the conditions in which personal relationships could mature. Whereas Henry knew that he had to build a level of businesslike connection with individuals as they controlled the local agencies of government, it was often at a private and personal level that a king needed to appeal directly for the trust and loyalty of men and women, to assess their personalities and employ subtle means to bind their future good fortune to the continuing success of a particular regime.

The king had some help in this direction from his mother. Margaret Beaufort, Countess of Richmond and Derby, seems to have been very effective in securing the loyalty of former Yorkists. She had stayed in England throughout the reigns of Edward IV and Richard III, even though she was identified as an increasingly ardent conspirator in favour of her exiled son. Her closeness to the centre of power, through the continuing prominence of her husband Lord Stanley, meant that Margaret did have first-hand knowledge of how allegiances could change and be secured with the right kind of support. The marriages of members of her extended St John and Welles families brought connections to the Scropes, Bigods, Zouches and Greys. Many of them had been solidly behind both Yorkist kings and a few, such as the Scropes of Bolton, had been caught up in the early conspiracies against Henry VII. The case of a man like Sir Ralph Bigod of Settrington in the North Riding of Yorkshire indicated how Margaret approached the issue of re-educating those men who probably fought against the Tudor army at Bosworth. Bigod had been a knight of the body to Richard III, a personal servant at the heart of his household. He transferred his service to the Tudors. As well as having some responsibilities as a Crown steward in his home county, he also entered the household of the Countess of Richmond. He seems to have been insulted for his previous allegiance, since the countess was obliged to intervene after Bigod got into arguments defending his former master. Margaret was happy to hold him up as an example of how loyalty could be transferred between opponents. She became well known for this skill in smoothing the causes of friction between her officers.[5] She encouraged her son the king to follow a similar path.

The Earl of Surrey might be the best example of Henry VII's achievement in this area. King Henry knew that he had to expand his pool of reliable servants. If he was to keep more of the Crown lands in his own hands, then he would require many more stewards and constables to run them. The people he really trusted either had specific and demanding roles within the household, such as the yeomen of the Crown, or else already found their contribution to the regime stretched by the king's reluctance to delegate power to a wider group. Henry's dilemma was to loosen the strings of control sufficiently to attract able Crown servants without, at the same time, enabling enemies to slip closer to the heart of the regime. Once there as the king's officers, they had greater means to attack the Tudor family directly. To enable this process of expansion to happen, the regime relied upon closer scrutiny of crown officers through administrative and accounting regulations managed by an offshoot of the inner royal council, the Court of General Surveyors. More generally, those people interacting with the Crown found themselves placed under bonds and obligations. Anyone tempted to make some advantage from their status as the king's representative and depart from what he required of them found that they risked a crippling fine as well as an end to all opportunity in Crown service. The threat of ruin hung over almost anyone serving the Crown at a level where disloyalty or poor performance had the potential to undermine the king's security. Such bonds became a standard condition of grants of office or licences to represent the king's power. The penalties would, however, only be demanded if the Crown considered that an office holder had broken the terms of his service agreement or otherwise damaged the status of the crown.

This uncertain environment was relevant to Prince Arthur's growing responsibilities because the prince's court and household could not escape the tensions that ebbed and flowed within the corridors of the king's palaces. Arthur might have been separated from his father by 150 miles, but the balance of service around the prince became crucial as the basis for the continuance of Tudor rule. If Henry VII was to leave the crown to an heir that was unchallenged and even loved by all subjects, then preparation for the inevitable change of leadership had to run in parallel to Arthur's development as a self-reliant lord throughout his extensive estates and dominion. Henry VII was too bruised by the continuing struggle to balance the crown on his head to relax so much as to inspire deep devotion. Arthur, on the other hand, presented a blank canvas. He offered a chance to shape the next generation of Tudor servants without being dragged back and stifled by the thorny branches of contending noble families and royal claimants.

When Arthur moved to Ludlow in the spring of 1493, the regime still had a narrow basis of key supporters. Perkin Warbeck's conspiracy had yet to achieve its full destructive impact. Rapidly after that date and over the following four years, the effort needed to contain and defeat the many manifestations of Warbeck's rebellion distracted Henry VII and absorbed his energies. He was unable to address the structure of his own group of reliable chief advisers because they were all working flat-out to support the regime in which they all had a major stake. There was little time for more considered policy changes as political firefighting became the recurring focus of the royal council. The need to destroy the threat from Warbeck inspired many other policy innovations, from taxation to the extension of bonds as tools of control. England even assembled a massive invasion army in the summer of 1497 to end Scottish support for the pretender. With such fundamental issues as the king's survival in the balance, implementation of a strategic programme to rebalance the personnel of the regime had to take a backseat for much of the decade. By the end of the decade, capacity had dwindled among Henry VII's oldest friends in their ability to sustain the demands made by the king in his struggles to defeat his enemies. The small cabal that were the foundation of Tudor power continued to retain a concentrated level of influence within government and in the projection King Henry's influence. The Tudors remained vulnerable while individuals like Cardinal John Morton, Archbishop of Canterbury and Lord Chancellor, or Sir Reginald Bray held so much direct power in their own hands on behalf of the king.

The composition of a group that emerged around Prince Arthur is therefore a telling indication of how Henry VII consented to the formation of the prince's affinity. This was a crown affinity in waiting. We should be slightly cautious in projecting broader influence upon the people noted as being present at Arthur's funeral, since the documentary evidence of a more regular association with the Prince has not yet surfaced. There are, however, clear suggestions of shifting and manoeuvring in some sections of the aristocracy to secure a closer attachment to the Prince of Wales. Can we even identify the type of family-court political dynamic more familiar in the 1520s and 1530s? At the front of the queue were the Greys.

When the connections of the family through marriage are included, the Greys represented a mixture of old and new loyalties, merged and reformed and placed at the service of the future king. Their role in this respect might also represent the king's attempt to widen the basis of his trust. With the right safeguards, there was a symmetry in the emergence of a network that included the 1st Marquis of Dorset and the 2nd Earl of Kent and their sons, but which was policed and monitored by Margaret Beaufort's men such as Bishop William Smith, or the king's men such as Sir Richard Croft. New opportunities also presented themselves if Prince Arthur's chosen friends were invited into the formation of a new royal affinity of young men all roughly the same age as their prince. A similar attempt to bring through the companions of the prince occurred when Henry, Duke of York's court friends stuck with him when he became Prince of Wales after Arthur's death. Many were still tight around the prince when he became King Henry VIII in April 1509. The complete supplanting of Arthur's friends and servants by Prince Henry's household friends indicates just how important this personal connection to the prince was. Henry's private servants formed the inner circle of the Privy Chamber during the first decade of the second Tudor reign.

The accounts of Arthur's funeral service at Ludlow and interment at Worcester Cathedral reveal the identities of the nobles who had been able to manoeuvre themselves close to Arthur in the final years of his life. The existence under Henry VII of a network based on family, marriage and political influence should come as no surprise. It has long been noticed as a major aspect of the way that Margaret Beaufort's political influence operated.[6] In fact, her links to the members of Arthur's household group remained robust through control over the king's wards from noble families. It was most likely to have been the king's mother that decided who reached the most private levels of Arthur's service. For that reason, it might be inappropriate to see the influence of the Greys wholly as a precursor to the type of power-politics that is much more familiar after 1509 in the activities of the Howard or Boleyn families during Henry VIII's reign. By the mid-1520s, the inability of the second Tudor king to produce a legitimate male heir gave rise to a very strong element of sexual politics around the manoeuvring of families competing for access to the king and influence over him. Nothing of this sort was prevalent around Prince Arthur, as his marriage had been negotiated and planned for most of his life before it actually occurred. He was married to a teenage beauty well before he would be king or old enough to be caught up in any sexual intrigue. Those who vied for close connection with Arthur were attempting to position themselves in preparation for the day when Henry VII died and the prince took the throne.

THE HAUNTING OF HENRY VIII

Arthur's place in history has stemmed almost completely from the consequences of his brief marriage to Catherine of Aragon in November 1501. Over twenty-five years after that, the lurid details of the married life of the fifteen-year-old prince and his wife were drawn out and raked over as Henry VIII attempted to get his divorce from Queen Catherine. Henry had married his brother's widow in June 1509. By 1525 Henry and Catherine had been unable to produce a male heir. Henry's numerous affairs had resulted in some illegitimate children but the continuation of the Tudor crown on King Henry's own terms required the birth of a legitimate prince. At the age of forty it was Catherine, rather than the king, who was blamed for this failure. To increase his chances of extending his dynasty, Henry felt he had no choice but to abandon the union with his queen and marry again.

Henry had known Catherine since he was ten years old. He had met her in the week before she had married Prince Arthur. His decision to break up this relationship at the age of thirty-seven was not something he would have undertaken without deep thought and prayer. It heralded a massive change in Henry's personal life. The longer-term effects of his decision still resonate around Britain today. To achieve the separation from his wife, experts in canon law were assembled to investigate the legitimacy of the king's marriage. Canon law was the international code that underpinned Catholic teaching and the Pope's authority. Since only the Pope could grant the annulment of the marriage, the King of England had to present evidence as to why his marriage was invalid. His principal focus was on whether Arthur and Catherine had consummated their relationship. Those former servants still alive at the end of the 1520s were dragged back into the limelight of a semi-public inquiry and encouraged to remember what they could of the few nights that Arthur and Catherine had spent together (or invent what seemed appropriate to the side of the argument they supported). Henry VIII intended to prove that Catherine was not a virgin when her husband died. Through study of the scriptures and the research of his theologians and lawyers, he could claim that his marriage had been invalid from the start.

The marriage of Arthur and Catherine had far-reaching consequences that could not have been imagined during the ceremonies in London in November 1501.[1] Many of the issues over the fullness of their married relationship would not have mattered at all or even surfaced in public had Arthur, Prince of Wales lived into adulthood and come to rule in his own right. Soon after he was dead, however, the king and his counsellors met to debate whether the Spanish alliance was sufficiently important to England that it should be continued through the marriage of Catherine and Arthur's brother, Prince Henry. When the king proclaimed that he was in favour, the discussion turned to consummation of Arthur's relationship with the Princess of Wales. The councilors believed it had been a full marriage and sought the appropriate papal dispensation in the summer of 1503. Catherine immediately protested that it was not true and that she was still a virgin. She wrote to her father, King Ferdinand, who asked Pope Alexander VI to issue a bull that said as much before any new treaty with Spain was agreed. The swift deaths of two popes meant that it was not until March 1505 that the papal dispensation was sent to England. The bull Julius II issued presented an element of doubt about the consummation of the marriage by including the Latin word *forsan* (perhaps) in the part of the text relating to the consummation. Instead of having a clear dispensation backed by unequivocal language, Henry VII had inadvertently created a document that would come back to haunt his son at the end of the 1520s. By the time the bull arrived in England, the planned marriage of Henry and Catherine was on hold. The delay had been too great and politics had moved on. Catherine began a period of very harsh treatment at the hands of King Henry. When the marriage issue was revived right at the end of Henry's reign the questions over Arthur's relationship with Catherine did not seem so relevant. The problem was, however, still lurking.

The terms of the dispensation and what it was actually absolving became central to the divorce debate. In canon law, when any two people had sexual relations another relationship was also created between their relatives. This was regardless of the state or nature of the people involved in the sexual relationship and the type of relationship that they had (married, unmarried, adultery, fornication, etc.). This connection was known as affinity and was similar to nearness of blood as a possible impediment to a marriage. It could also apply alongside nearness of blood, since many sexual relations emerged from within family groups. If a marriage then went ahead in full knowledge that the impediment existed, and it had not been removed by the Church authorities or no steps had been taken to remove it, the marriage could be judged as invalid. Some kind of acknowledgement of the impediment and dispensation would have to be obtained in those cases.

The initial arrangements for the marriage of Arthur and Catherine also established another impediment: public honesty, or, by the standards of the age, decency. This impediment to subsequent marriage was created between the husband and wife and any other of their relatives where negotiations, a contract and treaty of marriage, and a ceremony had taken place. This was clearly the case had the marriage of Henry and Catherine gone ahead without the dispensation. If the marriage was consummated, then public honesty would arise as an additional impediment to the affinity mentioned already. Public honesty could be resolved by dispensation but the correct request had to be made. Suitors only had a chance of getting what they asked for from the Pope's court; papal lawyers did not correct the omissions of suitors. Many late medieval canon law theorists would have expected impediments for affinity and public honesty to be addressed as separate issues. By the time Arthur and Catherine's case was under discussion in the 1520s, however, it was more usual for the impediment of public honesty to be dispensed with as part of a judgement on affinity in a marriage that had been consummated. If the marriage of Arthur and Catherine had not been consummated (and was, without disagreement, known to have existed in that state), then, if a remarriage of one of the partners was proposed after the death of the other, no dispensation for affinity would be required. Only a judgement for public honesty was needed. The problem for Catherine of Aragon and Henry VIII was that the key to their divorce was whether Catherine was still a virgin at Arthur's death. Based on how her status was adjudged in 1503, the dispensation acquired for her remarriage to Prince Henry would have dealt with the impediment of affinity if the marriage had been consummated.

The impediment of public honesty would have been accepted as part of the papal bull that allowed her marriage to Henry.

The bull that Pope Julius II was asked to issue suggested that the marriage of Arthur and Catherine might have been consummated but left the issue unresolved. The insertion of the word *forsan* revealed doubt in the Pope's mind and created an area where the lawyers could debate. Trying to prove that Catherine had been a virgin at the time of her second marriage was a very difficult thing to achieve within the canon law when Cardinal Wolsey's secret court was set up in May 1527 to give Henry's 'scruple of conscience' a legal basis. It was beyond the limits of proof. Catherine herself and her duenna, Dona Elvira, had protested that she was still a virgin in 1503 as soon as they learned of the new marriage negotiations. The princess claimed that although she and Arthur had lain together many times in the marriage bed, they had not consummated their relationship. Many of Catherine's ladies backed up their mistress. They made it clear that while it appeared to outside observers that the Prince and Princess of Wales had lived fully as man and wife, the reality behind closed doors was very different. When Henry VII was exploring what steps would be necessary before Prince Henry could marry Arthur's widow, he went so far as to assert that if Catherine's first marriage had never been consummated she was not truly Princess of Wales and should therefore not hold that status within the royal family. Ferdinand and Isabella had completed the transfer of the promised marriage payments, so Catherine was denied a dower share of Arthur's estate. King Henry seemed reluctant to make any provision for her at the level she had been accustomed to during her brief time with Arthur. This forced the debate as Henry VII sought to abandon Spain and align himself with the Hapsburgs. The prospect of being completely disendowed prompted Catherine to get her marriage to Prince Henry back on Henry VII's agenda. The issue of her virginity was put to one side as a bigger diplomatic picture was resolved during Henry VII's final weeks of life.

Since there was a wide difference of opinion as to whether Arthur and Catherine had managed to have sex together, any civil lawyer would have weighed probability in order to support a legal position. Either the view of events put forward by Arthur's friends or Princess Catherine's own recollections would prevail. It would not have been unreasonable to suppose that two young newlyweds spending winter and spring in a new residence, with little company other than themselves, would have slept together regularly and would, more than probably, have consummated their relationship over five months together as man and wife. Most of the memories of the ageing household friends of Prince Arthur confirmed that this assumption had been widely held in 1501–02. Catherine's own testimony was also a powerful factor. A solemn oath carried great weight, even if she was searching her memory of events at the start of the sixteenth century. It is unlikely that the Princess of Wales would have forgotten the circumstances of her first few months in a foreign country. Her marriage was a colossal and spectacular public state occasion which would have created private lifelong memories. In those circumstances, the first time that she slept with her husband and the loss of her virgin status would also have been a milestone that might well have been difficult to get confused about.

There would have been a little pressure but much more pleasant expectation that the first few months of married life would result in the princess becoming pregnant. Elizabeth of York's pregnancy had been a crucial factor in improving Henry VII's grip on the crown during 1486. The birth of children to build the next generation of Tudor royals would have been an important concern of the king and queen once Arthur and Catherine were married. There was also the health of the new alliance with Spain to consider. Arthur's Spanish marriage carried the assumption that a child would cement strengthen the friendship of the rulers of England and Spain. The arrival of a baby would demonstrate the fertility of the English royal couple. Equally important was the message sent by the production of heirs beyond the king's generation. Throughout Europe, the Tudor dynasty would be seen as more sustainable as a result.

Arthur's marriage came at exactly the time when the regime and its personnel required invigoration. The executions of November 1499 had cleared away the last real Yorkist candidate for the crown, the Earl of Warwick. The following year, however, some of the most diligent Tudor insiders started to get thin on the ground. By 1500, the people upon whom the king could implicitly rely were starting to die off. Against this background, the fulfillment of the years of negotiation for the Spanish marriage made it more than likely that Arthur and Catherine were *encouraged* to start a family as soon as possible. The extension of the Tudor line was their principal duty. There was certainly no reason why, like most teenagers, they would not have been curious about what was involved. What is far more difficult to perceive is whether Arthur was physically incapable of consummating his marriage. That is likely to have been the only reason on which Catherine could base her assertion that she was still a maid when she married Henry. There was a risk that revelation of some congenital issue might seriously damage Henry VIII's reputation and undermine his fitness to rule. No details of her knowledge on this subject therefore emerged during the investigations of 1527–8. Even at that stage of her life, Catherine was unwilling to reveal her most private information about the relationship she had with Arthur.

The witnesses called after May 1528 provided bawdy and graphic evidence of what went on in Arthur and Catherine's bed chambers. Its detail demonstrated that the king had lost love and respect for his wife.[2] Against that background, there was no possibility that the king would be denied what he wanted.

Crucially, the court proceedings and canonical debates related to the divorce forced Henry to look backwards into his own life. When he did, he saw his brother reminding him of circumstances that were emotional and painful and that Henry would rather have forgotten. The longer that Henry VIII went without a male heir, the more that the presence of his dead brother seemed to loom over the king's wellbeing. When Henry's agitation over his divorce was at its height, he was wracked by the guilt of transgressing divine law. He had been married to Catherine in the first place by the Pope's authority, but that dispensation was flawed. His reading and discussion of biblical texts, especially Leviticus 18:16 and 20:21, made him convinced that the Pope's decision in the matter made no difference to how God would judge him for staying within an invalid marriage for so long. Questioning the Pope's status as Vicar of Christ in this matter made it far easier for King Henry to doubt his efficacy more generally. The grains of belief that soon combined into the assertive dogma that fuelled the reformation and dissolution of the monasteries had origins in moments of private doubt where Arthur's legacy gripped Henry's consciousness.

Arthur was also present as the root of his brother's fear of infectious disease. Outbreaks of plague, fever, measles and, from the summer of 1485, the sweating sickness were a regular danger for those living in the close conditions of England's cities. The royal court had frequently moved from Westminster in the summer months to lessen the risk of infection. So there was nothing at all new or unusual about the royal family being concerned enough about epidemic disease to set off on a summer progress beyond the capital. For Henry VIII and Catherine of Aragon, however, fear of contagious disease had a more direct personal resonance. The queen's life in England had been thrown into turmoil at its very beginning by the death of Prince Arthur during the outbreak of sweating sickness around Ludlow.

It does appear that she was taken ill at the same time as her first husband, but recovered quickly. Several years followed in which the princess was shabbily treated by Henry VII before her marriage to Henry was agreed. We cannot know the strength of the direct legacy of Arthur's illness and the results of his death upon Catherine. Yet the fear of an early and unexpected death seems to have haunted King Henry VIII, especially as his stress levels rose in his search for a male heir.

King Henry's grip on the throne became more precarious the longer he went without a son. Queen Catherine was aged thirty by the end of 1515. The next few years would be crucial for the future of the regime; a fact that must have put pressure on her and her husband. Up to that point she had become pregnant many times and had given Henry four children. Unfortunately, all had been stillborn or had died in infancy. Princess Mary, who would be born on 18 February 1516 was the only offspring of Henry and Catherine to live more than two months. Another daughter, Catherine's last child, lived for a week in November 1518. That in itself would have maintained an awareness of mortality and sudden death. It might also have contributed to Henry's sense of vulnerability. Arthur's death had changed the course of his life. A repeat of an outbreak of virulent disease in which the royal family were ensnared would have dire consequences for as long as Henry VIII had no heir. Even after Princess Mary survived early infancy, the king's concerns about a son did not abate. He continued to have affairs with female courtiers. It was in the autumn of 1518 that Henry's mistress Elizabeth Blount became pregnant with Henry FitzRoy, Duke of Richmond and Somerset. The acknowledgement of his son and the titles conferred upon him indicate that Henry VIII was deeply conscious of the susceptibility of his regime. They might also have hinted that FitzRoy would have been made legitimate had he lived beyond his seventeen years. In June 1519 when FitzRoy was born, the survival of Tudor power depended upon the health of King Henry, Queen Catherine and the three-year-old Princess Mary.

After Prince Arthur's death, Henry VII was able to rule unchallenged because other male and female heirs survived the Prince of Wales. That is not to say that Arthur's death was not a heavy blow upon the royal family, as we have already seen that it was. The climate of the regime darkened further once Queen Elizabeth died in childbirth on her thirty-seventh birthday in February 1503. Henry VIII would have remembered how, even as they heard the news of Arthur's death, his mother and father had discussed having more children. Elizabeth's death just over ten months later was a direct consequence of the decisions made to extend the royal family. A manuscript illustration recently identified as showing Henry weeping in mourning for Queen Elizabeth does suggest the enormous emotional impact that the loss of his mother had on Henry. Even with healthy heirs, in the early summer of 1502, Henry VII and his queen did not feel that their family was in a strong position to withstand any further accident or epidemic. How much more precarious, then, was Henry VIII's situation in 1518–20?

Ordinances and proclamations for quarantine were produced for London and many other towns. The king became increasingly wary and morbidly fascinated by the disease. In October and November 1517 an outbreak was ravaging the royal household. Lord Grey and some of the servants of Henry's own chamber died suddenly. The king shut himself off from visitors. Henry was happy to abandon his residence at particular palaces as soon as outbreaks appeared. In April 1518 he opted to remain at Abingdon in Oxfordshire when news that London remained infected with sickness. His decision was explicitly blamed on a fear of the sickness by Wolsey's secretary, Richard Pace.[3] The effects of the 1528 outbreak were even more widespread. After almost twenty years as king, to Henry's way of thinking, a smooth succession of the crown still depended upon the son that he did not yet have. It is not difficult to see how Arthur's death still maintained a grip upon Henry VIII's thoughts almost thirty years after he died.

MEMORIES OF A PRINCE

Historians have given very little attention to Arthur in his own right. Many might claim with some justification that a fifteen-year-old boy, even by the standards of the later Middle Ages, could have achieved very little worthy of note. Little evidence survives that can supply the kind of details that all modern readers would love to find about his life in Farnham and Ludlow. His youthfulness has meant that Arthur has not been granted much individuality or agency even in comparison to other members of his family alive at the same time. His short life was, on the whole, conducted away from his siblings and the rest of the early Tudor royal family. He has a personal and geographical distance and separateness that has been hard to overturn because of this lack of evidence. Arthur's profile has been constrained by the controlling and meticulous reputation of his father, Henry VII. Since the prince predeceased his parents, his influence upon the political world of the first Tudor reign has been dismissed as negligible. It is true that his direct legacy as a lord was minimal. As a national figure, he was memorable only as the focus of very impressive state pageantry. Even on the Marches of Wales, he moved into a governing system that had been devised earlier in the century and was refined by his father to round-off Arthur's princely education. Arthur would have the benefit of it as an adult king, but its value must have been hard for him to accept during winters spent in Ludlow during the later 1490s. The dominant force of nature that his brother Henry was to become has also shunted aside the significance of Arthur's time as Prince of Wales. Yet as scarce as the information on Arthur's personal life might be, his role within the Tudor state and as the first child of a new ruling family was crucial: both directly to his close relatives, and also as a strategic impetus to the way that Henry VII's regime acted. Arthur's life also cast a long shadow over the reign of his brother, Henry. The second Tudor king's inability to shake off the consequences of Arthur's focussed preparation for kingship and, more disastrously, his marriage to Catherine of Aragon, had a far broader influence upon how English history was shaped in the sixteenth century and beyond.

Studies of the Tudor crown have presented Prince Arthur as a shadowy young man, and this description applies both to his contemporary status and to how he has appeared down the centuries. The first child of the Tudor monarchs did indeed become separated from his family almost as soon as he was born. Only weeks after his birth in September 1486, Arthur was set up in his own household. The rest of the royal children lived and learned together in close proximity to each other, their parents and the court within the nursery attached to Eltham Palace. Arthur, meanwhile, was educated and trained within his own establishment, a day's hard ride from Sheen Palace and even further from Westminster. In the spring of 1493 he moved to the Welsh Marches at Ludlow Castle, becoming even more distant from the centre of the crown's power and further removed from his family. It might appear to modern eyes that this was abandonment; that Arthur was separated and almost exiled within the kingdom. He certainly seems to have had few visits from his family, even when he was an infant at Farnham. But the surviving records might paint a false picture here.

There was nothing accidental or neglectful about the way in which the first Tudor prince was brought up. Henry VII had a comprehensive plan for Arthur. The preparations for his kingship combined the best of all elements of established royal education with the very latest knowledge of classical sources. As he mastered the meaning of these texts, Arthur simultaneously was learning how their ideas, lessons and techniques could be applied actively to the relationships and policy he was expected to become responsible for on the Marches. Henry VII's only gambles with Prince Arthur were that he would be able to bear the burden of this responsibility from such a young age, and that he survived to inherit the reward that his hard work merited. In this respect, the king's dynastic planning was a hazard of chance that all previous rulers had shared. The prince's inheritance of a secure and stable country was what all kings desired for their heirs. Kings had to hope and assume that their heirs would be competent and that they would live to take over their fathers' mantle. Arthur's intellectual abilities were obvious from the success of his classroom schooling. His skills in Latin and at formal social encounters were polished by the age of eleven. They were reflected in the letters and reports of ambassadors and chroniclers. These contemporary assessments from outside of the royal circle give greater weight to Bernard André's report on Arthur's accomplishments as a scholar. In order to build his competence and confidence still further, Arthur was given the support of a dedicated group of counsellors within his own sphere of influence on the Marches. Part of their role was to connect the abstract theory and example in texts and histories with the nuts and bolts of governing the March region and beyond.

Arthur's advisors and administrators were fully focussed on running the areas under the prince's control. Men like Sir Richard Pole or Sir Richard Croft were vastly experienced in the defending their friends, servants and lands, and in managing local issues for the crown. Their loyalty to Henry VII was also guaranteed in ways that are often opaque when viewed through the incomplete evidence that survives. The terror experienced by the king as some of the senior and junior men in his own household flirted with rebellion and treason in the 1490s could not be allowed to resurface around the Prince of Wales. Arthur's officers therefore had some leeway in how they behaved but their priority was to safeguard the prince. Some men took advantage of closeness to Arthur and occasionally abused the rewards they had access to. Others enhanced the power from their connection to Arthur and projected it further afield on his behalf. The benefit for the prince as he developed was that he received demonstration and instruction from the methods and behaviour of his servants in dealing with their duties and interests. As he learned, Arthur could then test his skills in addressing problems, finding solutions or bringing people to account based on observation. That arrangement offered a more precise, balanced and effective education than Arthur would probably have had access to had he stayed around the royal household. The security and military infrastructure that was built up around the prince at Ludlow and along the Marches was also stronger and more potent than that of almost any other senior noble. Arthur held the rights and responsibilities of a king in his own country and he also had the security to match.

In the century before Arthur was Prince of Wales, the sons of the king had energetically developed their own networks of servants, officials, merchants, clerics and companions without necessarily bearing a share of the wider responsibilities of running the state. Their impact was viewed by some royal advisors as a threat when the monarch was ageing or periodically became ill. Henry VII's other son, Prince Henry, had more in common with them than he did with Arthur.

Previous monarchs, like Henry IV, had required the Prince of Wales to serve in person within the Principality as a way of diluting the heir's influence at the centre of government. Any perceived threat to the crown from the prince grew from the fact that he had to be trained to rule but would usually be subject to limitations on his opportunities to exercise direct power. The English crown had to strike a balance between provision of the widest skills at the core of the royal role, and restraint on the prince's ability to apply that knowledge during the life of his father. As a second centre of gravity within the regime, the prince's household and service network might grow to undermine the policies or personal power of the monarch. Some mechanism to ensure that it remained loyal had to be put in place. Henry VII seems to have achieved a solution to this problem. He adapted the very robust plans that Edward IV and his councillors had created in the early 1470s for the heir to the Yorkist crown.

Princes such as Edward V and Arthur, who failed to reach full adulthood and died before they had ventured far beyond the schoolroom, are judged as less dynamic than those who were able to translate youthful learning into successful rule. These two princes shared an almost identical preparation for kingship. The lives of both the first Yorkist prince and the first Tudor prince might have ended prematurely, but they had already achieved considerable success in building the key skills of subtle and direct lordship. Edward IV's death in April 1483 when his heir was aged only twelve crucially came too early in Prince Edward's life for him to survive the ruthless struggle for political control that ensued. Once Prince Arthur was married at the age of fifteen in November 1501 there was every chance that he would have gone on to rule directly had Henry VII died around that time. Indeed, that was probably at the root of Henry VII's plan, since Arthur was brought up to be self-reliant and independent. An entirely separate governing infrastructure supplied the kind of regal and practical training that could have enabled him to sustain personal rule, even as a teenager. With Arthur and Catherine of Aragon marrying at such a young age and at a time when the king's health was still robust and the queen was able to have more children, it is probable that Henry VII felt he had time in which to dictate the pace at which Arthur was introduced to the responsibilities of the realm's highest office. Since the king was in his mid-40s when Arthur and Catherine were married, the prince might have expected to enjoy his semi-independent lordship along the Welsh Marches for at least a decade more before he succeeded to the crown. He would then have had twenty years in training to be king.

In the early part of his life, Arthur was a symbol for the hopes and aspirations of his father's regime. What stand out are the many set-piece ceremonies that he went through. All princes had endured very similar events and they would have become less conspicuous over time as children moved into adulthood. Modern appreciation of the importance of courtly religious ritual in the lives of medieval royal children has become obscured by the different challenges and achievements that became associated with them in later life. The lack of evidence of other aspects of their youthful private life tends to magnify the significance of the events in which they were centre-stage.

Henry VII would also have been aware that the previous three princes of Wales had not survived to reach their age of majority. In different ways, both Henry VI's son Edward of Westminster and Edward V were direct victims of civil war. Richard III's heir, Edward of Middleham, was kept in Yorkshire away from the spotlight of court life and died before the age of ten from an unspecified illness in April 1484. With these precedents in the background, Tudor leaders knew that if their regime was to endure in the next generation Arthur had to be protected from a resumption of conflict within England's aristocratic elite. That meant building stable loyalty and eliminating lingering attachment to previous rulers as a focus for conspiracy. It was why Henry placed so much emphasis on involving the surviving leading Yorkists in the showcase events of the early part of his reign, such as his coronation on 30 October 1485, his progress into the north at Easter 1486 and Arthur's christening in September 1486.

Arthur embodied a resolution of the quarrel between York and Lancaster. That particular status made him, and not his father or mother, the long-term focal point of the future of the Tudor crown. The constituent parts of Arthur's inheritance created an interesting dynamic within the regime as it progressed. Those who wished to earn a share of the opportunities that would become available as Arthur grew up had to demonstrate allegiance within an arena of competition. Loyal gentry, certainly along the border region, sought to be close to the prince as his abilities expanded and flourished. When this process was controlled effectively it was a healthy and supportive state for the prince to exist in. Henry VII was just the man to look at the detail and make obvious to all involved what his expectations were. Control was easier to manage if the people that shared Arthur's life had little or no independent power. Henry VII made appointments to Arthur's service through the filter of proven loyalty to the Tudor regime or the Beaufort family group. Nevertheless, the king had to be wily enough to control the dynamics of Arthur's training by offering him an increasing range of responsibilities. These had to absorb his attention and stretch the skills of his counsellors and officials, while at the same time providing enough incentives of status and reward to make Arthur's service an attractive aspiration. Initially, the rush to secure offices and posts led to jostling for status and attention in the region and then in the household and governing structure that would take shape around the prince. Those families of the March that were not already on the king's radar as potentially suspect, would have been wise to send all of the expected signals over their loyalty and commitment. That was the surest way that they would create the space in which to position themselves to benefit from the patronage on offer from the king and, further down the line, the prince.

Although there is no explicit evidence for it, once Arthur had been born with such strong reference to his Yorkist, Mortimer and more distant British heritage, King Henry was already tacitly announcing to the nation how his son's education would unfold. Re-establishing the Yorkist nursery set-up as the infant Arthur's household at Farnham made the first link to the example of Edward IV. In people's minds it followed that, at some point, the rest of the detail of Edward V's care and training would come into the picture. To many people within court and government circles, this meant that Arthur would move to Ludlow and learn to rule on the March in preparation for taking the crown after his father's death. Suggesting that Arthur's education would merge with and adapt the structures behind Edward V's upbringing cleverly gave the Tudor crown a number of years in which to manipulate the communities and individuals that had been most deeply associated with Edward V as Prince of Wales. Just how Henry VII would amend the blueprint of Prince Edward's upbringing was the fine detail that could not be predicted. The most important issue was resolved, however. If Yorkist convention was followed, then Prince Arthur would most-likely be moving to Ludlow Castle in the mid-1490s around the time he was aged about six. What ensued was a period of re-adjustment along the border as gentry and noble families began to prepare for the imminent future.

To guide them through the intervening years was the reconstituted Council of the Marches. Edward IV had already established protocols and jurisdictions, machinery and precedents for its function and interests. Many of the personnel that had been involved in its business, like John Alcock, Bishop of Worcester, were still around at the end of the 1480s to offer their advice and input to its Tudor evolution. Other, more political animals, like Sir William Stanley, saw openings for an extension of the gifts, power and influence that they had already secured for their part in putting Henry VII on the throne. The vacuum on the Marches left by the death of Edward V would soon be filled and people with interests to extend and defend were quick to stake a claim on what was on offer.

The process of securing a role in Arthur's service along the Welsh Marches generated its own disputes. Some of these quarrels were hanging over from earlier periods of the Wars of the Roses. The absence of an adult Duke of Buckingham, for example, had already created the room for scores to be settled around Brecon in 1486. Other clashes were directly connected to the opportunities and relationships that had been built up around the prince during the 1470s. That was a trickier issue to resolve since it drew in the formerly divided loyalties of men who had been on opposite sides at the Battle of Bosworth and earlier phases of the aristocratic civil war since 1455. Unless these figures were able to demonstrate how they had rid themselves of the old baggage of the Wars of the Roses, then Henry VII would consider them incapable of leaving the past behind. That would have impaired their chances of getting close enough to Prince Arthur to grasp meaningful opportunities in his service. This type of unrest and violence could have led to more serious disruption if it had been left unchecked. Henry VII and his counsellors with eyes and ears in the region (like Reginald Bray, who was born near Worcester) seem to have been more tolerant of the offences committed in the lands under Arthur's control. Unlike some other counties, the English side of the frontier with Wales had a highly evolved governmental setup. Arthur's presence would further emphasise that the king's influence was close by. Despite the geographical distance from London, the Council of the Marches and Arthur's household allowed for an interchange of personnel on the border and with Westminster. Any rough edges, lapses of security and negligence would be more apparent as the recycling of low-ranking officials took place. The first stages of many careers were formed in this way.

Just as Henry VII would not risk the security of the whole regime by collecting all his children in one place for too long a period of time, so he did not want a single powerful aristocratic figure in control of his heir's upbringing. With hindsight, it was obvious that Edward, Prince of Wales had been very vulnerable to a determined attack by the powerful figures within Edward IV's polity. The members of the governing committee – made up of Queen Elizabeth, her brother Rivers, other Woodvilles, churchmen, lords and experienced knights who on paper looked formidable – were rarely able to gather together around the prince; they had too many other responsibilities. Once he had decided on his purpose, Richard, Duke of Gloucester found it very easy to isolate Edward's guardians and take the twelve-year-old king into his care. Initially, the prince might not have been the direct focus of Richard in April 1483. Richard had seen that the influence of Earl Rivers and the Woodvilles around the prince had been too dominant for his own view of how Edward V's reign should progress. Edward's education was beyond Richard's control and with other nobles directing it, he was worried about the impact of their influence in the longer term. Getting control of the prince by eliminating his Woodville-dominated household was a first step towards resolving the situation. It was, of course, also the first step towards Richard seizing the crown and deposing his nephew. In Brittany, Henry Tudor had some leisure to observe this progression of events unfolding. The outline of his response was probably formed long before Arthur was born, since the structure for the prince's upbringing was established quickly during the spring and summer of 1486 and was put into practice as soon as Arthur was christened. Once the queen's first pregnancy was known to be progressing without incident then the king's intentions could be brought more directly to a conclusion.

After August 1485, the Tudors faced enough very visible enemies without making royal targets easy to pick off by vesting control in the hands of one or two high-ranking peers. Arthur's education was a collaborative effort that reflected what Henry VII hoped to achieve more widely by his kingship. Most people who had been prominent under the Yorkists and were not already committed rebels against the Tudor crown were at some point on the path to rehabilitation. Henry VII needed them to deliver their experience on his behalf. Even if they did not trust Henry personally, they might see that clearer opportunities would arrive by sowing the seeds of rewards that could be harvested under his heir, Arthur. The Prince of Wales embodied the union of previously competing royal claims. He was young enough to be looked after by specialists appointed for their skill and experience and not their rank and social status. That made Arthur's servants individually more dependent upon maintaining good relations with the king, his family and his direct representatives. Where it was necessary and desirable to involve more senior nobility, there was already a buffer of lesser loyalists in place around the prince and they answered directly to the king and his council. The role of trusted noble families such as Talbots and the wider Grey group, was one step removed from day-to-day contact with the prince. They were a presence that provided assurance to the king that a military force was readily available if needed to back up the troops readily to hand under Sir Richard Pole. That dormant threat diluted the impact of any lingering power struggles, such as the Cornewall and Croft dispute.

Placing a sixteenth-century King Arthur into the line of monarchs is not as improbable as it first sounds. Had Henry VII's eldest son escaped the outbreak of infection at Ludlow in the spring of 1502 we can be fairly sure that he would have gone on to inherit the crown from his father. If Arthur became king in his later teenage years (as Edward IV and Henry VIII actually did), then it is not too fantastic an assumption to think that he might have enjoyed a reign that lasted until he was aged past fifty – something that his father and brother also managed, despite many stresses and difficulties. Had Arthur lived then Henry VII might have been in a stronger position to hold off the ailments that began to debilitate him after 1500. Without the strain of having to reconstruct plans for the future succession of the crown, which Arthur's death brought on, the first Tudor king could well have had a more constructive and less oppressive role in preparing for the inheritance of the his heir. The crown would have passed in a way that had been planned for many years and to a king that had been trained explicitly to be his father's successor in style as well as fact. For that reason, we can speculate that Arthur's inheritance might have encouraged a balanced political environment as the more established and trusted families retained a stronger profile around the king and at court.

Since many factors had an impact on the decisions that monarchs made, there is a danger in taking this speculation too far, but in the case of Arthur it is worthwhile to pose a few more questions. In an age of personal monarchy, the personality of the ruler and how it was applied to or engaged with the responsibilities of leadership was the most important single factor in progressing the fortunes of the nation. It is quite easy to imagine the future Henry VIII as Duke of York or Prince of Wales galloping around with his gentlemen friends of the privy chamber. The evidence for the structure of Henry's circle is clear and strong. Its members quickly grew into a clique of the new king's closest companions after April 1509. In Arthur's case, the opposite is true. His early death, the evidence of his bookish education, and the fact that most of his friends were, after April 1502, unable to make any headway in the Duke of York's service, makes it far more difficult to see Arthur as a normal boisterous, privileged teenager. It would have been unusual if Prince Arthur did not at some point show some indication of wishing to be free of some of the severe and formal responsibilities that his father had saddled him with from a very early age. The fifteen-year-old bragging about sex with his new wife, but with a clever turn of phrase, is possibly much more like a true picture of Prince Arthur's character than we have previously thought.

By the same token, without deeper responsibilities, Prince Henry was fairly free to focus his energy on building friendships based around entertainment, pleasure and life around London. Even an eleven-year-old prince would have chosen friends that were good company rather than the worthy or learned advisors close to his father. Henry's thinking about relationships in this way would become more pronounced during the early years of his kingship. After 1502, the servants connected with him must have had a rapid realisation that they were on the fast track to becoming the core of the next group of royal favourites. That fact modified the dynamics of power around the royal family at a time when Henry VII was less able to deal with this shift personally. As things changed at the centre, so other senior nobles were also less than enthusiastic about finding places for Arthur's ex-servants. Very rapidly, the former Prince of Wales's network dissolved. There was nothing new in how influential people hoped to position themselves so that they got the best advantage possible from the succession of the crown. What is interesting is that political manoeuvring was such a strong theme of Henry VII's reign. It remains one that historians have been slow to investigate. Despite his best efforts to build allegiance to the institutional power of the crown (but obviously a crown worn by a member of the Tudor royal family), King Henry VII would probably have been disappointed to realise just how much the survival of his family's power depended upon personal power-broking and the deals built around prominence in the king's direct service.

If it still surprises people when they realised that England and Wales might have had a king named Arthur in the early part of the sixteenth century, that possibility makes it certain that Henry, Duke of York would not have become king at all. As a couple, had Arthur and Catherine survived their first year of marriage, they had every chance of becoming a long-living, happily married and productive king and queen of England. Many of the consequences of Henry VIII's first marriage and divorce would have been negated. England would have been very different in appearance in the later Tudor period had Henry VIII not come to the throne. The Reformation would still have taken hold across Europe, and it would have exerted influence within England and Wales. A reforming religious movement would have emerged, but without the need to secure an annulment of Henry VIII's first marriage, the break with Rome would almost certainly not have come to pass in the form that it did, if indeed it occurred at all. Without that event, the destruction of monastic life and the religious and social hold taken by Protestant leaders in the second half of the sixteenth century, the subsequent history of Britain would have taken a very different shape.

The value of singling out individual events and isolating the impact they had is debatable. Yet it should make us recognise that some events were momentous and that history has always shifted course on small, fateful decisions and incidents. We can see, for example, that the final few years of Henry VII's reign took shape because of the early death of Prince Arthur. After the change of regime in 1509 the consequences of his demise became diluted; but they might still have been set in motion by the tragic effects of an outbreak of infectious disease in the Welsh Marches in 1502. The premature end of Arthur's life put the king and queen under pressure to try and have more children. That, in turn, influenced the way that Prince Henry was encouraged to step into his brother's shoes and also how Henry VII was suddenly obliged to look to a future beyond his own death, with his second son Henry as the new king. After building a long-term strategy around Prince Arthur since the 1480s, this was no easy task.

Once Arthur died, and by the time Prince Henry was fifteen or sixteen, Henry VII was starting to struggle to control the flamboyant and extrovert man that his second son wished to become. Regardless of their inherent personalities, it was inevitable that the ways in which the two boys had been educated would produce differences in their character and demeanour. Prince Henry was aged almost eleven when Arthur fell sick. The shock of Arthur's death placed the regime in extreme danger. The threat was compounded further by the tragic death of the queen and the newborn Princess Catherine in February 1503. These losses forced Henry VII's regime into a tight corner. The king was unwilling to allow any actions that increased the danger to the fragile succession. In the 1490s he had already discounted any plan to create geographical power bases for each of his sons. Henry VII might have looked further ahead and seen a nightmare vision of his two princes competing as rivals in the same way that Edward IV's reign and legacy was beset by the conduct of his brothers George, Duke of Clarence and Richard, Duke of Gloucester. The deliberate establishment of rival territorial focal points for Arthur and Henry would be a source of friction, regardless of the specific ways in which their personalities emerged as a result. After 1502, there was no willingness within the febrile heart of the Tudor regime for Prince Henry to take over his brother's power base on the Welsh Marches; and insufficient time, anyway, to make a success of the transplantation of one son for another on the same terms. The king might have thought about a shorter tour of duty for Prince Henry. That would have taken account of his greater age and incomplete education in the palaces of the royal household. With the king as a widower, however, the safety net under Tudor rule had vanished. The king could afford to take no risks with the safety of Henry, his only surviving son. All of Henry VII's expectations and efforts had been invested in Prince Arthur; once he was dead then there could be no duplication of the process for Prince Henry. It had been essential that Arthur merged his physical growth and intellectual development with a simultaneous expanding awareness of his responsibilities as a lord, his direct relationship with ruling elites, and his expanding personal power. This had to be done in real time with real people, and it was why Arthur's marcher household and council were so carefully constructed. The most important formative years of Prince Henry, between the ages of six and eleven had denied him any personal governmental responsibility, however nominal, and had put little pressure on his faculties or stamina in the face of the mundane business of ruling.

These were indeed stressful times. In 1503 King Henry would have felt as vulnerable as at any time since the early 1490s. He was the first king of a new ruling family but it looked like he might be the last. Without Arthur pointing to the future, the path looked a lot less clear. Henry's sudden lack of reliable friends threw his reign back to the dark uncertainties of his early years as king. Princess Margaret had gone north at the end of June 1503 to marry James IV of Scotland. Any calamity befalling Henry would have brought to the fore a Scottish claim to the English crown through children of Margaret's Scottish marriage. Henry VII's reaction to a rapidly deteriorating dynastic situation was the initiation of a harsher set of controlling policies more generally. The ongoing dynastic threats from rivals and pretenders as well as fate's decimation of the familiar faces of the regime, suddenly seemed to have deeper menace. With more regular and lengthy periods of sickness after 1503 came Henry's probable realisation that he had a very few years available in which to alter this situation and provide Prince Henry with a basis for personal rule.

Henry VIII became king amid rejoicing that the dark days of his father's repression were ended. Henry was almost nineteen years old in April 1509. His prospects had changed spectacularly since he had danced so engagingly with Princess Catherine at his brother's wedding reception in November 1501. Henry had power, money and youth on his side. Within weeks of taking the throne he had married Arthur's widow. The future for England looked very bright indeed, as Arthur was already being forgotten by the Tudor elite and common people alike. Becoming king allowed Henry to fulfil all kinds of personal ambitions in emulation of the great English kings of the past. Managing the expectations of a nation seemed simple to a king used to smooth talking and looking good. Hiding beneath the lavish glamour of Henry VIII's first months as king, however, were the issues that Arthur's premature death had left unresolved.

Henry had taken up his brother's mantle when untrained and unprepared for it. Arthur had absorbed a great deal of his father's experience of the tribulations of holding onto the crown from his counsellors and household men, Prince Henry was not old enough to begin to appreciate these issues until he was plunged back into a crisis of control by 1503, following the deaths of family and friends. By then, Henry VII had little time or energy for training his only son. There is not much evidence that Prince Henry would have been very interested anyway. He wanted the opportunity to rule gloriously. As he saw it, the best preparation for his accession was not necessarily something that would come from books and time spent listening to councillors or judges explaining procedures and precedents. Henry's interests and skills had already swung too far in the opposite direction to those that Prince Arthur possessed.

Henry had learned to make decisions impetuously and without real consequence. He had struggled for very little. Responsibility as a ruler was not something that he had been forced to earn. Arthur personally had assembled the pieces of the puzzle that unlocked the inner workings of English government, both the institutions and the personnel. He had travelled up and down the Marcher counties and set about mastering the mundane responsibility of holding a kingdom together. When he died, Henry VII's long investment in the future of the country died with him. The kind of reign that came after Henry VII passed away would be very different from the one that had been planned by the old king since 1486. Britain is the way it is now because Arthur died.

NOTES

1 The First Tudor Prince from Birth to Independence

1. Henry VIII's failure to have a son created enormous pressure on his personal security for different reasons during the 1520s. See pp. 223–5.
2. E 404/79, no. 179 and various warrants for the privy seal in C 82/16.
3. O. J. Padel, 'Arthur *(supp. fl.* in or before 6th cent.)', *Oxford Dictionary of National Biography*, Oxford University Press, 2004; online edn, May 2007 http://www.oxforddnb.com/view/article/703.
4. D. Carlson, 'King Arthur and Court Poems for the Birth of Arthur Tudor in 1486', *Humanistica Lovaniensia*, XXXVI (1987), p. 147–83.
5. F. Madden, 'Genealogical and historical notes in Ancient Calendars', *Collectanea Topographica et Genealogica*, I (1834), 277–79.
6. E 404/79 unnumbered and undated warrant signed by the queen for a total payment of £9 16s.
7. The King's Household Act, 1487; 2 Henry VII c 14.
8. This information is found in N. Orme, 'The Education of Edward V', *Bulletin of the Institute of Historical Research*, lvii (1984), and his *Childhood to Chivalry*, p. 31.

9. M. W. Thompson, 'Recent Excavations in the Keep of Farnham Castle, Surrey', *Medieval Archaeology*, vol 4 (1960), p. 93; A. Emory, *Greater Medieval Houses of England and Wales, 1300–1500: volume 3, Southern England*, (Cambridge, Cambridge University Press, 2006), pp. 337–9.

10. *CPR, 1485–94*, pp. 152–3; C 66/569, m.18 (4).

11. E 101/413/1; transcribed in W. Campbell (ed), *Materials for a History of the Reign of Henry VII* (2 vols, London, Longman, 1877), ii, 495–500.

12. More details on medieval cloth are found at the Lexis of Cloth and Clothing project website: http://lexisproject.arts.manchester.ac.uk/index.html

13. *CPR, 1485–94*, pp. 220.

14. Nicholas Orme, *From Childhood to Chivalry: the education of the English kings and aristocracy, 1066–1530* (London, Methuen, 1984), p. 18.

15. Steven Gunn has traced the names between the original warrant in E 404/81/1 and estates records at TNA and the Duchy of Cornwall archives. Gunn, 'Prince Arthur's Preparation for Kingship, in Gunn and Monckton (eds), *Arthur Tudor, Prince of Wales* (Woodbridge, Boydell, 2009), p. 11.

16. E 101/413/9, fol. 8v; an account book of John Spelman, controller of the king's household.

2 Raising a Prince of Wales

1. Leland, Collectanea, IV, 251–2.

2. This section is based on D. R. Carson, 'Royal Tutors in the Reign of Henry VII', *The Sixteenth Century Journal*, vol. 22, no. 2 (summer 1991), 253–79.

3. Prince Henry might have inherited this copy from his brother after 1502, since an edition held at the Folger Shakespeare Library is inscribed with his autograph; PA6295.A3 1502 Cage.

4. Vergil came to England after Arthur's death in 1502, but he was exactly the type of scholar that Henry VII cultivated. Vergil was

deputy to the collector of papal taxes, Adriano Castellesi. Around 1505 he began a new history of England at the king's request. Carmeliano was a Lombard servant of five kings after and including Edward IV. He received a healthy income from English church livings and was adept at writing flattering poems praising whichever king he was serving. By 1490 he was Henry VII's Latin secretary. Giovanni Gigli, absentee bishop of Worcester after 1498, served as Henry VII's ambassador in Rome and left some impressive Latin writings composed to flatter and further his career in royal service.

5. M. M. Condon, 'An Anachronism with Intent? Henry VII's Council Ordinance of 1491/2', in R. A. Griffiths and J. Sherborne (eds), *Kings and Nobles in the Later Middle Ages* (Gloucester, Sutton, 1986), pp. 228–253.

3 The King-in-Waiting

1. *CPR, 1485–94*, p. 141, 22 September 1486.
2. E 404/79, no. 293; BL Cotton Julius B XII, fols 17r–17v; warrants in PSO 2/2 and C 82/10.
3. *Rotuli Parliamentorum*, V, 290–3; R. A. Griffiths, *Henry VI* (Berkeley, 1981), pp. 755–7.
4. This is the theme of Thomas Penn, *Winter King* (Allen Lane, London, 2011).
5. Owen and Blakeway, *History of Shrewsbury*, vol. 2, p. 449.
6. This information is collated in Gunn, 'Prince Arthur's Preparation for Kingshhip', p. 12.
7. See pp. 27–32.
8. M. Bennett, *Lambert Simnel and the Battle of Stoke* (Sutton, Stroud, 1987). See pp. 37, 119–20.
9. S. Cunningham, 'Henry VII and Rebellion in North-eastern England, 1485–1492: bonds of allegiance and the establishment of Tudor authority', *Northern History*, 32 (1996), 42–74.
10. See evidence of his letter to Sir Henry Vernon below, pp. 114–15.

11. J. Morgan-Guy, 'Arthur, Harri Tudor and the Iconography of Loyalty in Wales', in Gunn and Monckton, *Arthur Tudor*, pp. 50–63.

12. *CPR, 1485–94*, p. 488; on the commission of the peace for Herefordshire.

13. Physical comparison between the two sons of Henry VII and Elizabeth of York and speculation on their personalities is expertly made by David Starkey in *Young Henry* (London, 2008), p.134. The best discussion of Arthur's portraiture is F. Hepburn, 'The Portraiture of Prince Arthur and Katherine of Aragon', in Gunn and Monckton, *Arthur Tudor*, pp. 31–49, upon which this section is based.

14. *Calendar of State Papers Milan, 1385–1618*, vol. I (London, 1912), no. 539.

15. S. Thurley, *The Royal Palaces of Tudor England: Architecture and Court Life, 1460–1547* (New Haven, 1993), pp. 40–4.

16. See below, pp. 161.

4 *The Power of the Prince*

1. This section is based on M.E. Giffin, 'Cadwaladr, Arthur and Brutus in the Wigmore Manuscript', *Speculum*, vol. 16, no.1 (January, 1941), pp. 109–120. My thanks to Dr Paul Dryburgh for discussing this aspect of the Mortimer legacy.

2. *CPR, 1485–94*, p. 453.

3. C 255/8/5/54; C 54/376, m.3.

4. C. S. L. Davies, 'The Crofts: Creation and Defence of a Family Enterprise under the Yorkists and Henry VII', *Historical Research*, vol. 68, no. 167 (October 1995), 241–65.

5. E 28/93, no.89; STAC 2/27/84.

6. KB 9/402, no. 20.

7. BL Lansdowne 639, fol. 24.

8. For background on the organisation of government on the Welsh Marches see, C. A. J. Skeel, *The Council in the Marches of Wales:*

a study of local government during the sixteenth and seventeenth centuries (London, 1904); R. A. Griffiths, 'Wales and the Marches in the Fifteenth Century', in S. B. Chrimes, C. D. Ross and R. A. Griffiths (eds), *Fifteenth Century England, 1399–1509* (Manchester, 1972), pp. 145–72.

9. WAM 32850A.

10. BL Additional Charter 79647.

11. W. R. B. Robinson, *Early Tudor Gwent, 1485–1547* (privately printed, Welshpool, 2002), p. 12.

12. C 66/527, m. 1.

13. WAM 5474.

14. PROB 11/18, fol. 67v.

15. C 54/376, m. 42.

16. WAM 16045.

17. S. Cunningham, 'National War and Dynastic Politics: Henry VII's Capacity to Wage War in the Scottish Campaigns of 1496–1497' in A. King and D. Simpkin (eds), *England and Scotland at War, c.1296–c.1513* (Leiden, 2012), pp. 297–328.

18. E 36/285, fols 29v–30r.

19. E 405/79, rot. 36d.

5 The Royal Wedding of the Century

1. BL Cotton Vespasian C. XIV, fols 94r–103v. This entire section is based on the transcripts and commentaries collected in G. Kipling, 'The Receyt of the Lady Katheryne', *Early English Text Society*, no. 296 (Oxford, 1990). Manuscript references are given there and discussed in detail.

2. This section is based on S. Anglo, 'The London Pageants for the Reception of Katherine of Aragon: November 1501', *Journal of the Warburg and Courtauld Institutes*, vol. 26, no. ½ (1963), pp. 53–89; which in turn analyses the record of the pageants in *The Receyt of the Lady Katheryne*, pp. 12–36.

3. BL Egerton MS, 2358.

4. Simeon had a revelation that he would not die until he had seen the messiah of the Lord; and he would see Jesus if he went to the Temple.

5. *Letters and Papers Foreign and Domestic of the Reign of Henry VIII*, vol. 4, part III, no. 5773; BL Cotton Vitellus, B XII, fol. 80.

6. BL Egerton MS 2358, fols 24r–36v.

7. D. J. Guth, 'Richard III, Henry VII and the City: London Politics and the 'Dun Cow", in R. A. Griffiths and J. Sherborne (eds), *Kings and Nobles in the Later Middle Ages* (Gloucester, Alan Sutton, 1986), pp.185–99.

8. Douglas Gray, 'Guy of Warwick (*supp. fl. c.930*)', *Oxford Dictionary of National Biography*, Oxford University Press, 2004 http://www.oxforddnb.com/view/article/11797.

9. Detailed discussion of these tournaments is in S. Anglo, 'Financial and Heraldic Records of the English Tournament', *Journal of the Society of Archivists*, ii (1962), p. 185.

10. BL Cotton Julius, B XII, fols 93r–103r.

11. D. Starkey, *Young Henry*, pp. 221–233.

6 A Sudden End

1. BL Egerton MS 616, fol. 14 is a letter sent from Arthur to Katherine on 30 October 1499 from Ludlow. Arthur wrote in Latin to his 'most beloved wife' and his 'most illustrious and excellent lady, his most dear'.

2. BL Cotton Vitellius A XVI, fol. 176.

3. As recently as 1499 the king had founded six houses of friars, with the chief ones being at Greenwich and Richmond. Their church was built adjacent to Greenwich palace, and received support from Henry VII during his life and in his will.

4. Si bona de manu Dei suscipimus mala autem quare non sustineamus.

5. Kipling, *Receyt of the Ladie Kateryne*, p. 81.

6. This section is based on M. A. Faraday, 'Mortality in the Diocese of Hereford, 1442–1541', *Transactions of the Woolhope Naturalists' Field Club*, vol. 42 (1977), 163–74. Locally-proved wills might

provide a clearer pattern than those from the Marcher region proved at the Prerogative Court of Canterbury.

7. The wills of people dying in close geographical and chronological proximity to Arthur might supply some clue to the prevalence of disease, e.g., the will of Walter Hubolde of Ludlow of 1 Aug 1501 (PROB 11/13/17).

8. Kipling *Receyt*, p. 91.

9. Kipling, *Receyt*, p. 79.

10. Of the kind that led to the death of Arthur's grandmother Margaret, countess of Richmond on 29 June 1509. She had endured the funeral of her son Henry VII at the end of April 1509, the marriage of her grandson Henry VIII to Catherine of Aragon on 11 June and their coronation on 24 June. In what was probably an exhausted condition, the sixty-six-year-old countess died at Westminster Abbey possibly after symptoms resulting from eating a cygnet at the coronation feast. M. K. Jones and M. G Underwood, *The King's Mother* (Cambridge, CUP, 1992), pp. 235–6.

11. L. Carroll, *Notorious Royal Marriages: a juicy journey through nine centuries of dynasty, destiny and desire* (Penguin, London, 2010), p. 58.

12. J. A. Guy, *The Children of Henry VIII* (Oxford University Press, Oxford, 2013), p. 4.

13. See below, pp. 186, 188.

14. See below, p. 195.

15. *Beati mortui qui in Domino moriuntur.*

16. See the photograph in Gunn and Monckton, *Prince Arthur*, facing page 69.

17. Kipling, *Receyt*, p. 91.

7 *Friends and Family Politics*

1. T. Penn, *Winter King*, pp. 85–7.

2. W. R. B. Robinson, 'Prince Arthur in the Marches of Wales, 1493–1502', *Studia Celtica*, 36 (2002), pp. 89–97.

3. R.E. Horrox and P. W. Hammond, *British Library Harleian Manuscript 433* (4 vols, Gloucester, 1979), I, pp. 10–15.

4. The Earl of Kent also had another blood-link to Elizabeth Woodville. Around the time of the battle of Agincourt, his great-grandfather, Reginald, 3rd Lord Grey of Ruthin, had married for a second time to Joan Ashley. One of their grandsons was Sir John Grey, lord Ferrers of Groby who had been Elizabeth Woodville's first husband. They were the parents of Thomas Grey, Marquis of Dorset and Sir Richard Grey, executed by Richard, Duke of Gloucester as he seized the crown in June 1483. The relationship was distant, but the Greys of Ruthin and earls of Kent were nevertheless cousins to Queen Elizabeth of York's half-brother, Thomas Grey, 1st Marquis of Dorset.

5. Jones and Underwood, *The King's Mother*, pp. 179–80.

6. Jones and Underwood, *The King's Mother*, pp. 66–92.

The Haunting of Henry VIII

1. For a clear explanation of Henry VIII's divorce proceedings and a simplified summary of the canon law issues, see J. J. Scarisbrick, *Henry VIII* (London, 1988), pp. 163–197. This section is based on Scarisbrick's discussion.

2. BL Additional MS 4622, fol. 104: a compendium of information to impugn the matrimony of Henry VIII and Queen Catherine; For statements of witnesses, see L&P 21 H8 (1529–30), vol. 4, part 3, no. 5791 and 5774.

3. L&P, II, pt 2, nos.4060–61, 3788

BIBLIOGRAPHY

Printed Primary Sources

'Historical Notes of a London Citizen, 1483–1488', ed. R. F. Green, *English Historical Review*, 96 (1981), 585–90.

'The Petition of Edmund Dudley', ed. C. J. Harrison, *English Historical Review*, 87 (1972), 82–99.

Bacon, Francis, *The History of the Reign of King Henry VII*, ed. Roger Lockyer (London, 1971).

Bishop Percy's Folio Manuscript, ed. J. W. Hales and F. J. Furnival, 3 vols (London, 1867–8).

British Library Harleian Manuscript 433, ed. Rosemary Horrox and P. W. Hammond (4 vols, Gloucester, 1979–83).

Calendar of Inquisitions Post Mortem, 1485–1509, 3 vols ed. H. C. Maxwell-Lyte (London, 1898–1955).

Calendar of the Fine Rolls, 1485–1509, ed. P. V. Davies (London, 1962).

Calendar of the Patent Rolls, 1485–1494, ed. H. C. Maxwell-Lyte (London, 1914).

Calendar of the Patent Rolls, 1494–1509, ed. H. C. Maxwell-Lyte (London, 1916).

Calendar of the State Papers Milanese, 1385–1618, ed. A. B. Hinds (London, 1912).

Calendar of the State Papers Spanish, 1485–1509, ed. G. A. Bergenroth (London, 1862).

Calendar of the State Papers Spanish, 1554–1558, ed. Royall Tyler (London, 1954).

Calendar of the State Papers Venetian, 1202–1509, ed. Rawdon Brown (London, 1864).

Chronicles of London, ed. C. L. Kingsford (Oxford, 1905).

Excerpta Historica, or Illustrations of English History, ed. S. Bentley (London, 1833).

Foedera, Conventiones, Literae, ed. Thomas Rymer, 3rd edition. (10 vols each in 4 pts, London, 1739–45; reprinted Farnborough, 1967).

Four Years at the Court of Henry VIII, ed. Rawdon Brown (2 vols, London, 1854).

Hall, Edward, *The Union of the Two Noble and Illustrious Families of Lancaster and York* (London, 1550; facsimile reprint, Menston, 1970).

Holinshed's Chronicles of England, Scotland, and Ireland (6 vols, London, 1807–8).

Joannis Lelandi…Collectanea, ed. Thomas Hearne (6 vols, Oxford, 1774).

Letters and Papers Illustrative of the Reigns of Richard III and Henry VII, ed. James Gairdner (2 vols, Rolls Series, xxiv, 1861–3).

Letters and Papers, Foreign and Domestic, of the Reign of Henry VIII, ed. J. S. Brewer, J. Gairdner, and R. H. Brodie (21 vols with 2 vols of *addenda*, London, 1862–1932).

Letters of the Kings of England, ed. J. O. Halliwell (London, 1848).

Mancini, Dominic, *The Usurpation of Richard III*, ed. C. A. J. Armstrong (Oxford, 1969).

Materials for a History of the Reign of Henry VII, ed. W. Campbell, 2 vols (London, 1873).

Memorials of King Henry VII, ed. James Gairdner (Rolls Series., x, 1858).

More, Thomas, Sir, *The History of King Richard III*, ed. R. S. Sylvester (New Haven, 1963).

Original Letters and Papers Illustrative of English History, ed. Sir H. Ellis, 2 vols (London, 1824–27).

Plumpton Correspondence, ed. Thomas Stapleton (Camden Society, old series, iv, 1839).

Rotuli Parliamentorum, ed. J. Strachey et al, 7 vols (London, 1767–1832).

Select Cases before the King's Council in the Star Chamber, ed. I. S. Leadam (2 vols, Selden Society, xvi, xxv, 1903–11).

Select Cases in the Council of Henry VII, ed. C. G. Bayne and W. H. Dunham (Selden Society, lxxv, 1958).

State Papers Henry VIII (11 vols in 5 parts., London, 1830–52).

The Anglica Historia of Polydore Vergil, A.D. 1485–1537, ed. Denys Hay (Camden Society, 3rd series., lxxiv, 1950).

The Crowland Chronicle Continuations: 1459–1486, ed. Nicholas Pronay and John Cox (London, 1986).

The Great Chronicle of London, ed. A. H. Thomas and I. D. Thornley (London, 1938).

The Household of Edward IV, the Black Book of the Ordinances of 1478, ed. A. R. Myers (Manchester, 1959).

The New Chronicles of England and France...by Robert Fabyan, ed. Henry Ellis (London, 1811).

The Parliament Rolls of Medieval England, ed. Chris Given-Wilson, Paul Brand, Seymour Phillips, Mark Ormrod, Geoffrey Martin, Anne Curry, and Rosemary Horrox (Leicester, 2005).

The Paston Letters, ed. James Gairdner (6 vols, London, 1904; facsimile reprint, Gloucester, 1983).

The Plumpton Letters and Papers, ed. Joan Kirby (Camden Society, 5th series, viii, 1996).

The Reign of Henry VII from Contemporary Sources, ed. A. F. Pollard (3 vols, London, 1913–14).

The Statutes of the Realm, ed. Alexander Luders, T. E. Tomlins, J. France, W. E. Taunton, and John Raithby (11 vols, London, 1810–28).

Three Books of Polydore Vergil's English History, ed. Sir H. Ellis (Camden Society, 29, 1844).

Tudor Royal Proclamations, ed. P. L. Hughes and J. F. Larkin (3 vols, New Haven, 1964–9).

Secondary Sources

Anglo, S., 'The London Pageants for the Reception of Katherine of Aragon: November 1501', *Journal of the Warburg and Courtauld Institutes*, vol. 26, no. ½ (1963), pp. 53–89.

Anglo, S., 'Financial and Heraldic Records of the English Tournament', *Journal of the Society of Archivists*, ii (1962), p. 185.

Anglo, S., *Images of Kingship* (Seaby, 1992).

Anglo, S., *Ill of the Dead*. The Posthumous Reputation of Henry VII', *Renaissance Studies*, 1 (1987), pp. 27–47.

Anglo, S., 'The Foundation of the Tudor Dynasty: The Coronation and marriage of Henry VII', *Guildhall Miscellanea*, 2 (1960), pp. 3–11.

Archbold, W. A. J., 'Sir William Stanley and Perkin Warbeck, *English Historical Review*, 14 (1899).

Arthurson, I., 'Espionage and Intelligence from the Wars of the Roses to the Reformation', *Nottingham Medieval Studies*, 35 (1991), pp. 134–54.

Arthurson, I., 'The King's Voyage into Scotland: The War that Never Was', in Daniel Williams (ed.), *England in the Fifteenth Century* (Woodbridge, 1987), pp. 1–22.

Arthurson, I., 'The Rising of 1497: A Revolt of the Peasantry?', in Joel Rosenthal and Colin Richmond (eds.), *People, Politics and Community in the Later Middle Ages* (Gloucester, 1987), pp. 1–18.

Arthurson, I., *The Perkin Warbeck Conspiracy, 1491–1499* (Stroud, 1994).

Baker, J. H., *The Oxford History of the Laws of England, 1483–1558* (Oxford, 2003).

Barron, C., 'Chivalry, Pageantry and Merchant Culture in Medieval London', in Peter Coss and Maurice Keen (eds.), *Heraldry, Pageantry and Social Display in Medieval England* (Woodbridge, 2002), pp. 219–41.

Bellamy, J. G., *Bastard Feudalism and the Law* (London, 1989).

Bennett, M. J., *Lambert Simnel and the Battle of Stoke* (Gloucester, 1987).

Bennett, M. J., *The Battle of Bosworth* (Gloucester, 1985).

Bernard, G. W., *The Power of the Early Tudor Nobility: A Study of the Fourth and Fifth Earls of Shrewsbury* (Brighton, 1985).

Brown, A. L., *The Governance of Late Medieval England, 1272–1461* (London, 1989).

Bryan, D., *Gerald Fitzgerald, the Great Earl of Kildare, 1456–1513* (Dublin, 1933).

Busch, W., England Unter den Tudors I (Stuttgart, 1892), English translation by A. M. Todd, *England Under the Tudors*, I, *Henry VII* (London, 1895).

Cameron, A., 'Complaint and Reform in Henry VII's Reign: The Origins of the Statute of 3 Henry VII, c. 2?', *BIHR*, 51 (1978), pp. 83–9.

Cameron, A., 'The Giving of Livery and Retaining in Henry VII's Reign', *Renaissance and Modern Studies*, 18 (1974), pp. 17–35.

Carlson, D., 'King Arthur and Court Poems for the Birth of Arthur Tudor in 1486', *Humanistica Lovaniensia*, XXXVI (1987), pp. 147–83.

Carpenter, M. C., 'Henry VII and the English Polity', in Benjamin Thompson (ed.), *The Reign of Henry VII* (Stamford, 1995), pp. 11–30.

Carpenter, M. C., 'Introduction: Political Culture, Politics and Cultural History', in Linda Clark and Carpenter (eds.), *The Fifteenth Century IV: Political Culture in Late Medieval Britain* (Woodbridge, 2004), pp. 1–19.

Carpenter, M. C., *The Wars of the Roses: Politics and the Constitution in England, c. 1437–1509* (Cambridge, 1997).

Carrol, L., *Notorious Royal Marriages: a juicy journey through nine centuries of dynasty, destiny and desire* (London, 2010).

Carson, D. R., 'Royal Tutors in the Reign of Henry VII', *The Sixteenth Century Journal*, vol. 22, no. 2 (summer 1991), pp. 253–79.

Cavell, E., *The Herald's Memoir, 1489–1490: Court Ceremonial, Royal Progress and Rebellion* (Donington, 2009).

Chrimes, S. B., *English Constitutional Ideas in the Fifteenth Century* (Cambridge, 1936).

Chrimes, S. B., *Henry VII* (London, 1972).

Chrimes, S. B., *Henry VII*, in Chrimes, S. B., Ross, C. D. and Griffiths, R. A., eds, *Fifteenth-Century England 1399–1509* (2nd edition, Stroud, 1995), pp. 67–85.

Cokayne, G. E., *et al.*, *The Complete Peerage* (14 vols, London, 1910–59).

Colvin, C. M., *The History of the King's Works* (London, 1963).

Condon, M. M., 'An Anachronism with Intent? Henry VII's Council Ordinance of 1491/2', in R. A. Griffiths and James Sherborne (eds.), *Kings and Nobles in the Later Middle Ages* (Gloucester, 1986), pp. 228–53.

Condon, M. M., 'Ruling Elites in the Reign of Henry VII', in Charles Ross (ed.), *Patronage, Pedigree and Power in Later Medieval England* (Gloucester, 1979), pp. 109–42.

Coote, L. A., *Prophecy and Public Affairs in Later Medieval England* (York, 2000).

Cunningham, S., 'National War and Dynastic Politics: Henry VII's Capacity to Wage War in the Scottish Campaigns of 1496–1497' in A. King and D. Simpkin (eds), *England and Scotland at War, c.1296–c.1513* (Leiden, 2012), pp. 297–328.

Cunningham, S., *Henry VII* (Abingdon, 2007)

Cunningham, S., Henry VII and Rebellion in North-Eastern England, 1485–1492: Bonds of Allegiance and the Establishment of Tudor Authority', *Northern History*, XXXII (1996), pp. 42–74.

Currin, J. M., '"To Traffic with War"? Henry VII and the French Campaign of 1492', in David Grummitt (ed.), *The English Experience in France, c. 1450–1558: War, Diplomacy and Cultural Exchange* (Aldershot, 2002), pp. 106–31.

Currin, J. M., 'England's International Relations, 1485–1509: Continuities amidst Change', in Susan Doran and Glenn Richardson (eds.), *Tudor England and its Neighbours* (Basingstoke, 2005), pp. 14–43.

Davies, C. S. L., 'Bishop John Morton, the Holy See and the Accession of Henry VII', *EHR*, cii (1987), pp. 2–30.

Davies, C. S. L., 'The Crofts: creation and defence of a family enterprise under the Yorkists and Henry VII', *Historical Research*, lxviii (1995), pp. 241–65.

Davies, C. S. L., 'The Wars of the Roses in a European Context' in A. J. Pollard (ed), *The Wars of the Roses* (London, 1995), pp. 162–85.

Duffy, E., *The Stripping of the Altars: Traditional Religion in England, 1400–1580* (2nd edition, New Haven, 2005).

Dunham, W. H., 'Lord Hastings' Indentured Retainers, 1461–1483', *Transactions of the Connecticut Academy of Arts and Sciences*, 39 (1955).

Dunlop, D., 'The "Masked Comedian": Perkin Warbeck's Adventures in Scotland and England from 1495 to 1497', *Scottish Historical Review*, 70 (1991), pp. 97–128.

Ellis, S. G., *Tudor Ireland* (London, 1985).

Elton, G. R., 'Henry VII: Rapacity and Remorse', in *Studies in Tudor and Stuart Politics and Government* (4 vols, Cambridge, 1974–92), i. pp. 45–65.

Elton, G. R., 'Tudor Government: The Points of Contact', in *Studies in Tudor and Stuart Politics and Government* (4 vols, Cambridge, 1974–92), iii. 3–57.

Elton, G. R., *England under the Tudors*, (2nd edition, London, 1974).

Emory, A., *Greater Medieval Houses of England and Wales, 1300–1500: volume 3, Southern England* (Cambridge, 2006).

Faraday, M. A., 'Mortality in the Diocese of Hereford, 1442–1541', *Transactions of the Woolhope Naturalists' Field Club*, 42 (1977), pp. 163–74.

Gairdner, J., *Henry VII* (London, 1892).

Giffin, M. E., 'Cadwaladr, Arthur and Brutus in the Wigmore Manuscript', *Speculum*, vol. 16, no.1 (January, 1941), pp. 109–120.

Given-Wilson, C., *The Royal Household and the King's Affinity: Service, Politics and Finance in England, 1360–1413* (New Haven, 1986).

Goodman, A., *The New Monarchy: England 1471–1534* (Oxford, 1988).

Grant, A., *Henry VII* (London, 1985).

Gray, D., 'Guy of Warwick (*supp. fl. c.930*)', *Oxford Dictionary of National Biography*, Oxford University Press, 2004, online edition, 2007 [http://www.oxforddnb.com/view/article/11797].

Griffiths, R. A., '"Ffor the Myght off the Lande, Aftir the Myght off the Grete Lordes thereoff, Stondith Most in the Kynges Officers": The English Crown, Provinces and Dominions in the Fifteenth Century', in Anne Curry and Elizabeth Matthew (eds.), *The Fifteenth Century I: Concepts and Patterns of Service in the Later Middle Ages* (Woodbridge, 2000), pp. 80–98.

Griffiths, R. A., *The Reign of Henry VI* (Berkeley, 1981).

Griffiths, R. A., 'Public and Private Bureaucracies in England and Wales in the Fifteenth Century', *Transactions of the Royal Historical Society*, 5th series., 30 (1980), pp. 109–30.

Griffiths, R. A., 'Wales and the Marches in the Fifteenth Century', in S. B. Chrimes, C. D. Ross and R. A. Griffiths (eds), *Fifteenth Century England, 1399–1509* (Manchester, 1972), pp. 145–72.

Griffiths, R. A., and THOMAS, R. S., *The Making of the Tudor Dynasty* (Stroud, 1985).

Grummitt, D. A., 'Henry VII, Chamber Finance and the "New Monarchy": Some New Evidence', *Historical Research*, 72 (1999), pp. 229–43.

Gunn, S. J., '"New Men" and "New Monarchy" in England, 1485–1524', in Robert Stein (ed.), *Powerbrokers in the Late Middle Ages: The Burgundian Low Countries in a European Context* (Turnhout, 2001), pp. 153–63.

Gunn, S. J., 'Dudley, Edmund', in H. C. G. Matthew and Brian Harrison (eds.), *The Oxford Dictionary of National Biography* (60 vols, Oxford, 2004), xvii. 66–9.

Gunn, S. J., 'Prince Arthur's Preparation for Kingship, in S. J. Gunn and L. Monckton (eds), *Arthur Tudor, Prince of Wales* (Woodbridge, 2009).

Gunn, S. J., 'Sir Thomas Lovell (*c.* 1449–1524): A New Man in a New Monarchy?', in J. L. Watts (ed.), *The End of the Middle Ages? England in the Fifteenth and Sixteenth Centuries* (Stroud, 1998), pp. 117–53.

Gunn, S. J., 'The Accession of Henry VIII', *Historical Research*, 64 (1991), pp. 278–88.

Gunn, S. J., 'The Courtiers of Henry VII', *English Historical Review*, 108 (1993), pp. 23–49.

Gunn, S. J., *Early Tudor Government, 1485–1558* (London, 1995).

Guth, D. J., 'Richard III, Henry VII, and the City: London Politics and the "Dun Cowe"' in R. A. Griffiths and J. Sherborne (eds), *Kings and Nobles in the Later Middle Ages* (Gloucester, 1986), pp. 185–204.

Guy, J. A., *The Children of Henry VIII* (Oxford, 2013).

Guy, J. A., *Tudor England* (Oxford, 1988).

Harris, B. J., *Edward Stafford, Third Duke of Buckingham, 1478–1521* (Stanford, 1986).

Harriss, G. L., 'The Dimensions of Politics', in R. H. Britnell and A. J. Pollard (eds.), *The McFarlane Legacy: Studies in Late Medieval Politics and Society* (Stroud, 1995), pp. 1–20.

Harriss, G. L., *Shaping the Nation, 1360–1461* (Oxford, 2005).

Hepburn, F., 'The Portraiture of Prince Arthur and Katherine of Aragon', in S. J. Gunn and L. Monckton (eds), *Arthur Tudor, Prince of Wales* (Woodbridge, 2009).

Hicks, M. A., *Bastard Feudalism* (London, 1995).

Hicks, M. A., 'Attainder, Resumption and Coercion, 1461–1529', *Parliamentary History*, 3 (1984), pp. 15–31.

Hicks, M. A., 'Dynastic Change and Northern Society: The Career of the Fourth Earl of Northumberland, 1470–1489', *Northern History*, 14 (1978), pp. 78–107.

Hooker, J. R., 'Notes on the Organization and Supply of the Tudor Military under Henry VII', *Huntingdon Library Quarterly*, 23 (1959–60), pp. 19–31.

Horrox, R. A., *Richard III: A Study of Service* (Cambridge, 1989).

Ives, E. W., *The Common Lawyers of Pre-Reformation England: Thomas Kebell: A Case Study* (Cambridge, 1983).

Jones, M. K., 'Sir William Stanley of Holt: Politics and Family Allegiance in the late Fifteenth Century', *Welsh History Review*, 14 (1988), pp. 1–22.

Jones, M. K., and Underwood, M. G., *The King's Mother: Lady Margaret Beaufort, Countess of Richmond and Derby* (Cambridge, 1992).

Jones, M. K., *Bosworth 1485, Psychology of a Battle* (Stroud, 2002).

Kipling, G., 'The Receyt of the Lady Katheryne', *Early English Text Society*, no. 296 (Oxford, 1990).

Lander, J. R., 'Attainder and Forfeiture, 1453–1509', in *Crown and Nobility, 1450–1509* (London, 1976), pp. 127–58.

Lander, J. R., 'Bonds, Coercion and Fear: Henry VII and the Peerage', in *Crown and Nobility, 1450–1509* (London, 1976), pp. 267–300.

Lindley, P., 'Collaboration and Competition: Torrigiano and Royal Tomb Commissions', in Lindley, P., *Gothic to Renaissance: Essays on Sculpture in England* (Stamford, 1995), pp. 47–72.

Lindley, P., and Galvin, C., 'Pietro Torrigiano's Portrait Bust of Henry VII', in Lindley, P., *Gothic to Renaissance: Essays on Sculpture in England* (Stamford, 1995), pp. 170–187.

Lloyd, D., *Arthur, Prince of Wales, 1486–1502* (Ludlow, 2002).

Macdougall, N., *James IV* (Edinburgh, 1989).

Madden, F., 'Genealogical and historical notes in Ancient Calendars', *Collectanea Topographica et Genealogica*, I (1834), pp. 277–79.

Madden, F., 'Documents Relating to Perkin Warbeck, with Remarks on his History', *Archaeologia*, 27 (1838), pp. 156–8.

Mattingley, G., *Catherine of Aragon* (Boston, 1941).

Mcfarlane, K. B., 'Bastard Feudalism', *BIHR*, 20 (1943–45), pp. 161–80.

Mcfarlane, K. B., *The Nobility of Later Medieval England* (Oxford, 1973).

Miller, H., *Henry VIII and the English Nobility* (Oxford, 1986).

Morgan, D. A. L., 'The King's Affinity in the Polity of Yorkist England', *Transactions of the Royal Historical Society*, 5th series, 23 (1973), pp. 1–25.

Morgan-Guy, J., 'Arthur, Harri Tudor and the Iconography of Loyalty in Wales', in S. J. Gunn and L. Monckton (eds), *Arthur Tudor, Prince of Wales* (Woodbridge, 2009).

Orme, N., 'The Education of Edward V', *Bulletin of the Institute of Historical Research*, lvii (1984).

Orme, N., From Childhood to Chivalry: the education of the English kings and aristocracy, 1066–1530 (London, 1984).

Owen, H., and BLAKEWAY, J. B., *A History of Shrewsbury* (2 vols, London, 1825).

Padel, O. J., 'Arthur (*supp. fl.* in or before 6th cent.)', *Oxford Dictionary of National Biography*, Oxford University Press, 2004; online edition, May 2007 [http://www.oxforddnb.com/view/article/703].

Penn, T., *Winter King* (London, 2011).

Pennington, K., *The Prince and the Law, 1200–1600: Sovereignty and Rights in the Western Legal Tradition* (Berkeley, 1993).

Pickthorn, K., *Early Tudor Government: Henry VII* (Cambridge, 1934).

Plucknett, T. F. T., 'The Lancastrian Constitution', in R. W. Seton-Watson (ed.), *Tudor Studies* (London, 1924), pp. 161–81.

Pollard, A. J., *North-Eastern England During the Wars of the Roses* (Oxford, 1990).

Pugh, T. B., 'The Indentures of the Marches between Henry VII and Edward Stafford, Duke of Buckingham, 1477–1521', *EHR*, 71 (1956).

Pugh, T. B., 'The Magnates, Knights and Gentry' in S. B. Chrimes, C. D. Ross and R. S. Griffiths (eds), *Fifteenth Century England, 1399–1509* (2nd edition, Stroud, 1995)

Rawcliffe, C., 'Baronial Councils in the Later Middle Ages', in Charles Ross (ed.), *Patronage, Pedigree and Power in Later Medieval England* (Gloucester, 1979), pp. 87–108.

Rawcliffe, Carole, *The Staffords, Earls of Stafford and Dukes of Buckingham, 1394–1521* (Cambridge, 1978).

Richmond, Colin, F., '1485 And All That, or what was Going on at the Battle of Bosworth', in P. W. Hammond (ed.), *Richard III, Loyalty, Lordship and Law* (Gloucester, 1986).

Robinson, W. R. B., 'Prince Arthur in the Marches of Wales, 1493–1502', *Studia Celtica*, 36 (2002), pp. 89–97.

Robinson, W. R. B., *Early Tudor Gwent, 1485–1547* (Welshpool, 2002).

Ross, C. D., 'Rumour, Propaganda and Popular Opinion during the Wars of the Roses', in R. A. Griffiths (ed.), *Patronage, the Crown and the Provinces in Later Medieval England* (Gloucester, 1981), pp. 15–32.

Ross, C. D., *Edward IV* (London, 1974).

Ross, C. D., *Richard III* (London, 1981).

Ross, J. A., *The Foremost Man of the Kingdom: John de Vere, thirteenth Earl of Oxford (1442–1513)* (Woodbridge, 2011).

Rosser, G., *Medieval Westminster: 1200–1540* (Oxford, 1989).

Saul, N., *Richard II* (London, 1997).

Scarisbrick, J. J., *Henry VIII* (London, 1968).

Schofield, R., *Taxation under the Early Tudors, 1485–1547* (Oxford, 2004).

Skeel, C. A. J., *The Council in the Marches of Wales: a study of local government during the sixteenth and seventeenth centuries* (London, 1904).

Somerville, R., 'Henry VII's "Council Learned in the Law"', *English Historical Review*, 54 (1939), pp. 427–42.

Somerville, R., *History of the Duchy of Lancaster* (2 vols, London, 1953–70).

Starkey, D., *Young Henry* (London, 2008).

Starkey, D. R., 'Intimacy and Innovation: The Rise of the Privy Chamber, 1485–1547', in Starkey (ed.), *The English Court: From the Wars of the Roses to the Civil War* (London, 1987), pp. 71–118.

Starkey, D. R., *The Reign of Henry VIII: Personalities and Politics* (London, 1985).

Storey, R. L., *The Reign of Henry VII* (London, 1968).

Thurley, S., *The Royal Palaces of Tudor England: Architecture and Court Life, 1460–1547* (New Haven, 1993).

Thompson, B. (ed.), *The Reign of Henry VII* (Stamford, 1995).

Thompson, M. W., 'Recent Excavations in the Keep of Farnham Castle, Surrey', *Medieval Archaeology*, vol. 4 (1960).

Thurley, S., *The Royal Palaces of Tudor England* (New Haven, 1993).

Tremlett, G., *Catherine of Aragon, Henry's Spanish Queen* (London, 2011).

Virgoe, R., 'The Recovery of the Howards in East Anglia, 1485–1529', in E. W. Ives, R. J. Knecht, and J. J. Scarisbrick (eds), *Wealth and Power in Tudor and Stuart England* (London, 1978), pp. 1–20.

Watts, J. L., '"A Newe Ffundacion of is Crowne": Monarchy in the Age of Henry VII', in Benjamin Thompson (ed.), *The Reign of Henry VII* (Stamford, 1995), pp. 31–53.

Watts, J. L., *Henry VI and the Politics of Kingship* (Cambridge, 1996).

Wedgwood, J. C., ed., *History of Parliament, Biographies of the Members of the Commons House, 1439–1509* (London, 1936).

Wolffe, B. P., *Henry VI* (London, 1981).

Wolffe, B. P., *The Crown Lands, 1461–1536: An Aspect of Yorkist and Early Tudor Government* (London, 1970).

ACKNOWLEDGEMENTS

My warmest thanks to Kate Cunningham for reading drafts of this book and for keeping it focussed when I began to wander. Prof. Ralph Griffiths read the manuscript and saved me from several errors, as well as providing brilliant insight and support. Jonathan Reeve and Alex Bennett have made the editorial and production process run very smoothly and I am very grateful to Amberley for asking me to write this book. Thanks also to Dr Paul Dryburgh, Dr Samantha Harper, Amy Licence, Dr Tom Penn, Dr James Ross, Chris Skidmore and Dr Laura Tompkins for reading, commenting and/or discussing the text and Prince Arthur general. All contributions have helped to shape this book but all published opinions and errors are my own.

INDEX

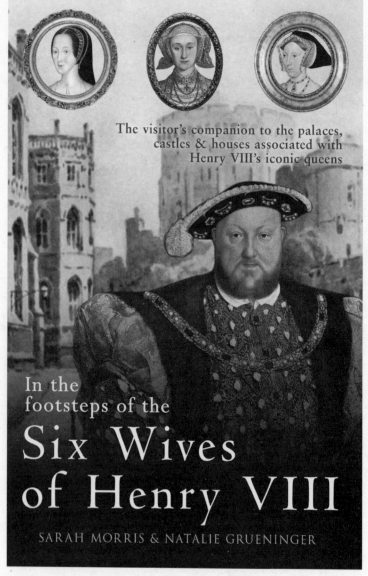

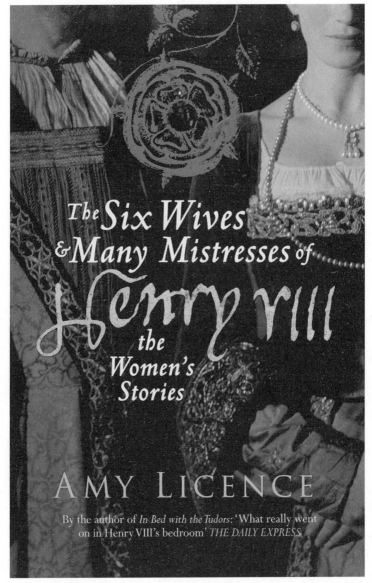